T0091958

WINNING WITH DATA SCIENCE

Howard Steven Friedman
and
Akshay Swaminathan

WINNING
WITH
DATA
SCIENCE

A HANDBOOK
FOR BUSINESS
LEADERS

 Columbia Business School
Publishing

Columbia University Press
Publishers Since 1893
New York   Chichester, West Sussex
cup.columbia.edu

Library of Congress Cataloging-in-Publication Data
Names: Friedman, Howard Steven, author. | Swaminathan, Akshay, author.
Title: Winning with data science / Howard Steven Friedman and
Akshay Swaminathan.
Description: New York : Columbia University Press, [2024] |
Includes bibliographical references and index.
Identifiers: LCCN 2023024328 | ISBN 9780231206860 (hardback) |
ISBN 9780231556699 (ebook)
Subjects: LCSH: Management—Statistical methods. | Databases. |
Data mining. | Electronic data processing.
Classification: LCC HD30.215 .F74 2024 | DDC 658.4/033—dc23/eng/20230714
LC record available at https://lccn.loc.gov/2023024328

Printed in the United States of America

Cover design: Noah Arlow

HOWARD FRIEDMAN

TO ALAN FRIEDMAN—WHO, FOR DECADES, HAS ALWAYS
EAGERLY READ MY VERY FIRST DRAFTS.

AKSHAY SWAMINATHAN

TO MY BROTHER, GOUTHAM, WHO REMINDS ME OF
WHAT IS TRULY IMPORTANT.

CONTENTS

ACKNOWLEDGMENTS

This book represents the culmination of years of brainstorming, discussion and revision.

We would like to thank the many people who provided comments, suggestions, and support to the writing, review, and ideation, including: Alan Friedman, Jerry Friedman, Alysen Friedman, Arthur Goldwag, Daniel Guetta, Caroline Bastian, Jeff Chen, Kim Sweeny, Paul Thurman, Sam Natarajan, Lathan Liou and Tina Seelig

We would like to thank Shreya Parchure, Matt Swanson, and Christian Caravaglia for compiling references throughout the manuscript.

We would also like to thank Myles Thompson and Brian Smith for their guidance and feedback as we moved this project from a rough draft to a final product.

We appreciate the editorial skills of Ben Kolstad and Marielle T. Poss.

AS:

I would like to thank my co-author Howard Friedman for the opportunity to collaborate on this important project. Learning from Howard's years of experience as an author and an educator has been truly enlightening. His patience, generosity, and mentorship have shaped me as a writer and as a person.

I want to thank my immediate family for providing ever-present support and encouragement: Priya Swaminathan, Sam Natarajan, Goutham Swaminathan, Raji Natarajan, Veeraswamy Natarajan, and Kamala Natarajan (the namesake for the protagonist Kamala).

Thank you to my friends Lathan Liou, Lucia Tu, Iván López, and Menaka Narayanan for providing invaluable feedback and inspiration throughout the development of this book. A special thank you to Pranay Nadella, with whom I developed the 30-day text based course "Spotting Fake Statistics in Real Life," which was a big inspiration for many of the chapters of this book.

Last but not least, thank you to my mentors, colleagues, and collaborators from whom I have learned so much about statistics, data science, writing, communication, and interdisciplinary collaboration: SV Subramanian, Vikram Patel, Arthur Kleinman, Daniel Corsi, Gidon Eshel, Tinku Thomas, Olivier Humblet, Jeremy Snider, Arjun Sondhi, Blythe Adamson, Brian Segal, David Mou, and Sid Salvi.

HF:

I would like to start by thanking my co-author Akshay Swaminathan who has been a brilliant inspiration and wonderful co-author. Without his vision, this book would have been mired in the wilderness for years.

I warmly thank Shui Chen and Howard Chen Friedman Jr for their love, encouragement, and support.

I am grateful to Arthur Goldwag, who has been a friend and mentor throughout the development of this book.

Much of this book was inspired by the great leaders and collaborators that I have worked with in the past. I wish to thank Prakash Navaratnam, Joe Gricar, Kim Heithoff, Nathan Hill, Dorie Clark, Mark Jordan, David Todd, Nelson Lin, Whit Bundy, Jack Harnett, Kyle Neumann, Xena Ugrinsky, Afsheen Afshar, Charles Solomon, Armen Kherlopian, Emma Arakelyan, Armen Aghinyan, Arby Leonian, Conner Raikes, Derrick Perkins, Gavin Miyasato, Mohit Misra, Vamsi Kasivajjala, Wlad Perdomo, Mark Jordan, Rachel Schutt, Brandt McKee, Jason Mozingo, Daniel Lasaga, Russ Abramson, Natalia Kanem, Diene Keita, Julitta Onabanjo, Will Zeck, Anneka Knutsson, Arthur Erken, Ramiz Alakbarov, Frank Rotman, and Peter Schnall.

WINNING WITH DATA SCIENCE

INTRODUCTION

Whether you are a newly minted MBA, a business development manager at a start-up, or a project manager at a Fortune 500 company, working with data science and data scientists is going to be part of your career. How well you work with this team and what value you can jointly develop will determine much of your own career success and that of your company.

You cannot thrive in a modern corporate environment without having some understanding of data science and its applications. This doesn't mean that every job will require you to become a Python programmer, develop your own cloud-based solutions, or become a PhD-level expert in machine learning algorithms.

It means that you need to learn the subject well enough to speak the language and ask good questions. What do we mean by good questions? Questions that increase the chances that the proposed solutions will solve your problems while avoiding unnecessary expenses and wasted effort.

The challenges of working with data science teams are similar to those of working with other technical teams. The customer needs to understand what they want and to be able to communicate those goals. The data science team needs to be able to communicate back what possible solutions can be developed as well as their advantages and disadvantages. The customer and the data science team need to collaborate to deliver value. Doing so requires each to understand the other well enough to ask the right questions and to actively listen to the other's concerns, whether the data science team sits next door or on the opposite side of the world.

This book prepares you to be a good customer for data science teams, helping you get the most value out of their expertise and hopefully avoid major pitfalls where money and time are wasted. This book will walk you through many of the key ideas you need to know to introduce data science at your company, to improve the data science team's effectiveness and efficiency, and to give you the basic background needed to communicate well with your technical teams. You will be able to understand the basic lingo, recognize the types of talent on the data science team, and pose good questions to your data science team to create insights and opportunities. By the end of this book, you will be able to answer key questions, including what the main hardware and software tools used to analyze data are, who the different players on the data science team are, and which models should be considered for specific projects.

Most importantly, you will also be armed with critical questions that you can use to further probe data analysts, statisticians, data scientists, and other technical experts. To gain the most value from this book, you should have a basic understanding of descriptive statistics (means, medians, and modes), be able to read simple graphs, and have some experience with spreadsheet programs such as Excel or Google Sheets. Programming experience, advanced knowledge of statistics, and other computational skills are not necessary. We will dig into some of the fascinating methods that have been developed by data scientists through practical examples, but we won't saddle you with equations and concepts that you don't need to understand.

With that scope in mind, we want to state very clearly what this book is definitely not.

This is not a textbook for those hoping to gain the skills or knowledge necessary to become a data scientist. There are plenty of excellent textbooks and online materials available that teach technical data science concepts. We will introduce many of the basic concepts from the point of view of the customer so that it is clear how each idea is relevant for solving the customer's problem.

This is not a programming book. Again, there is a wealth of great materials already available for those who want to learn programming languages such as Python, R, SQL, Java, and others. Online resources, like Kaggle contests and coding academies, to name a few examples, are easily accessible for those wishing to learn.

Our book will start by discussing tools of the trade, basic information you need to become a good data science customer. Whether you are an internal customer or someone who needs to hire an external data science team, your project budget should not include the expenses of investing in the wrong software and tools. This will waste precious time and money. Using the right tools is a critical step, since you can't do data science without appropriate data storage and analytic software. By understanding the basics of data systems, such as cloud versus local storage and data lakes versus data warehouses, you will grow comfortable with the technical language, concepts, and applications. When your data science team proposes how it will analyze a dataset or deliver a solution, you can probe further to increase the chances that the deliverable will fit your needs. Programming languages and software are the basic tools of the trade for any data science team. In order to help you work effectively with the team, we will introduce some basic concepts involving key proprietary and nonproprietary languages.

Data science projects are, simply put, projects. We will walk through the basics of managing a data science project, including the key steps necessary for success. People are fundamental to the success of any project. Bring in the wrong staff, and your data science project is going to be dead in the water. With job titles like data scientist, data engineer, data analyst, machine learning engineer, and statistician, it is often difficult to figure out who has the skill sets needed to deliver success. Just as a baseball team has different players with different skills, a data science team is composed of different specialists. We will meet the players involved in a data science team, understand their skill sets, and see how they work to deliver products and services. We will explain the roles of data engineers, machine learning specialists, data visualization experts, and other specialists. We will also walk through how to prioritize projects so that the limited resources of time and money are allocated appropriately.

A common failure when companies begin their first foray into data science is trying to hunt mosquitoes with a machine gun. Deep learning and artificial intelligence (AI) are getting so much attention that many key decision makers are getting distracted by the buzz. A dirty little secret about data science is that the most advanced, cutting-edge modeling methods are often not necessary to gain most of the value from the data. We'll explore how data science customers working in companies, organizations, and governments can move from basic analysis to simple predictive models to advanced modeling most efficiently. This pathway will be introduced by explaining what some of the foundational concepts of data science are and how they are applied.

One of the goals of this book is to teach you the key approaches to different data problems. Later we'll describe some of the main modeling techniques. This is not intended to turn you into a fully fledged data scientist or even a medium-level programmer. Instead, we will focus on making sure you are well equipped to have discussions with data scientists, understand some of the commonly used jargon, recognize the solutions might be most appropriate for different problems, and are ready to ask good questions.

We'll survey unsupervised machine learning techniques. These methods do not try to predict an outcome but rather group people together based on the data. For example, rather than treating millions of customers as one big group, data scientists can find clusters of customers that share similar likes, patterns, and other key features. Customer clusters in the restaurant industry can include the weekly night-outers, the anniversary diners (who indulge in a few expensive meals infrequently), the family mealers (groups of, say, four or more who often eat at the same few restaurants), and the one-and-doners (who go once to each restaurant and then never return). Patient clusters in the health insurance industry can include older, sick patients with major surgical needs; younger, healthy patients with limited medical needs and almost no health resource use; active, healthy seniors requiring only routine doctor visits; and accident-prone, young risk takers with frequent ER visits. These clusters are subgroups of the total customer base that have important things in common. By thinking about these clusters of customers, rather than the entire customer base, advertising, cross-sells, and other recommendations can be better targeted.

We'll move on to supervised machine learning, whose methods are applied to predicting an outcome of interest. Whether we are trying to predict who will respond to an ad, how long a patient will stay in the hospital, or if a customer will pay their credit card bill on time, the key concepts for modeling and the methods used are often similar across industries. Methods including linear regression, logistic regression, classification and regression trees, random forests, and gradient-boosted machine learning will be introduced along with some tricks data scientists use to improve model prediction.

This book will touch on a few specialized topics within data science in one chapter that pulls together many of these interesting topics, including network analysis, spatial analysis, deep learning, and AI. The analysis of group behaviors using tools such as network analysis—a critical part of Facebook, LinkedIn, and Twitter analytics—will be introduced. This will help you identify how different users are related, who the key connectors in a group are, and whether the network is tightly linked or very loosely connected. We will discuss key metrics for understanding networks, including concepts like density and centrality. We will introduce spatial analysis, which looks at how different items are related to each other in physical space. Uber drivers aren't the only ones who need to be concerned about how to get from one location to another. Ambulance drivers need to know the best routes to get patients to the hospital. People looking to buy apartments may prefer those closest to subways or buses, and knowing if there is shopping nearby is important for most.

Of course, no discussion of data science is complete without discussing AI and deep learning. Whether we are talking about autonomous vehicles, language translation, chatbots, or tumor detection, incredible advances are constantly being made in these cutting-edge areas. We'll introduce the basic concepts behind the most powerful of these methods, including convolutional neural networks, recurrent neural networks, and large language models. We'll then describe one of the more common applications of AI, involving computer vision. Consider the incredible technological advances that allow computers to accurately tag images as being malignant or benign. Similarly, millions of handwritten documents can be scanned and the information extracted digitally using computer vision rather than having massive teams trying to decipher someone's scribbled handwriting.

Many senior managers are less interested in understanding the details of the data structure and modeling decisions and more interested in seeing results. You'll need to be prepared to answer this simple question: "Are the millions of dollars we spend on our data science investments providing a good return on the investment?" You'll need to measure impact through simple methods like A/B testing as well as more advanced methods of causal inference like difference in difference, interrupted time series, and regression discontinuity to demonstrate the impact of policies and programs. This book will introduce the basic concepts of measuring impact and then provide important questions to consider related to the more advanced methods.

An important issue that is often ignored in data science is ethics. The last thing your company wants is to land on the front page of the *New York Times* because your algorithm is reinforcing racial, sexual, or other biases. Your data science team will need to be aware of the ramifications of its modeling to ensure no explicit or implicit bias is included in the models. For example, credit-scoring models may inadvertently and indirectly include factors like race and sex, which is illegal. And talent prediction models may create closed loops, where students applying to schools and job applicants applying for positions are unfairly penalized for not fitting historical patterns. You'll learn some of the basic ethical concerns, ways to avoid these issues, and some best practices in ethics.

The journey in our book will be taken along with two people, Steve and Kamala. Both are looking to progress in their careers, and both need to extract value from the data science expertise in their companies. Steve works in consumer finance, with rotations in the Fraud Department, Recoveries Department, and Real Estate Division. Kamala, a junior executive at a health insurance company, is tasked with roles in both clinical strategy and marketing, where she needs to balance delivering good patient care with keeping her company profitable. While we will dig deeply into consumer finance and health insurance in this book, the lessons about being a good customer are general across industries, so you will find relevant guidance regardless of your professional focus.

What are you waiting for? Let's get started.

1

TOOLS OF THE TRADE

STEVE AND SHU MONEY FINANCIAL COMPANY

Steve was always a bit of a handyman at home. He did minor plumbing, some electrical work, and his pride and joy was a set of cabinets he designed, built, and installed himself. His workbench had almost every tool you could imagine: power sanders, a full drill bit collection, routers, planes, over thirty types of screwdrivers, and a table saw. He used each tool skillfully and knew when and where each one should and shouldn't be used.

But Steve wasn't sitting at home now. He was staring at his computer screen, midway through his two-year rotation at Shu Money Financial. Fresh out of his MBA program at Columbia Business School, this was his first real job. Why did he take this job in consumer finance? Shu Money Financial was constantly ranked one of the best companies to work for in the United States. The company invests heavily in its staff and treat its over 20,000 employees like a very large family. The "Shusters" pride themselves on being on the cutting edge of technology, tossing around acronyms and lingo that Steve barely understood.

Steve's main task was to lead the development of a new strategy for prioritizing cases sent to the Recoveries Department. The flow of accounts into the department is straightforward. If the customer has not paid anything owed in the previous six months, the debt is charged off. This is true for any financial product offered by Shu Money Financial, be it a credit card, a line of credit, a car loan, or a mortgage. The charged-off account is then transferred to the Recoveries Department, whose task is to collect as much of the debt as possible.[1]

This morning Steve met with the company's data science team. As a primer, they shared with him a bewilderingly long list of programming languages, software tools, and deployment methods used in the last three years. His eyes glazed over as the team members recounted their inventory of data products delivered to other parts of the company. This was the data science team's first project in the Recoveries Department.

Steve felt overwhelmed. He wanted to understand everything that the data science team members mentioned and not embarrass himself. He wanted them to view him as a well-informed future leader of the company. He started thinking about the data science discussion and again felt a tightness in his chest.

But then Steve remembered that he wasn't building the solution. He was the customer.

Instead of lining up different grades of sandpaper, wood, drill bits, and saws, he needed to act like a customer. If he was buying cabinets and having someone install them, he would know how large the cabinets had to be, where they would be installed, and how exactly he would use them. He would let the cabinet professionals build the solutions for him, while he made sure that the products met his needs.

Steve relaxed a bit. He didn't need to become an expert on every tool in the data science toolbox. What he needed to do was focus on the problem he was trying to solve. While it is true that different tools are better for different situations, he was not going to make the decisions in terms of which data storage devices, software, programming languages, and other tools were being used. He needed to understand the options and implications of the data science team's recommendations. If he had specific needs or restrictions, then he had to make sure that the data science team members understood this clearly so that his project requirements were incorporated in their recommendations and solutions. For example, he may need to put a solution in place in the next two months, have a clear set of milestones and deliverables, and keep the entire project cost below $50,000.

Steve's priority was solving his business problem. In this case, he was tasked with improving how the Recoveries Department prioritized its work.

Thinking about the Recoveries Department as a business, with its own profit and loss statements, Steve wanted to maximize the total dollar amount collected while minimizing the necessary operational costs. The department had only enough resources to make substantial efforts on a limited percentage of the cases. In the other cases, customers simply received an automatic email or a phone call, usually resulting in no connection with the customers and, not surprisingly, no money collected. Most of the accounts were sold to third-party collection agencies.[2] With limited resources, Steve couldn't simply double or triple the Recoveries Department staff, as that would likely make the department less profitable.

Steve first wanted to understand the current method for prioritizing accounts and assigning them to associates in the Recoveries Department. He found the current method was rather simple. Every account that had ever made a payment was assigned to tier 1. Every account that had never made a payment but had some email or phone contact with the Customer Service Department, Collections Department, or any other department was assigned to tier 2. All accounts that had never made a payment and had never had any contact with those departments were assigned to tier 3. These assignment rules were created by the previous director of the Recoveries Department based on their intuition and decades of work experience.

Steve understood that his goal was to increase the profitability of the Recoveries Department by improving the work prioritization. He immediately recognized that the current rules-based prioritization did not take a data-informed approach to predicting which customers are most likely to pay as well as how much they are likely to pay. The current policy takes a simplified approach to workload prioritization by using some past customer behaviors to decide how to collect debts in the present and future. There may be some merit to the variables used in these business rules, such as the assumption that customers who previously paid Shu Money Financial are probably more likely to pay in the future. But there may be many other factors that are predictive of the probability of receiving future payments, how much those future payments are likely to be, how responsive the customer is likely to be, and what the most profitable way of working with the customer is likely to be. These questions can be explored in a data-informed approach by gathering the appropriate data about the customers and then systematically analyzing it rather than relying solely on intuition and experience. Steve realized that if he could predict which customers were most likely to pay the highest recovery amount, he would be able to optimize how he prioritized accounts in terms of his department's human resources, time, and money. In this framework, the cases with the lowest expected recovery amount would be given a low priority or sold to a third-party collections agency.

Steve scheduled another meeting with the data science team to discuss his problem and understand the team's proposed solutions. Before the meeting, he brushed up on some of the basics of data, data systems, and data architecture with the modest goal of understanding the key concepts so that he would be able to ask good questions.

DATA WORKFLOW

Basic data workflow consists of five stages: data collection, storage, preparation, exploration, and modeling, including experimentation and prediction (figure 1.1). Throughout this data workflow, the data science team looks at key considerations and makes key decisions that will impact the final product. Data pipelines move data into defined stages by automating data collection and storage. The automation can be scheduled regularly or triggered by an event. Data quality and data transfer processes are monitored with

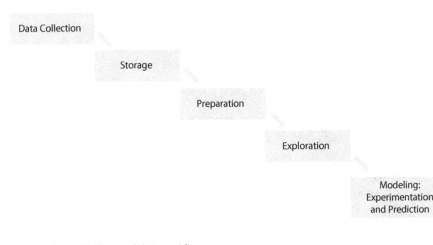

Data Collection

Storage

Preparation

Exploration

Modeling:
Experimentation
and Prediction

Figure 1.1 Stages of data workflow

generated alerts, but decisions need to be made regarding which quality checks are required. An understanding of both the data and the business is necessary to implement data standards.

The standard approach to gathering data elements from various sources and then bringing them to a single location is known as extract, transform, and load (ETL).[3] The extraction stage is when the data is first extracted from its source. These sources can range from existing databases to newly created data sources, from purchased data warehouses to web-scraped data to standardized customer relational databases. The Recoveries Department has internal data on a customer's purchases and payments as well as their contact history, such as phone calls, emails, and letters. It has external data from credit bureau reports, databases of people who change locations, social media records for some customers, and even inputs from a death registry. It also has specific information about the demographics of different geographic neighborhoods and local economic indicators such as foot traffic patterns. All of this data can be extracted from the sources and potentially fed into the analysis.

The data transformation step is critical to ensuring data quality. This can include identifying and resolving inconsistencies and missing values, standardizing formatting, removing duplicate records, and deleting erroneous data inputs. In Steve's case, he has to ensure that the data science team has applied proper controls to the inputs. He must be confident there are no entries that are clearly erroneous or that misidentify customers with the same name. This can require the data science team to perform logical checks between data sources as well as for individual variables coming from the data sources. We know that a person in the database is not going to be more than 130 years old. That is a very simple example of a data error, but what about the person who calls Customer Service every day? Is this a real data point or an error? While we know the 130-year-old person is an error, it is best to have the data science team work closely with the subject-matter experts in the business to develop some of the quality checks. Quality checks are needed to ensure not only that the retained data is correct but also that we don't discard true data points even when they are strikingly different from the rest of the data set. In a situation where the number of calls is orders of magnitude higher than the average, we can retain the information (if it is correct) and then apply a transformation by defining a new variable with categories for how frequently the customer called.

Using data that hasn't been processed can lead to incorrect results. Issues with the input data such as inappropriate handling of missing values, data input errors, or misformatted data can result in modeling errors and poor predictions. Consider the simple situation in which a customer's personal information is occasionally misentered. Shu Financial doesn't actually have customers that are 130 years old, yet the database includes a few of these input errors. Without cleaning the data, these incorrect inputs could potentially have a negative impact on the accuracy of the predictions for all customers, not just the misentered ones.

This transformed data must be loaded into its destination. The data can be loaded at once in a full load or at scheduled intervals in incremental loads. Incremental loading adds additional records to the destination only if the transformed data has new information compared with what is already in the destination.

In some situations, a customer can provide great insight into the processes and decisions; in other cases, there are often corporate standards that the data science team will be required to follow. While Steve has specific requirements and challenges for his particular project, good data architectures all have some basic features and share some key requirements. They need to have a method to enable scaling, be available for the users (with minimal downtime), be secure, have performance that supports the customer's needs, and be cost efficient.

DATA STORAGE

Looking back a few decades, the world of data was much simpler. The volume and velocity of data were limited to events when the customer directly interacted with the company by sending in a check, calling Customer Service, or using a credit card. Data remained in silos and was linked only if the same identifier, such as the customer identification number, appeared in two tables so that the tables could be joined.

Data storage was local, using physical storage devices such as hard disk drives, solid-state drives, or external storage devices. This worked fine until there was a physical disaster or the physical devices simply failed, something that happened quite often. Backups would need to be loaded to replace the lost data, but one would often be quickly disappointed to learn that the files were not backed up with any degree of consistency.

In business school, Steve was assigned a data analysis project that had to be solved using hard drives and external storage devices for backup. He presented the results and received a solid B+ on what turned out to be only part one of the project. Part two required the students to complete the same data analysis project using a cloud provider of their choice, with nearly all choosing Google Cloud, Amazon Web Services, or Microsoft Azure. Part two resulted in solutions that were more quickly trained and automatically backed up online. The lesson from this exercise was clear—that cloud computing had major advantages—and Steve earned a solid A on that second part.

Steve had absorbed the lesson about some of the advantages of cloud computing. Shu Money Financial and many other companies either have migrated to cloud solutions or are cloud-native in that they were designed and built to run in the cloud.

Steve recognized that he needed to learn more about cloud computing. A little networking led him to Brett, a data scientist with years of experience at Shu Money Financial. Their discussion was short and productive, with Steve leading with the question "What exactly is the difference between local computing and cloud computing?"

Brett smiled, as he had responded to questions like this nearly once a month. "Think about it as the difference between creating an Excel spreadsheet and creating a Google sheet that you can share.[4] The Excel spreadsheet is stored locally, so if anything happens to that computer, then you have lost your work unless you have a recent backup stored on a separate device or in the cloud. If it is a huge spreadsheet, then your local computer's power is the limit in doing the computation. Also, you can access the spreadsheet only from wherever the spreadsheet is stored."

Steve picked up on the thread. "I see, so the Google sheet is stored in the cloud, meaning that I can access it from anywhere I have internet access, track changes, add comments, and easily share it with colleagues, requesting their input in specific areas."

"Exactly—the computing power for that Google sheet does not depend on your local laptop but rather on the cloud server that supports it," interrupted Brett. "Now think about the old days of data storage. Here at Shu Money Financial, storage devices used to be purchased to meet our anticipated needs, and as the needs increased, we bought more storage devices. We always had to prepay to have storage capability, no matter how often we accessed that stored data. We were responsible for routinely backing up our data and for ensuring that the data environments were secure. We were

100 percent responsible for defending the integrity of our systems. It was completely our problem when someone attacked our data with ransomware (where criminals block access to our computer system until a sum of money is paid) or malware (where criminals insert software that disrupts, damages, or misuses our computer system)."

"What about data portability? Does cloud computing have any advantages in situations when the data is required to stay in one country?"

"Definitely. In the past, we had to house the physical storage devices in countries where the data wasn't allowed to cross borders. Sometimes analysts flew to that country to do their work. That meant we needed to purchase servers to support our computing needs all around the world. The server capacity was often much larger than the normal usage in order to handle those brief moments when there was a lot of demand placed on the system. With cloud computing, we can assign the servers to be in the country of interest with the push of a button. This way the data can remain on servers in that country, yet it can still be accessed by users in other locations.[5] This is a far more flexible solution than one that would restrict users to individuals physically in the country."

Steve's confidence was growing. "It seems like the world of cloud computing has created a lot more options: options related to different ways of storing data, accessing information, and analyzing data as well as to security and costs."

"Exactly. Cloud computing describes the delivery of different services, including data storage, servers, databases, networking, and software, through the internet. Cloud computing gives us scalable access to computing resources and IT services so we pay for what we are using. Cloud computing is elastic. Users can adjust how many or how few services they need at any given time without having to lock themselves into a specific amount of storage space or number of servers. We can achieve cost savings by paying only for storage that we need and not paying for servers that are much more powerful than what we require 99 percent of the time. Of course, security risks still exist. Accounts can get hacked, and data can be stolen from even the most respected cloud providers, so we need to be vigilant by not responding to spam, not sharing passwords, and taking all of the standard security measures."

Steve wrapped up the discussion with Brett and then moved on to some more self-study. He learned that major cloud vendors, such as Google Cloud, Amazon Web Services, and Microsoft Azure, can provide data storage at a much lower cost than if Shu Money Financial was purchasing its own storage.[6] Also, all cloud storage providers offer some type of tiered storage pricing, so data that would not be accessed often would cost less than data that might be used on a daily basis. These providers perform backup services automatically, including having copies in different parts of the world, simplifying the customers' responsibilities. Using cloud storage also means that Shusters can access data from anywhere. Cloud providers have protections against ransomware and malware, as they are responsible for maintaining up-to-date defenses.

One disadvantage of cloud storage is that there may be delays in transferring data and in creating backups due to internet speeds. In situations of internet failure, Shu Money Financial will have a lot of unplanned downtime as employees wait to access the data and services. Also, performance may suffer if there are major bandwidth limitations, since cloud computing uses internet bandwidth at the same time as other internet-related activities. Bandwidth rules can and should be established to prevent one internet application from slowing down a higher-priority process. In addition, some cloud users worry about not having total control, since the data is held off-site by another company.

Another concern is vendor lock-in. Once you've committed to one specific cloud storage provider, it is often difficult to migrate. Hacking can happen to cloud service providers as well as local storage services, where cloud providers might be considered a good target for top hackers, since those providers pitch their security advantages. There have been many famous cases of leading cloud providers being hacked, including Dropbox, Apple's iCloud, and Codespace.

Decisions regarding whether to use cloud computing and, if so, which service provider and services to use are usually made at the corporate level, not at the individual project or department level.

For a large company like Shu Money Financial, Steve isn't going to make these decisions. At a smaller company, he may be one of the key customers that helps drive this decision. What he may want to know is what the advantages are for him in this specific case. If he has a very small analytics project, one that can be readily run on a local computer, then he won't need major computing power or storage capability. He may be more focused on addressing issues such as version control, data security, and backup for critical files.

DATA SOURCES

Today a great deal of effort is expended on creating data architectures that integrate standard application programming interfaces (APIs) to enable data sharing across different systems, processes, organizations, and locations. APIs are sets of rules that explain how computers or applications communicate with one another.[7] They act as an intermediary between an application and the web server. If a data scientist wants to extract data from an API, they have to review the API specifications to understand how that API can be engaged to extract data. Typically, the programmer initiates an API call (or request), and the API ensures that the request is valid. If valid, then the API makes a call to the external program or server, which sends the requested information, and the API transfers the data. APIs are available from companies willing to share some information—for example, the popular Google Analytics, Google Maps, Facebook, and Twitter APIs—and they are also often available from federal, state, and local government entities such as the U.S. Census Bureau, state-level health administrations, and even local police departments.

This is a reflection of the fact that the variety of data has increased—due to both the amazing breadth of data sources now available and the type of content itself. Today a company can obtain far more information about customers from their public computer footprint on social media as well as from data vendors who sell detailed information about customers, neighborhoods, industries, and any other content areas where there is a market. Much of this information is scraped from the web, while other information is aggregated from public records, APIs, and private data sources.

There is a world of difference between the data elements captured from a company's prespecified inputs and the wide assortment of data that comes from social media, customer emails, chatbots, or other external sources. In the past, nearly all data was structured, with predefined values, ranges, and formats for information, such as how old the customer was, where they lived, or how much they spent last month. This information was company data in that it reflected information about the relationship between the customer and the company. The information was stored in data warehouses, where a substantial effort was made to clean the data and make it readily amenable to analysis. This type of structured information is readily stored in relational databases, since the data points are related to one another and can be thought of as a large data table.[8] The columns hold attributes of the data, and each record has a value for each attribute. Different files could be merged using a variable that was common to each file, such as a customer's unique identification number.

Today there are vast quantities of unstructured data (data that is not captured in traditional relational databases), such as the content of email communications, online chatbot exchanges, video files, audio files, web pages, social media sites, and speech-to-text conversions from interactions with a customer service representative. This type of data is often stored in a document database, or it can be stored as a data lake and later processed and stored as a data warehouse. Data lakes are data storage mechanisms that hold the raw data in its native format until it is required for use.[9] The data has some tagging, such as keywords that are added to the records. These tags are useful later when there is a need to use the information, enabling the correct records to be extracted, cleaned, and then used.

Some useful information can be automatically extracted from unstructured data. Years ago a human was required to manually convert this unstructured data to structured data. Now technologies such as text-to-speech conversion and natural language processing

(NLP) can take a recorded conversation between an agent and a customer and extract information such as the customer's concern, how it was resolved, and how satisfied the customer was.[10]

From a data science customer perspective, it is very important to identify all of the possible data sources that can be used for the project. This challenge of identifying possible data sources is shared among the customers, data scientists, and others involved in the project and is critically important. The breadth and richness of the data are primary factors in determining how insightful a piece of data analysis is or how accurate a predictive model is.

DATA QUALITY

The breadth and richness of the data are going to provide only limited value if the data quality is not assured. A truism for data science, and for analytics more generally, is "garbage in, garbage out." As a result, the data preparation and cleaning stages are critical and usually involve many steps. That said, many data sets have their own idiosyncrasies, so the data scientist will need to understand the input data well enough to know what kinds of data cleaning are the highest priority.

Removing duplicate records is necessary so that observations do not receive excessive weighting because they were accidentally repeated in the database. The data types have to be verified to prevent the same field from being represented as both a number and a character or as both a date and a text field. The range of possible values needs to be understood so that misentered values can be readily detected and corrected. Also, the relevance of missing values needs to be understood. How frequently is there missing data in each field? Does the fact that data is missing have meaning? If so, then that should be considered in the data quality checking. Are missing values allowed, or does there need to be some imputation method (a data-driven method for making a guess when the data is missing) in situations where the data is not available?

The data preparation steps provide a great opportunity for the data science customer to get directly involved. After all, Steve and others in the Recoveries Department are well positioned to discuss with the data science team what each field represents, what values are expected, what ranges of values are possible, and what relevance, if any, the missing values have. This dialogue between the data science customer and the data science team is critical to ensuring that the data preparation steps improve the quality of the data to be used later for modeling purposes. This exchange can help increase the chances that plausible, but surprising, data will be retained for further analysis rather than being incorrectly discarded.

CODING LANGUAGES AND REPOSITORIES

Steve knew that when planning to work on improving his kitchen, he needed the right tools at the right time. He used power sanders sometimes and hand sanders at other times. He reached for his power tools when appropriate and used manual screwdrivers and hammers at other times.

The array of software and programming languages overwhelmed him, so he decided to buy Brett a coffee and chat. Brett led off: "Data scientists are humans. We form habits with preferences on how we work and what problems we prefer tackling. Of course, we are reliant on corporate policies and standards, so this isn't the Wild West of programming. Some data scientists tend to use the same tools and languages over and over regardless of the problem. Others scan the horizons far and wide to explore all tools and, to be honest, end up unable to decide a way forward. As the customer, you should ask the data scientists what software solutions are being considered and why."

Steve nodded his head. He wasn't going to tell the cabinetmaker how to build, and he wasn't going to dictate tools to the data science team. But he would ask the cabinetmaker why they chose that type of wood, and he should ask the data science team to explain the advantages and disadvantages of the proposed software solution.

Moreover, he should understand whether those decisions will lock him into a solution that may have expensive ongoing costs such as software licensing fees.

"So what are the basics about programming languages that I need to know?" asked Steve.

Brett responded: "Any book that mentions the most common coding languages will find itself quickly dated. That said, one of the most dominant languages for decades has been SQL (Structured Query Language).[11] It is fundamental to numerous applications that involve building tables, querying, and obtaining summary outputs from relationship databases. SQL (along with its variations) is the standard language for relational database management systems. SQL statements are used to perform many key tasks such as updating data, creating new data tables, linking between tables, retrieving data, and even doing basic statistics and reporting from a database. The most basic commands in SQL can be read almost like regular English statements."

Steve had learned some simple SQL in business school. He remembered that the basic commands of CREATE TABLE, SELECT, FROM, and WHERE do exactly what you think they would do. SELECT defines what fields to extract, FROM states which database or databases to use, and WHERE states the conditions that have to be met for the records to be extracted. For example, if Steve wanted to extract the customer's account number and debt amount from the data table called "customer_database" for debts over $1,000, he could use a simple query like

```
SELECT account_number, debt_amount
FROM customer_database.accounts_table
WHERE debt_amount>1000
```

Different tables can be linked very easily using SQL. The user simply has to identify the tables in the FROM statement and specify exactly what fields need to be the same in the two tables in a JOIN statement. There is a wide variety of ways to join tables that specify which of the records needs to be in which of the tables.

Brett was thrilled to see that Steve had a working knowledge of SQL. "Basic programming in SQL is straightforward. Many of our business partners like you readily use it to extract some information without even calling the data scientists. For developing more advanced reporting, doing statistical analysis, and building data models, two of the most popular languages are Python and R.[12] Other commonly used languages include Scala, Julia, JavaScript, Java, and C/C++."

"Should I learn Python and R in addition to SQL?" Steve asked.

"Will you program in it as part of your work, or are you thinking about it as a hobby? If you don't actually use a programming language regularly, then, like a foreign language, you will probably forget much of it quickly. That said, if you want to learn, then there are great online resources to get you started. Also, these languages have a wealth of free content that is constantly being improved."

Many programmers have developed useful Python libraries and R packages that greatly facilitate programming along with documentation to help other programmers understand how to implement these libraries and packages. In fact, these libraries and packages are the basis for why users find these languages so helpful. They include built-in functions that can readily be called in the programming language. Whether you are trying to develop a complicated graph, a regression model, or a neural network or to perform a statistical analysis like a t-test, there is often a library or package that can be leveraged as a starting point or possibly as the solution itself.

While both Python and R are popular among data scientists, they have specific use cases. R is often more popular with those having a greater focus on statistical analysis, such as statisticians. Common applications include performing statistical tests, modeling, analyzing spatial and time series data, classifying, and clustering. Two popular integrated development environments for R users are RStudio and R Tools for Visual Studio. Those tools enable users to quickly write, debug, and test code. They empower programmers by allowing them to program, track which packages are installed, and view output and data tables.

There is a large swath of integrated development environments for Python developers. Much of Python's early development was supported by Google, and the work was released to the open-source community for free. A key strength of Python is that it can be easily integrated with other programming languages.

Because Python and R are available for free and have extremely large networks of developers, they have grown in popularity over the past decade, taking market share from proprietary programming and data analytics software.

At one point, SAS was a dominant language for statistical programming and software not only in Steve's field of finance but also in other industries such as health, telecommunications, and retail and in the public sector. It still retains a large set of users in a number of industries and sectors, including the pharmaceutical industry, health care, and the public sector. Other major proprietary language and software options include Matlab, STATA, and SPSS.

It is a good idea for the customer to ask what languages are being used by the members of the data science team. If they are using a proprietary software option such as SAS, Matlab, STATA, or SPSS, then follow-up questions can include how long the company's current license lasts and what the plans for renewal are. While simple programs can be readily rewritten in a new language such as Python or R, this can still be time consuming and create delays. More-complicated programs may require substantial time to recode from a proprietary language to a freely available language, and in some cases, the proprietary software may not be perfectly replaceable. Also, the programming languages currently being used may become a consideration in future hiring when the need arises to replace team members who leave or to bring in new team members.

The world of data science programming is changing rapidly, especially with automated machine learning (AutoML) solutions gaining market share as more companies see the value in these products. These solutions have the flexibility to be used in either point-and-click mode or hands-on programming in Python, R, or other programming languages. This flexibility enables a wider population to readily derive value from analytical software tools instead of continuing to limit data analysis and modeling to those with advanced programming skills. This "democratizing" of the development of advanced models is part of the value proposition of AutoML software. This software can import data sets from different sources and then merge them. Feature engineering is performed automatically, so that new potential input variables are explored by the software itself. Numerous possible predictive modeling solutions are examined by the software, and the best performing models are reported. Data quality checking is performed by the software, though some review of the process is appropriate.

Code repositories are another basic tool of the data science trade. Whether your company is using Github, Bitbucket, or some other code repository, it is important to understand their value. Essentially, they allow multiple programmers to work on a project while tracking their contributions. Not only are these online file storage systems, but also they are specifically designed to enable collaboration among different programmers on a project. The contributions of one programmer can be easily identified, and versions of the code can be quickly traced. The data science team can isolate specific parts of the programming to work on and check them without negatively impacting other parts of the project. It greatly facilitates teamwork and allows different team members to not only contribute but also check each other's work. It allows users to create markdown files, which allow programmers to readily add notes with text formatting such as bold, highlighting, italics, and headers to their programs. These notes are critical, since they serve as reminders of what the programmer was thinking at the time as well as communicating with other programmers on the purpose of each section of the code—anyone reading their own code one month or one year later is grateful for having used as many detailed notes as possible.

As a customer, Steve should request access to the code repository. This will let him see how often people are checking their work in and out of the system and, more importantly, how well they are documenting their work. The code should be documented sufficiently that a nonprogramming customer such as Steve should be able to read through the notes and understand the purpose of the program and, step-by-step, how it works. If the documentation is not at that level of detail, then the project risks having a major issue if the main programmer leaves or there are significant staff transitions.

These code repositories are a useful tool regardless of the coding language used. From the point of view of the customer, a more relevant question is whether the choice of languages will limit the potential solution options, future maintenance, and portability. Languages themselves are continuously being updated and expanded, with new capabilities built into packages and libraries. This means that while languages are constantly being created to more efficiently address data needs, simplify coding, or enable the programmer to have more control over the modeling, legacy code may be rendered less functional or may be less understandable to programmers familiar with more current coding paradigms and languages.

DATA PRODUCTS

Data science customers like Steve may be curious about decisions regarding data storage, software, and programming languages. But their primary interest is having their problems solved with products developed by the data science team. These data products are the translation of the raw data science project into a practical solution that is tailored to the end user's needs.

A key step for Steve is to work with the data science team to define the exact data product he needs (figure 1.2). Does he need a basic deliverable like raw data, an advanced product such as automated decision-making, or something in between?

What data product he needs depends on the problem he is trying to solve. In Steve's case, he is trying to maximize the profitability of the Recoveries Department by improving the prioritization of the caseload. The solution also depends on the resources that are already in place. These resources can include the human talent, software, hardware, and money that are readily available to use the output of the data science team. Is the customer a lean operating department that is best suited to implementing black-box solutions

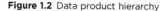

Highest Level of Data Product:
Automated decision-making

Decision Support tools leveraging
algorithms

Data reports, visualizations, and analyses

Quality-checked, document-derived databases

Lowest Level of Data Product: Raw Data

Figure 1.2 Data product hierarchy

its employees receive from outside the department? Does it have its own tech-savvy team with analysts, modelers, and programmers who are ready to build solutions for their associates, provided the right raw data is piped into their data systems? Does it have enough funds and business justification to use external data science consultants or data solutions? Even if the talent does exist within the department to begin its work from the raw data stage, another consideration will be whether that is the optimal use of time and money (a question we will visit later in the book). If the department hires external talent to develop code, then who owns the code?

Raw data is a useful deliverable if the Recoveries Department is already well staffed with a team that can perform data cleaning and quality checks, document the data elements, and make sure the data is fully prepared for the statistician's use.

One level of sophistication above this raw data deliverable are quality-checked, documented derived databases. Imagine that the Recoveries Department already has a talented staff that includes a traditional statistician, Sylvia. Sylvia is highly skilled at building strong predictive models when given a well-prepared data set. Her focus has always been on ensuring that the statistical properties of the data are well captured in the model and that the model makes accurate predictions. As reliable as she is in creating models, she is not used to working with dirty data. For her entire career, she has worked with data engineers, data analysts, and others who were skilled at all of the tasks needed to prepare data sets for modeling. In this project with Steve, Sylvia doesn't have this team to support her. As a result, Steve needs to make sure that the product developed by the data science team and delivered to Sylvia is not the raw data but rather the cleaned data set. It would include the information that was directly provided by the original sources, but it also could include derived data fields. Derived data fields can include more-complex terms such as an indicator of whether the customer did all of their transactions in less than a year or whether they called Shu Money Financial to ask how much more credit they could get.

One critical product that should be included in the development of this cleaned data set is a data dictionary. This data dictionary identifies for Sylvia the fields that are contained in the database as well as how each field is defined.[13] The format of the field may be numeric, categorical, text, date, or something else. Better data dictionaries will also include information about the source of the field, the acceptable ranges, and links to any references related to the field. The data dictionary is often a key starting point for those analyzing the data (some prefer to begin by chatting first with the database developers or others who have some experience with the database before touching the data). If the data-set delivery does not include a data dictionary, then, as the customer, Steve should insist on one being provided.

More-advanced data products are algorithms. Here Steve and his team would receive predictive models. These models could estimate the probability that the Recoveries Department will be able to contact the customer, the probability that the customer will pay any money, the expected amount that the customer will pay, the expected costs associated with collecting from this specific customer, and other useful modeled information that can support the recovery process. A different algorithm process might be developed to identify optimal ways to contact the customer by doing web scraping, searching public online records, licensing private databases, and exploring employer-based information. The output of this type of algorithm would be an enhanced set of contact information and mechanisms that the Recoveries Department could use to connect with the customer and attempt to recover money that was owed. The business unit would receive the output of these models and then develop its own data analytics, visualizations, and decision-making rules based on the outputs of these models as well as other, readily available information.

Moving along the data products pathway, Steve can consider decision support tools. These provide information that can help support business decisions regarding work prioritization, such as who is the most important to try to contact and what is the best way to try to contact them. The data science team is responsible for providing critical information to the business unit, but the actual business decisions themselves are left to people, not algorithms. Decisions about how to collect the data, develop new data fields, and create algorithms and about what data to display and how to display it will all influence the key business decisions. What should be displayed and how it should be displayed are data visualization decisions, ones that should involve the customer as well as the data science team.

The highest level of data product is an automated decision-making tool. Here all of the elements described in the decision support tools exist, but the algorithm is making the decision itself. Automatic recommendations for a movie on Netflix, a product on Amazon, and a song on Spotify are examples. In the realm of customer communications, think of chatbots that do their best to help solve customer problems. In the physical world, self-driving vehicles are a good example. In each automated decision situation described above, humans (currently) can choose to override the automatic decision by opting out of the chatbot, searching for their own movie interests, or manually driving the vehicle.

In Steve's application, the automated decision-making algorithm would identify the highest-priority recovery cases, the way those cases should be handled, and perhaps even the associate who should handle them. The entire work-prioritization process would be handled by the data product, while routine monitoring of performance by Steve and others would allow them to better understand how the process is performing and when adjustments should be considered.

KEY TOOLS

There are many important questions a customer can ask the data science team, including the following:

- Overall Project
  - o What are the business's priorities in terms of solutions?
  - o What are the business's key constraints?
  - o Does the business have institutional policies regarding data storage, programming languages, and software choices?
  - o What are the advantages and disadvantages of each tool option?
- Data Workflow
  - o What steps are you taking to handle data cleaning and preprocessing tasks?
  - o How do you handle data integration or merging from multiple sources?
  - o How do you handle missing or incomplete data?
  - o What tools and alerts have you implemented to monitor and maintain data pipelines?
  - o How do you handle updates or changes to the underlying data sources?
- Data Storage
  - o What are the advantages and disadvantages of our current data storage system?
  - o What other data storage options have you considered?
  - o How are data security and privacy concerns addressed in our current data storage solution?
  - o What techniques are being used for data backup and disaster recovery?

- Data Sources
  - o Is all the source data structured, or is it a mix of structured and unstructured data?
  - o Is there a list of the data sources that can be shared?
- Data Quality
  - o Is there an up-to-date data dictionary?
  - o What data quality checks are being implemented for specific data sources and fields?
  - o Would the data quality checking be improved by linking the data scientists with the subject-matter experts?
  - o What is the frequency of missing data for different data fields and sources?
  - o Is there a pattern to the missing data, or is it random?
  - o Are missing values allowed, or does there need to be some imputation method?
- Coding Languages and Repositories
  - o What coding repository is being used?
  - o Can the customer have access to the project repository?
  - o What coding languages are being used and why were those languages chosen?
- Data Products
  - o What is the level of data product that is appropriate for the business given its IT capacity and human resource skill set?
  - o Why is the specific data solution being proposed?

2

THE DATA SCIENCE PROJECT

KAMALA AND STARDUST HEALTH INSURANCE

Kamala was the pride and joy of her family. Her parents had moved from Bangalore to New Jersey when her mom was pregnant with her. As the eldest of three children, she was always the one to break new ground. She was named both "the top entrepreneur" and "the one most likely to be retired by age 40" by her high school class.

Kamala was the first in her family to go to college and, just a few years later, had finished her MD and MBA from Stanford. She settled into the Bay Area after graduation to work at a med-tech start-up. She figured they would IPO in less than 5 years. With her fortune, she could coax her parents into an early retirement so they could finally enjoy themselves instead of working night and day to pay for the other kids' education. But the start-up folded in less than a year.

With her degrees in hand and over a quarter of a million dollars of debt, she soon found herself looking for stable employment. At age 28, she joined Stardust Health Insurance, a medium-sized insurance company working primarily in California and Florida. Within 4 years, Kamala was promoted to become the director of clinical strategy and marketing. This position perfectly matched her passion for health care and her talent for growing businesses. Her position was considered to be one that would put her on the fast track to joining the C-suite. As long as Kamala could show some big wins, she would quickly move even higher up the corporate ladder.

Kamala was given a budget of a few million dollars to spend on a diverse set of projects as broad as her job title.

As her boss, Annie, told her on day one, "Your goal is to increase the profitability of Stardust Health Insurance by taking data-driven decisions on which drugs and procedures are the most cost effective. Given the choice among drugs that are commonly used to treat pneumonia, lung cancer, high blood pressure, or other medical conditions, Stardust needs to know which one is most likely to achieve better outcomes after accounting for the patient's demographics, other medications, medical history, and family medical history. If there is a difference in the expected outcomes of the drugs, we need to know the total expected treatment cost of each option. And if the drugs are expected to achieve the same outcomes, then we need to know which one is the least expensive."

Kamala nodded her head. "I understand completely. Sometimes the more cost-effective decision involves a drug that is more expensive but leads to better health outcomes as well as to less future health care resource utilization, such as reduced future outpatient visits, emergency room visits, or inpatient admissions. Other times the increased drug costs are not offset by reduced expenses or better health outcomes, so they are not worth the additional expenses. If my team finds data in support of one of the drugs, we will advise the medication formulary team at Stardust to add that to the list of generics and brand-name prescription drugs we cover. Also, we can incentivize the patient to use this more cost-effective drug by reducing the co-pay for the preferred drug."

Annie added, "Ultimately, the patient still has an option regarding which treatment they choose, but your team plays a very strong role in nudging the patient in one direction or another. Your job function includes the marketing title as well. You will lead promotional campaigns that build awareness of Stardust within the target population. I expect you to manage the negotiations with advertisers regarding the different media outlets, including billboards and TV, radio, and online advertising. Stardust has always pitched its campaign as 'the fair insurer,' so reaching populations who are traditionally underserved, such as immigrant and non-English-speaking communities, is a core value of the company."

"This means that when the data is analyzed, the demographics of the patients need to be strongly considered," interjected Kamala. "These populations in need will continue to receive good medical care."

"Yes, those populations need to receive good medical care at an affordable price, while our jobs require us to keep Stardust solidly in the black with strong profit growth," said Annie.

PROJECT MANAGEMENT

A key lesson that Kamala took from her med-tech start-up failure was the importance of project management. That business was pitched as delivering an end-to-end system for taking MRIs, reading the images via artificial intelligence algorithms, and delivering the results online, followed by chatbot-based customer support to answer patient questions. The main issue was that the product was never built. No functional prototypes were ever produced. Sure, they had some algorithms that could be coaxed into making accurate predictions on a specially selected set of images, but that wasn't going to get them a product that could work in the marketplace. Rather, it became an academic exercise led by the founder, a professor of data science, and a data science team whose members were too focused on seeing what cool things they could do rather than on delivering what they needed to produce to become profitable. One of the main reasons that this academic exercise never left academia was the lack of basic project management supervision. Since her arrival at Stardust, Kamala has insisted on aggressive project management for all projects, especially data science projects, which she feared could cost her money and time but yield few usable products. Her mantra for her team is "Measure twice, cut once," and her personality is such that she usually plans diligently by lining up the critical steps rather than trying to sprint into the wind.

In her first meeting with the data science team, she asked, "So which one of you is formally trained as a project manager?" The dead silence was eventually broken by someone coughing up, "I've managed a few projects before, and, well, most of them did OK." Kamala's confidence was deflating by the second, but she quickly rebounded. "I have some great project managers on my team. Phil has worked on many IT projects and is a pro at planning, organizing, staffing, and leading projects from concept to completion. He'll be working with you on a day-to-day basis, and we will do weekly check-ins. Of course, I am always checking emails and available for a quick call." Kamala understood that, as the project sponsor, she needed to stay informed of the progress and key decisions but didn't need to get into the day-to-day minutia, as Phil would take care of those details.

The second meeting featured Phil walking the team through the paces of his project management training with the precision that one expects from a military officer with 20 years' experience. Following Kamala's lead, he insisted that data science projects are just like any other projects, with four basic phases and milestones: concept, planning, implementation, and closeout (figure 2.1).[1] Other companies have their own standard sets of definitions for the different project phases. These may include more phases and have different names. The key is to ensure that the project team members agree on what

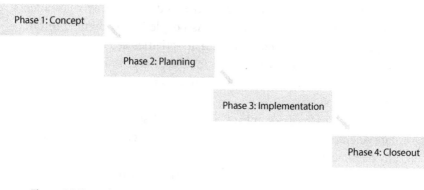

Figure 2.1 Four phases of project management

they will call the different phases of the project and what exactly those phases represent. Agreeing on definitions is critical, since a large percentage of the disagreements that people have about projects stem from simply working off of a different set of definitions.

Phil explained, "The concept phase refers specifically to defining the project requirements and its desired outcomes. This is necessary, since a project can never succeed if everyone involved—from the sponsor, Kamala, to the project manager to the data science team—doesn't agree on the project's requirements, goals, and scope." There was plenty of head nodding around the room, as everyone understood that if the project's scope and objectives continue to change, it will constantly be a moving target for everyone involved. Clearly, these questions had to be answered: What exact data product will be produced? How are the products expected to be used? How will success be measured? How will the utility of the deliverable be assessed? What are the constraints on human resources, time, cost, equipment, and other resources? What are the risks associated with the data product and this project? How can those risks be mitigated?

Kamala took over at this point. "The planning phase includes laying out many of the key activities for the project along with the resources required, risks identified, and risk mitigation steps needed. It also includes discussing what the final deliverables are, who will review those final deliverables, and what the timelines and budgets are for the work."

"Let's review the planned activities and then clarify roles and responsibilities," Phil announced. As people began chiming in on suggestions, Phil reminded them that activities are the tasks that need to be accomplished in order for the project to be completed. Sequencing refers to the fact that some activities have to happen before others.

"Here's a perfect example of sequencing," said David, the senior data scientist. "You have to first acquire data before you can begin any data-cleaning process."

"And, similarly, you need to clean the data before you begin doing any modeling work," added Kamala.

Different activities have different resource requirements in terms of budget, skill sets, equipment, and other resources. All of these resource requirements need to be reflected in the project budget. It is critical that the budget be agreed on between the customer and the project team. Often the customer doesn't have the budget for the perfect data solution, so some interim deliverables should be established that provide functionality within the resource constraints.

Phil then smiled as he said, "Now we get to my favorite part, the implementation phase. This step requires considering human resources, quality control, and risk management. In terms of human resources, job titles are often not very helpful. For the purposes of delivering a final product, it is critical to know exactly who is performing what tasks."

The activities for any project have specific skill requirements. These skill requirements determine the terms of reference you might want for recruiting people for the project, the qualities most critical in selecting candidates, and any additional training that the team might require. It is important not only to understand who does what but also to have backup plans. As a customer, it is perfectly acceptable to ask the question "What happens if she gets hit by a bus?" Or, a bit less graphically, "What is the contingency plan in case XYZ is unable for some reason or another to do the work?"

"Quality control is a critical aspect of project management," added David. "We need to establish quality standards and clearly communicate them to all involved in the project from developers to clients using the output."

Kamala saw that everything was coming together nicely. She reminded the team, "It is necessary to identify who will assess the data products against those quality standards and how. The developing team itself is often the most qualified to perform the quality tests, though the customer should explicitly be involved in discussing what the standards of quality are and how they will be tested."

Risk identification and management are critical to project success. Risk management includes an assessment of potential future risks along with an identification of how these risks can be quickly spotted and mitigated. Human resource risk is one of the first risks that most teams consider. Looking around the room, they assess whether the team has the appropriate skills to do the job and, if not, what should be done to address gaps. Steps needed to address gaps often include hiring other staff or consultants, providing training, and planning for unexpected departures.

Beyond these human resource risks are cost risks, where the project costs exceed the planned budget; schedule risks, where the activities take longer than planned; performance risks, where the data product doesn't produce results that meet the business needs; operational risks, where the implementation of the data product is not successful, resulting in poor outcomes; and legal risks, where the project violates specific regulatory requirements or legal restrictions. Other risks relate to governance, strategy, and external hazards and risks outside of the scope of the project team or company, such as natural disasters or changes in the regulatory framework or the competitive landscape. Risk assessment is often subject to human biases, so some consideration of the biases that are implicit in the assessments is useful.[2] For example, "Do we have data to support our risk assessment?" is a fair question, though it may result in some blank stares.

Phil liked to open up the discussion about risks by asking the simple question "What can go wrong with this project?" and developing a systematic list of categories of risk such as those mentioned above. For each risk, he would ask the team to guess the likelihood of the risk becoming a problem as well as the expected impact. For risks that are worth attending to, the team members would then develop mitigation strategies as well as ways of detecting whether those risks are becoming more likely.

The key take-home regarding project management of data science projects is that these are projects and should be treated similarly to how one would treat other important projects. The best practices of project management should be applied so as to reduce the chances of project failure and increase the chances that the data product will solve the customer's needs.

Phil drafted a project plan design document that listed the key activities, roles and responsibilities, task sequencing, risks, mitigation plans, and final product specifications. He then circulated the document to everyone involved in the project, and for the extracurious, he provided a link to the Project Management Institute so the team could learn more about formal project management methods.[3] Each person contributed their additional thoughts, and then they moved to a sign-off stage. After the sign-off by all involved in the project, the work began with everyone on board. The closeout phase involved everyone reviewing the project plan design that they had signed off on and agreeing that the project had been completed.

ROLES AND RESPONSIBILITIES

In Phil's kickoff meeting, he set the tone immediately by announcing "My role is to keep everything on track for delivering the product at the expected level of quality at or below the costs and timelines projected. I will focus on risk management and actively document the team's activities. This means I will be distributing meeting minutes as well as reaching out to team members to discuss issues you are struggling with or foresee in the future."

Kamala jumped into the discussion by stating that "we all know that job titles are not always very informative. We will need to dig below the surface of each of our backgrounds to understand how we fit and add value into this project."

From a human resources perspective, the project manager needs to understand the exact skill sets needed for the project at each stage. In the real world, job titles exist, so it is good to understand some of the common job titles and what they are generally supposed to reflect in terms of skills sets and common applications.

Phil, David, and Kamala started discussing the team and titles. David led off by stating "Let's start with the rarely discussed fact that the title of data scientist has no clear definition in terms of scope. This title is generally overused by recruiters and human resources departments, often with little attention paid to the necessary skills and experience."

Phil agreed. "It is best to focus on using much more specific titles and detailing the exact skills and experience required rather than creating a wish list that is not tied to the necessary tasks. There is a multitude of skills and tasks that can fall into the broad swath of activities referred to as data science, so we will focus on some of the main areas only."

David continued. "Data engineers are fundamental to any data science project. Simply put, if there is no data, then there is no project." Phil turned to Kamala to clarify: "Data engineers play the critical role of designing, building, and maintaining the data structures used. They create the data pipelines and storage solutions that are later used by the other members of the data science team. Their engagement is necessary to ensure that the data solutions will support the users and business needs while staying within the constraints of the organization's policies and standards."

Data errors that can be readily identified, such as format issues, range issues, and other impossible or illogical values, can be addressed at this stage before the data is stored within the organization's data systems. While the tools they use change rapidly, as of today, data engineers have expertise in cloud computing solutions as well as deep programming experience in SQL, Scala, Java, Python, and other languages, where SQL is specifically used for storing and organizing data. The title of data architect is often used synonymously with data engineer, as they both design and create new database systems to support the business's requirements.

Kamala added, "In my previous work, we had data analysts. They were the first line in the analytics process and played a major role in data preparation processes such as data cleaning."

David replied, "Yes, we have that role here as well. Data analytics can be viewed as a second round of quality checking to correct mistakes or errors in the data itself. Ideally, most of the data errors are detected and addressed in the data engineering steps before data analysts view the data. In addition to this function, they are often the main people involved in data wrangling, also called data munging. This is the process of exploring and developing ways to transform the data into formats that are more valuable for doing further analysis and modeling work."

"What are some examples of these common data transformations?" asked Kamala.

David explained, "Common data transformations include taking values that have very large ranges and using log transformations to map them to a space with a smaller range. For continuous variables, there are sometimes advantages to converting, creating, and using categorical variables. For example, consider the patient's age. While it could be measured in days or years, often it is more useful to use age groupings such as 5-year increments. In that case, the data analysts might identify which new variables should be created and then add those to the database for future use. In addition to this data preparation, data analysts' work includes doing basic querying of the data, retrieving data for specific questions, and preparing output used for reporting. Their work is often displayed using business intelligence tools and data visualization tools such as Tableau and Power BI or, more simply, using spreadsheets."

Kamala asked, "What about specialized roles like data visualization specialist or data storyteller?"

David smiled as he replied, "There is often little distinction between the role of a data analyst and that of a data visualization specialist or data storyteller. They all use data as inputs to communicate results, often to a nontechnical audience. They are the link between the data science team and you, Kamala, or perhaps they produce the key communications content that you use to explain the project's value and the utility of its deliverables to the board and senior management like Annie. Ideally, this work goes beyond the charts, tables, and graphs to develop a narrative that can support effective storytelling."

David finished off by providing some more details on other titles, including machine learning scientist, natural language processing (NLP) expert, and statistician. He explained that machine learning scientists focus on creating and using the newest technology and innovative approaches. They can be engaged in developing and applying new algorithms and data manipulation approaches. Because their work sits at the cutting edge of research and application, they often work in research and development departments. Some of their work may be published in research papers. They actively read and engage with the data science community to understand new innovations through user groups, scientific journals, and conferences. In some companies, this position may have a title such as research scientist or research engineer.

Many companies use the data scientist title to refer specifically to those who are engaged in designing, building, and implementing machine learning models. These individuals are experienced in the main programming languages and routinely do tasks such as feature engineering (creating new variables from available data), feature selection (selecting input variables that are the most informative for the task), and dimensionality reduction (removing variables that are not useful for the task or creating compact projections of the data that can be readily used).

Some of these data scientists have a particular specialty, such as network analysis, computer vision, NLP, or spatial data, while others are more generalists. The network analysis specialist focuses on technologies used to analyze the structure of networks to determine, for example, how different customers are connected to each other or to different health care providers. The computer vision specialist could focus on using algorithms to automatically detect cancers or other medical conditions in an image. The NLP expert looks at ways to automatically extract usable clinical information from free-form text fields—for example, by converting clinical notes into clinical codes for diagnoses, procedures, and drugs. They can also be involved in translating texts to other languages and in using text-to-speech conversion processes, where the recorded audio files of a doctor's notes could be converted into written text from which usable clinical information could be extracted. Today the task of NLP has become vastly simpler by the release of large language models like GPT, BLOOM and LaMDA. Relatively simple programs leveraging these large language models can perform many of the tasks that previously required deep NLP experience. The spatial data scientist leverages GPS and other location data to create systems used for site selection (the best place for a new store), navigation (the best route to take), and other geospatial-specific tasks.

Some "old school" titles that may appear in your data science team and still are used in the corporate world include mathematician and statistician. Mathematicians often have degrees in operations research or applied mathematics and tend to focus on optimization problems. Statisticians would have experience in theoretical and applied statistics. They would have a deep understanding of how to apply specific statistical tests or models and to quantify uncertainty, for example using confidence intervals. The statistical tools and tests will need to be well matched to the specific problem and data set. Before implementing the statistical test, the statistician should verify that the key assumptions in the statistical test are valid. The medical field and health care industry tend to employ many statisticians, since their work is often scrutinized by governments and scientific committees.

The list of typical data scientist job titles above is meant to be only a rough guide, since often titles don't reflect the actual job function as well as the experience and skill sets required. A key step in the project management of a data science project is to identify what skills are needed at different phases of the project. When exactly will we need data engineers and for how long? In what specific areas of machine learning do we need expertise? Do we need someone with experience in NLP or geospatial data?

This listing of the skill sets required for the project and when they are required needs to be mapped against the actual available resources. In areas where there are skills gaps, a decision needs to be made regarding where to source those resources. Internal transfers can be a short-term option, though in many cases staff are already well utilized in their current roles and have little availability. When they can't find additional resources internally, the project manager needs to look externally. External sourcing can involve either internal human resources or headhunters to identify both short-term consultants to work on a project or a time-and-materials basis and new employees if the need is expected to be permanent.

PRIORITIZING PROJECTS

Kamala is lucky enough to have a solid team supporting her as she develops projects to support both clinical strategy and marketing. With a long list of possible projects, she will need to prioritize. Her team doesn't have the resources to work on every project at once, nor would it make sense, since some projects are more appropriate to complete sooner rather than later.

To begin the prioritization process, Kamala has asked Phil to be her brainstorming partner. They recognize that the project prioritization process generally tries to get a sense for a return on investment for the different projects. Because of data limitations, they don't have the detailed input to estimate the expected benefits and costs in terms of human resources, time, and other expenses.

As a way to begin the process, they have listed the problems they are trying to solve as well as any known opportunities. For each of the opportunities, they want to get some understanding of how advanced Stardust Health Insurance is in this area. For example, have there been other data-related projects in this area before? What were the results of those previous projects? From a benefits point of view, they want to understand exactly how each project will benefit the customers and the company. Will it increase sales or reduce customer attrition? Will it increase revenue or reduce operating expenses? It is helpful to understand whether the solution is readily testable so they can see if the solution is driving value before doing a large-scale rollout. The problem or opportunity can be rated with respect to the different considerations to get a qualitative sense for its relative importance. It is important to try to quantify the impact itself, even if this is done mostly through guesswork along with some sensitivity analysis. The sensitivity analysis could probe what the corresponding change in the benefits to the company will be if the impact turns out to be 50 percent less than expected or 50 percent more than expected. Factors that go into this estimate of the benefits for a problem or opportunity that relates directly to the customer include the volume of customers impacted, the impact per customer, and the frequency of the issue that is being addressed.

In some cases, the project can be classified as *mission critical*. For those small sets of projects, success on the project is necessary for the company to be successful. In other situations, an industry average solution or an off-the-shelf solution might be sufficient where the area involved is not considered a competitive advantage.

Many within Stardust Health Insurance have adopted the objective and key results (OKR) framework for project management.[4] This framework requires the team to define an objective, which is a significant, clearly defined goal that can be readily measured. The key results are used to track the achievement of the objective. These key results should be SMART: Specific, Measurable, Assignable (state who will accomplish the goal), Relevant, and Time-related.[5] This isn't the only formulation of this acronym; you may see examples where the *A* stands for Achievable or Attainable and the *T* stands for Time-bound.

The data should be explored to understand the current status of the in-house data as well as to identify external data sources that could be useful for the project. For each possible data source, it is necessary to understand information such as the data availability, the data limitations, the time required to acquire the data, and the costs for both initial data acquisition and ongoing data use. Even data that is publicly available for free, such as that on government websites, may still involve some costs related to the staff time needed to acquire the data, do any necessary cleaning, and monitor the data source, as changes can often be made to variable names, formats, and other quality control processes.

For the data itself, an assessment should be made regarding its potential utility. Is the level of resolution appropriate for your needs? Do you need geographic information accurate to the street block, but the data provides information only by zip code? Do you need age information accurate to the year, but the data is provided only in 5-year age groupings?

Is the sample size sufficient for your purposes? If you already know that a model like the one you want to develop requires thousands of different observations, then a database of only a few hundred is going to be insufficient. In Kamala's world, she has access to the health care records of Stardust Health Insurance customers, which gives her some limited information about tens of thousands of patients. She also can leverage a very rich clinical trial data set that has many more useful data fields for modeling, and while the data is nearly 100 percent complete, there are fewer than five hundred patients in the database. Along with the question of the volume of data comes the question of sampling. How representative is this data set of the population of interest? Does it overweight certain parts of the population? If so, are weightings provided (or can they be computed) so you can obtain more accurate estimates by weighting the population in the database when doing the analysis?

The data quality should be understood. What mechanisms are in place to ensure that the data you acquire is accurate? What quality control measures have already been performed? Also, how recent is the data? Some databases are updated on a daily basis, while others may be updated quarterly, annually, or even less frequently.

The incremental value of a new data set is also critical to understand. Are there fields that you don't already have access to that make this database particularly valuable? Is this database standard in your field already, or is there something special or unique about it that others haven't identified yet? If leveraging this data set will become a unique asset for Stardust Health Insurance, then how can this competitive advantage be maintained when others discover the potential use of this data?

Businesses need to be able to have flexibility in their planning. As such, any project should also include some consideration of what the alternatives are if the project turns out to be unsuccessful or later becomes far more costly than originally anticipated. Can the data sources, models, and other elements be easily migrated to other systems?

Feasibility is a key consideration in any project prioritization. Can the project be delivered with the expected quality in the expected time? Some projects are considered low risk. They involve using data, methods, and software that are well established and have degrees of feasibility. Others are risky. Perhaps there is risk associated with a new data source or new software. Perhaps there is personnel risk as staff are tasked with developing and utilizing new skills.

On the costs side of the equation, it is important to understand what the project will cost in terms of both initial and ongoing costs. For the data itself, what are the costs of acquisition, including not just the licensing fees but also the human resources costs and other expenses, such as supplies and equipment? Accessing the data itself can become its own miniproject, so it is important to understand the process, time, and costs to obtain the data and get it in a format that can be readily analyzed. Time associated with data acquisition and preprocessing needs to be accounted for in the costs of the project and may become an ongoing expense that lasts for years to come.

One area where Phil reached out to brainstorm with Kamala related to the critical question of whether to buy software or build in-house solutions.

As Phil stated, "The buy-or-build question can be reduced to another cost-benefit analysis where the two scenarios are compared. For example, consider the decision of whether to purchase automated machine learning (AutoML) software. This software is meant to help facilitate the process of data merging, data cleaning, model development, model deployment, and model performance monitoring. The costs of licensing the software can be readily estimated by the software vendor. The benefits are likely to be more difficult to quantify."

Kamala responded, "Some of these benefits could include reducing the time for data quality checking, possibly obtaining higher-quality models, developing models more quickly, and monitoring models automatically."

"Fully agree," said Phil. "What I am struggling with is quantifying the part of the cost-benefit analysis that involves the potential for human resources savings where the software is more efficient at model development (so less data scientist time is required for model development) and can be effectively leveraged by less technically advanced personnel."

Kamala's suggestion was simple. "Let's assume in the cost-benefit analysis that future staff costs would be reduced by the use of AutoML due to both efficiency and less need for more advanced, and expensive, data science talent. But also do a sensitivity analysis that doesn't include this assumption, just in case it doesn't bear fruit. By the way, any concerns from your end on whether we will feel less confident in the output of AutoML programs, since we will be using a black box to produce answers?"

"No concerns. The AutoML software isn't a black box. It gives us details on the variables that are important, the factors that drive individual decisions, the reason a specific model was chosen, and many other pieces of information we have trouble getting from our programmers."

With that guidance, Phil developed a few rough cost-benefit analysis estimates for the AutoML software. The sensitivity analysis showed that purchasing the software was not necessarily a major win for the organization, so they decided to stick with their current Python and R programming approach.

MEASURING SUCCESS

In one of the classic jokes in project management, the final step is said to be "celebrations, bonuses, and promotions for the nonparticipants." While this is hopefully just a joke, it is true that one of the final steps is measuring success. Did the project fulfill its expectations in terms of time, money, and performance? Measuring the quantitative impact of a program on an outcome or of a new model requires careful design of the model rollout. Here we will focus on the more basic aspects of measuring a project's success and pick up the discussion about how to measure the impact of a model later in the book.

The sign-off agreement that Phil developed provides a basis for measuring success. As you recall, the different people and groups involved in the project signed off on the project's key activities, roles and responsibilities, task sequencing, risks, mitigation plans, and final product specifications.

There are many ways to measure success, but a simple way is to evaluate the five key dimensions shown in figure 2.2: schedule,

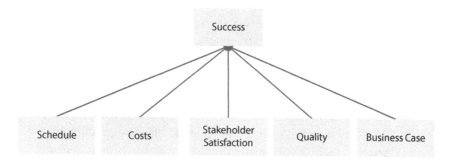

Figure 2.2 Five dimensions of measuring success in data projects

costs, stakeholder satisfaction, quality, and the business case itself.[6] Most of these ideas are self-explanatory. For example, measuring success with respect to the schedule or costs asks whether the project was delivered within the timeline or the costs that were planned, respectively.

Stakeholder satisfaction is a bit more nebulous, since we need to define who exactly are stakeholders. While stakeholders technically include anyone who has an interest (or stake) in the project's success, not all stakeholders are created equal. The broad set of stakeholders can include the project team itself, the project manager, the senior management supervising the project, the senior management sponsoring the project (whose budget is supporting the project), and the customers who are the direct users of the product. Other stakeholders can be identified both internally and externally, including governments, vendors, sellers, contractors (and subcontractors), the company's customers, and even potentially society itself. This is a very long list, but in most cases, the most critical stakeholders are readily identified. In a corporate environment, they will tend to be the senior managers who are involved in the project and who are responsible for the budget used in the project.

Quality can often be quantified. If you are developing a new piece of software to replace a previous one, then there are previous performance standards. How much better is the new project than the previous standard? How does the performance compare with the expected performance? How does it compare with the assumptions in the business case?

Perception in measuring success is sometimes removed from reality. A project that met all the agreed-on expectations in terms of time, cost, and quality may be viewed as a failure by the key stakeholders if the project goals change. For example, if the project originally was supposed to deliver a model with an accuracy of at least 95 percent, then an on-time, on-budget project with an accuracy of 96 percent should be deemed a success. But perhaps while the project team members were working on their deliverable, a new model with an accuracy of 98 percent was released by another group within the company or by a vendor. While the project delivered everything it was supposed to achieve, it may still be viewed as a failure by many because the expected standard for quality has changed. Keeping the management team informed of the project's status in terms of the time and cost as well as the expected product standards can help manage expectations. Also, if expectations change, as in the example of a higher standard being established midway through the project, then the timelines, costs, and other project aspects should be reestablished.

Another way to think about success is through the balanced scorecard approach.[7] This approach looks at the project from different perspectives: the customer perspective, internal perspective, innovation and learning perspective, and financial perspective: From the customer perspective, it asks "How do customers see us?" while from the internal perspective, it asks "What must we excel at?" From the innovation and learning perspective, it asks "Can we continue to improve and create value?" while from the financial perspective, it asks "How do we look to shareholders?" This balanced scorecard approach focuses on just a few measures and is popular in many business applications, since it requires the performer to think carefully about what is most important.

As Kamala seeks to achieve success in her work, she needs to ensure that her team does a thorough job not just on the technical aspects of data modeling but also on the critical aspects related to project prioritization and project management. After all, data science projects should be considered as one specific example of a project where all of the best practices of project management should be applied.

KEY TOOLS

Phases of Project Management:

1. Concept
2. Planning
3. Implementation
4. Closeout

Common Skills Associated with Data Scientists, Divided Into Technical Skills and Softer Skills:

TECHNICAL SKILLS

- Math and Statistics
- Data Manipulation, Including Data Wrangling and Feature Engineering
- Analytics and Modeling
- Machine Learning Methods
- Experimentation
- Programming (SQL, Python, R, Java JavaScript, Scala, Julia, C/C++)
- Data Visualization (Tableau)
- Software Engineering
- Version Control (Github, Bitbucket)

SOFTER SKILLS (NOT SPECIFIC TO DATA SCIENCE)

- Intellectual Curiosity
- Communication Skills
- Business Acumen
- Collaboration

Project Prioritization Questions:

COST-BENEFIT ANALYSIS

- Do you have sufficient information to develop a cost-benefit analysis?
- What information is missing, and can it be obtained or estimated?
- What sensitivity analysis can be performed?

PROJECT PURPOSE

- Is it considered mission critical by the company?
- Have there been other data-related projects in this area before?
- What were the results of those previous projects?
- How will this project benefit the customers and the company?
- Will it increase sales or reduce customer attrition?
- Will it increase revenue or reduce operating expenses?

DATA SOURCES

- What are the expected acquisition and ongoing costs?
- What are the limitations on availability?
- Is the level of resolution appropriate?
- Is the sample size sufficient?
- How representative is this data set of the population of interest?
- Are weightings provided to adjust for populations that are overweighted or underweighted?
- What mechanisms are in place to ensure that the data you acquire is accurate?
- What quality control measures have already been performed?
- How recent is the data?
- Are there fields that you don't already have access to that make this database particularly valuable?
- Is this database standard in your field already, or is there something special or unique about it that others haven't identified yet?
- Can the data sources, models, and other elements be easily migrated to other systems?

- Can the project deliver the expected results in the expected timeline?
- What are the risks involved in the project?
- How can these risks be mitigated?
- Are there new data sources, new software, or new skills required from human resources that add uncertainty to the project's chance of success?

Measuring Success Dimensions:

1. Schedule: Did the project get completed within the expected timeline?
2. Costs: Was the project's actual spend in line with the expected spend?
3. Stakeholder Satisfaction: How are the stakeholders in the project feeling about the project deliverables? Did it meet their signed-off expectations?
4. Quality: Did the project's deliverables meet the quality standards, whether measured by the modeling performance, the improvement over current processes, or some other benchmark?
5. Business Case: How did the benefits of the delivered project compare with the expected benefits as established in the cost-benefit analysis developed as part of the project planning?

Project Implementation Questions:

- What are the phases of the project called in your company?
- What are the milestones (deliverables) and timelines associated with your project?
- What happens if an important member of the project team gets hit by a bus? Or, a bit less graphically, what is the contingency plan in case XYZ is unable for some reason or another to do the work?"
- What are the standards of quality, and how will they be tested?
- What can go wrong with this project?

3

DATA SCIENCE FOUNDATIONS

Kamala's MD gave her a valuable clinical background that helps her understand the importance of effective medical care—that is, which drugs and procedures have positive impacts on the patient's outcomes and which have little or no value. But her current job at Stardust Health Insurance requires her to think about not only effective medical care but also cost-effective medical care. Care that is cost effective produces desirable outcomes at a reasonable cost. After all, Stardust is a business—it has to be profitable to support its mission of providing affordable access to high-quality health care. As head of clinical strategy, Kamala's goal is to ensure that the company's patients receive the most cost-effective care possible.

A big part of Kamala's job is understanding the patient population her company serves. This includes everything from patients' age and gender distributions to their most common conditions and medications. She uses this information about the patient population to make decisions about what partnerships to pursue, what services and products to provide, and what areas to invest in.

The company's biggest source of expenditure is health care reimbursement. When patients receive health care that is covered under their insurance plan, Stardust Health Insurance will reimburse the health care provider for all or part of that care. The company recently determined that 80 percent of its reimbursements went to care for just 20 percent of its patients. These patients represent the most costly clients, and many of them are unprofitable from Stardust's point of view. Kamala's assignment is to understand who these patients are to see if there are opportunities to improve the cost effectiveness of their care. This 80/20 rule is not so unusual. Often called the Pareto principle, named after economist Vilfredo Pareto, this type of relationship occurs in many areas of data, where it may appear as an 80/5 rule or 95/1 rule or some other ratio where the vast majority of results come from only a small percentage of the causes.[1]

Tasked with a large, abstract project, Kamala starts by breaking down the problem into smaller pieces. Her goal is to understand who is contributing the most to reimbursement costs. From prior internal research, she knows that patients who undergo inpatient surgery tend to be a particularly expensive group to manage. This is not only because surgery can be expensive but also because the hospitalization as well as the follow-up care for surgery can be particularly costly. While some surgeries demand less oversight, others require longer postoperative hospitalizations, discharge planning, physical therapy, home nursing, and follow-up appointments, all of which can impact cost effectiveness.

She decides to focus her analysis on patients who have received surgery. If she can figure out what aspects of postsurgical care are most expensive, she may be able to identify ways for providers to deliver more cost-effective care.

With a goal and a target population in mind, Kamala sets up a meeting with the data science team to scope out a plan for her project. In the rest of this chapter, we will look at how Kamala interacts with the data science team, focusing on what types of results the data science team produces and how Kamala interprets and acts on those results.

EXPLORATION

As someone who doesn't usually use the company's claims database, Kamala needs to better understand the data set. A good first step in understanding data is an exploratory data analysis. Such an analysis will generate key insights into the data set, such as its limitations, summary statistics, and relationships between variables. All of these features will yield greater insight into what data is available to answer the question "Who are the most costly patients, and what is driving their costs?"

Data Scope

Maya, a junior data scientist who reports to the team lead, David, provides an overview of the claims database that the team used for the exploratory analysis.

"The database we used includes claims made by all covered patients from 2015 to 2023. Note that clients below age 18 at the time of the claim are not included in the data set due to privacy concerns. If we want data on pediatric patients, we'll have to use another data source. We can be pretty confident that the data set is comprehensive and accurate, since the data is collected automatically whenever a claim is made. One important caveat is that the database does not include claims for dependents for certain employers whose contracts stipulate that data on dependents must be stored in a high-security data lake. For these folks, we need to tap into a separate database if we want to look at their claims."

There are a few key points from the data exploration that help Kamala frame her analysis:

- *The time period of the data.* The data set covers claims from 2015 to 2023, but Kamala is mainly interested in claims patterns from 2017 to 2023 because Stardust made some major changes to reimbursement rates in 2016. Data before that policy change is less relevant.
- *Data inclusion criteria.* Since the data set contains only claimants who are 18 or older, Kamala may have to access different data sources to understand cost patterns in child claimants.
- *Missing data.* It's important to know that the database doesn't include claims for certain dependents. Kamala asks the data science team to

investigate how many claimants this omission would impact and the total reimbursement for those claimants to determine whether it is worth the effort to get access to the high-security data lake.

Next Maya provides an overview of the types of data available in the database. "The main table in this data set is called the *procedures table*. Each row in the table represents a unique procedure that a patient underwent. Each patient is represented by a series of letters and numbers that acts as a unique identifier. If we need to identify a certain patient, we have a separate table where we can look up their name, date of birth, social security number, address, and employer information based on their unique identifier. This process of dei-dentification is used to secure the patient's personal information and is common across many industries.[2] As for the other data in the procedures table, we have the procedure and diagnosis codes associated with the procedure (these are codes used throughout the industry to facilitate analysis and billing), the date of the claim, the date of the patient encounter, a unique identifier for the provider organization, and the reimbursement amount."

Data Limitations

"We also found some data quality issues that you should be aware of," Maya points out. "The 'Date of patient encounter' field is empty 17 percent of the time. For these cases, we assumed the date of the encounter was the date of the claim."

Kamala interrupts. "A missing patient encounter date is not uncommon, since many services are reimbursed without a patient encounter. For example, some patients have a health plan that reimburses gym visits. For those folks, a claim is triggered 3 months after they buy their gym membership, and it wouldn't have an associated patient encounter, since they're not interfacing with their health care provider. The reason we wait 3 months before we trigger the claim is that many folks cancel their gym membership within the first month. So if we want to know when they activated their gym membership, we'd have to go back 3 months from the date of the claim. Similarly, we delay the claim date by several weeks or months for all subscription services or nonmedical purchases that we reimburse, like yoga classes, wellness apps, and online vitamin purchases. In these cases, it probably doesn't make sense to impute the claim date to the patient encounter date."

One common approach to dealing with missing data is called imputation.[3] Imputation means replacing a missing value with a nonmissing value. In this case, the data science team chose to replace all missing values in the "Date of patient encounter" field with the values in the "Date of claim" field. Upon first glance, this seems like a reasonable assumption. If the date of the patient encounter isn't captured, it makes sense to use the date of the claim as a proxy, since the date of the claim is probably close in time to the date of the patient encounter.

But every data set has its own nuances. Although Kamala is not a data scientist, she is the domain expert when it comes to this particular data set. She knows the details of her company's health plans, and she may be able to understand some of the apparent data gaps that are observed in the data set. In this case, she correctly pointed out a flaw in the imputation approach.

Maya continues. "We're also seeing that some clients switched employers during the course of their coverage. And for about 13 percent of clients, the 'Employer' field seems to be missing—we excluded these folks from the data set."

This is another common approach for dealing with missing data: exclusion, or removal of records with a missing value.[4] Let's see what Kamala thinks of this approach.

"Hold on. Why are we excluding these folks?"

Maya explains, "We assumed that folks with an empty 'Employer' field may not have filled out all their documentation and would therefore have less available or accurate data. So we decided to exclude them to improve the overall quality of the data set."

Kamala interrupted. "I see a major issue with that approach. It's possible that someone doesn't have an employer listed because they are unemployed, self-employed, or retired. These are all patients that we are interested in understanding! Instead of excluding these folks, let's figure out who is unemployed, self-employed, or retired. We can figure out who is retired based on their health plan: retirees qualify for our Medicare Advantage plans. Is there a way we can track down who is unemployed or self-employed?"

"Yes, we do capture that data when new patients fill out their intake form. That data is stored in a separate table that we can use for this analysis," Maya answers.

Excluding and imputing missing data require careful consideration and a nuanced understanding of the data. An inappropriate approach could lead to a lot of data issues down the road. Imagine what would have happened if the data science team had accidentally excluded all Medicare Advantage patients because they had a missing employer field! Luckily, Kamala recognized that the team's approach to imputation and exclusion was problematic. With her suggestions, the data science team can course correct for the next iteration of analysis.

In this brief intro to the data science team's analysis, Maya has given an overview of the data scope, including what type of data is available, how it is collected, what limitations the data set has, and what considerations will be important for analyses.

After hearing about what data is available, Kamala thinks about what questions she can answer using this data. Her main question is "Are there certain clients that contribute disproportionately to costs, and if so, who are these clients?" She also wants to know what the demographics and clinical characteristics are that make these high-cost patients different from the lower-cost patients in the database. It seems like Kamala's question can be answered using this data set, since it captures all claims from nearly all clients.

There are also a number of other questions that could be answered using this data. For example, she could use this data set to find the average number of claims per claimant over time. She could also look at whether patients from certain employers or regions file more claims than others. Are certain times of year associated with more claims? What diagnosis and procedure codes are most costly for her company? These are all questions that she can answer with this data set.

Importantly, Kamala realizes that she *cannot* use this data set to answer certain questions. For example, she wouldn't be able to look at whether patients with a family history of chronic illness incur higher costs because there is no data on family history captured.

After hearing about the scope of the data set from the data science team, Kamala has a better understanding of how this data set can be used to answer the question she's interested in.

Summary Statistics

Now that they've reviewed the scope and limitations of the data, the data science team members dive into their key results from the exploratory data analysis.

Maya begins. "We saw that the total number of patients in our network has been increasing over time. The total number of claimants in 2018 was 1,003,123, and in 2019, this number was 1,014,239. We also saw a drastic increase in the average number of claims per claimant: this increased by 20 percent from 2018 to 2019. Digging into this result a bit more, we found that in 2018, the number of claims per claimant ranged from 0 to 368. In 2019, this number ranged from 0 to 199,093. We also saw an increase in the average age of claimants from 46 to 50 from 2018 to 2019. Lastly, we looked at the relationship between the age of claimants and the number of claims they filed. We made a scatterplot of these two variables that shows a positive slope."

There are typical ways results from exploratory data analyses are reported. One key feature is reporting a measure of central tendency, like an *average* or *mean*. Other measures of central tendency include *median* and *mode*.[5] These metrics boil down large amounts of data into a single number. With over 1 million claimants, it's useful to understand general patterns in a few simple numbers. For Kamala, it's useful to know that the average age of all 1 million claimants was 46 in 2018 and that this average increased to 50 in 2019. This shows that the claimant population got older on average.

There are times when using an average can be misleading and when a measure like a median is more appropriate for understanding the overall makeup of a set of numbers.[6] Consider a group of ten people for whom the average net worth is about $10 million. The high average makes you think that this is a group of extremely wealthy individuals! In reality, nine of the people have net worths of $100,000, and only one of them has a net worth of $100 million. The one megamillionaire inflated the average of the entire group. In this case, the average does not represent the overall population well. This example illustrates a limitation of averages: they are sensitive to extreme values (like the net worth of the megamillionaire). A more appropriate measure of central tendency for this example would be the median, or the middle value when all the data points are sorted from lowest to highest. In this case, the median is $100,000, which represents the overall population much more realistically.

How do you know whether the mean or the median is more appropriate? One simple way is to calculate both and see if they are different. If the mean and median are substantially different, it may mean that the distribution of the variable is not symmetric or that there are outliers. It can also be useful to think about whether the variable of interest is likely to have extreme values or "long tails." For a variable like age, where the natural range of the variable is restricted from 0 to approximately 120, the mean may often be an adequate measure of central tendency. For a variable like annual income, the vast majority of people will have a value less than $200,000, but there will be a long tail of individuals whose incomes range from $200,000 to upwards of $50 million. Even though the people in this long tail are the minority, they will skew the average in the positive direction.[7]

Another approach is to plot the distribution of the data (in a histogram or a boxplot, for example) and see if it is symmetric. A bell curve is an example of a symmetric distribution. In symmetric distributions, the mean and median are usually pretty close to each other (figure 3.1). In asymmetric distributions, the median is a better choice, since the mean can be influenced by the extreme values.[8]

While measures of central tendency are often useful, they can be dangerous because they mask variation.[9] For example, Kamala sees that the average age of claimants in 2018 was 46, but it would be a mistake to assume that most claimants are around age 46. It could

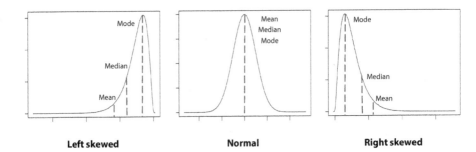

Figure 3.1 Comparison of the mean, median, and mode for normal, left-skewed, and right-skewed data distributions. In normally distributed data, the mean, median and mode are equal. In right skewed distributions, the mode is less than the median which is less than the mean. In left skewed distributions, the mode is greater than the median, which is greater than the mean. In skewed distributions, the mean is pulled towards the tail

be that half of all claimants are 26 and half are 66; in this extreme case, the average age of claimants would be 46 even though none of the claimants was actually 46! This example (albeit extreme) shows that understanding variation is just as important as understanding measures of central tendency. It's like the joke about the person who has one leg in an ice bath and the other in scalding hot water and who says, "The average temperature is very comfortable."

Some typical measures of variation include range, percentiles, interquartile range, standard deviation, confidence intervals, and variance.[10] Each of these measures (figure 3.2) is useful in different scenarios. The range is the difference between the minimum and the maximum observed values. It can be useful in identifying outliers and errors in data entry. For example, Kamala notices that the range of claims per claimant goes almost as high as 200,000 in 2018. That's over 500 claims per day! She flags that unrealistic result for the data science team to investigate.

Percentiles are a great way to understand variation. The nth percentile value means that n percent of all data points have a value less than or equal to that value.[11] For example, if the 50th percentile for claims per claimant is 20, that means 50 percent of claimants have less than or equal to 20 claims per year. The 0th percentile is the same

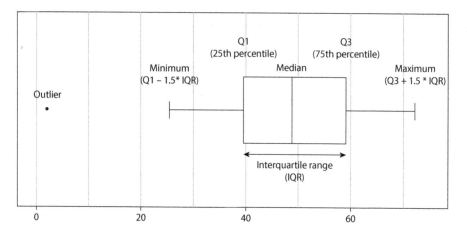

Figure 3.2 Components of a boxplot

as the minimum, the 50th percentile is the same as the median, and the 100th percentile is the same as the maximum. Another related measure of spread is the interquartile range, which is the difference between the 75th and 25th percentiles. This corresponds to the "middle half" of a data set. The interquartile range can be more helpful than the range (minimum to maximum), since the interquartile range typically excludes outliers at both ends of the distribution.[12]

Kamala explains to the data science team, "The range of 0 to almost 200,000 claims in 2019 makes me think that the upper values are outliers—maybe there was some issue in how the claims were being recorded that is making this number so unrealistically high. Do we know the interquartile range for the number of claims per person? That may give us a better sense of the data, since it would minimize the impact of outliers."

Luckily, one of the data analysts has their computer on hand, ready to field on-the-fly questions from Kamala. The analyst calculates the interquartile range for the number of claims per person for both 2018 and 2019 and recalculated the range and average number of claims for both years after excluding the outliers. "This makes a lot more sense." The analyst goes on to explain, "In 2018, the interquartile range was 3 to 123, and in 2019, it was 5 to 148."

In this case, the outlier was due to data quality issues: there must have been something wrong with the data entry because it's impossible to have that many claims. However, there may be situations where outliers arise legitimately, not owing to issues with data integrity. We saw this in our discussion of wealth, where a high-net-worth individual may have wealth that is many orders of magnitude greater than that of most of the population. This is an example of an outlier that cannot be attributed to data quality issues.

Quantifying Relationships Between Two Variables

A key step in any exploratory data analysis is to examine the association between the variables. They may be correlated due to some causal relationship where changes in one variable drive changes in another or due to some other explanatory factor. Kamala asked the data science team to examine the relationship between the claimant's age and the number of claims filed. David immediately responds, "It has a correlation of 0.4, which we would call a moderately positive relationship, so the average number of claims increases with increasing claimant age."

David has just reported the correlation coefficient, a number between −1 and 1 that quantifies the relationship between two continuous variables.[13] A continuous variable is a quantity that can take on many possible values across a continuum.[14] Money, time, age, height, and weight are all examples of continuous variables. Continuous variables can typically be measured with high precision. For example, money can be measured in dollars and cents, time can be measured in days or hours or seconds, and height can be measured in feet or inches or fractions of inches. Categorical variables, on the other hand, are variables that can take on only a few values.[15] For example, a patient's race would be a categorical variable because there is a finite number of values that a patient's race can be.

A correlation coefficient of 1 or −1 indicates a perfect positive or negative relationship, respectively. For example, your age has a perfect positive correlation with the date. As the date increases by one unit (1 day), your age increases by an equal unit (about 1/365 of a year). Another way of putting this is that given the date, we can precisely determine your age. An example of a moderate correlation (-0.4 to -0.7 or 0.4 to 0.7) is the relationship between height and weight. In general, taller people are heavier, but this is not always the case. If we were to plot the relationship between height and weight for everyone in the United States, the points would have a positive slope to them, but it would be a messy scatterplot, not a clean line. Something with a weak correlation (-0.2 to 0.2) may be the relationship between the number of steps you take in a day and the number of minutes you spend listening to music in a day. If we plotted these two quantities, we would expect to see a random cloud of points that do not show any clear linear pattern. Situations where there are only weak correlations can still be useful. For example, using variables that are only weakly correlated still allows the data science team to develop predictive models that will do better than random guesses.[16]

It's important to keep in mind that the most popular correlation coefficient, called a Pearson correlation coefficient, assumes linear relationships, while there are other types of correlations—such as the Spearman coefficient, which looks at the rank order of values—that are more robust to other relationships.[17] Calculating a correlation coefficient is similar to fitting a line to a scatterplot (figure 3.3). For some scatterplots, a line cannot be easily fit, and for these types of plots, calculating a correlation coefficient may be misleading.[18] For example, the relationship between the amount of carbohydrates eaten and overall health may not be linear—it may look more like an upside-down U. If you eat very few carbohydrates, you may not be getting enough energy, and your health outcomes may be negatively impacted. Similarly, if you eat too many carbohydrates, you may develop insulin resistance and associated metabolic conditions like diabetes. In between the two extremes is the "Goldilocks zone" of carbohydrate consumption that maximizes health. Let's assume that these two variables, carb consumption and overall health, have a strong upside-down-U relationship (also known as a quadratic relationship). If we were to calculate a correlation coefficient for these two quantities, we may get a coefficient of 0.1. The key is that this indicates a weak *linear* relationship, not necessarily

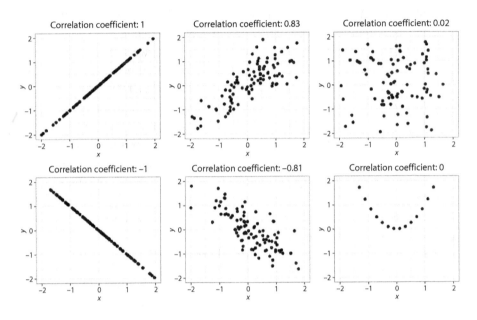

Figure 3.3 Scatterplots with associated correlation coefficients

a weak relationship in general; if you try to fit a straight line to a U-shaped curve, it won't fit that well! In this case, it's important to visualize the relationship between variables because a linear correlation coefficient is not the best way to quantify the relationship.

Another good reason to visualize the data is to quickly identify outliers and their role in estimating the correlation.[19] For example, a simple scatterplot of the patient's number of claims versus the patient's costs would have shown not only that the patient with 199,093 claims was a data error but also that leaving that number in could have led to a spurious Pearson correlation (Spearman would not have been impacted much by this data issue).

There are other methods available to quantify the strength of nonlinear relationships, like Spearman and Kendall correlations that can be discussed with the data science team to see if they are appropriate.

FROM EXPLORATION TO TARGETED ANALYSIS

After presenting the scatterplot, Maya goes on to provide a business proposal. "We're seeing that older people are filing more claims, likely because they're sicker. We should consider raising premiums for this population of patients."

Kamala interjects, "Whoa, let's slow down here. This was just an exploratory data analysis. We don't want to mistake correlation for causation. All we've seen is a general trend across the entire population. We don't know if this relationship holds for everyone, and we certainly don't know why we're seeing this trend." Kamala begins to form some explanations for these findings. "We brought on several employers that employ older workers in 2019. I wonder if this increase in average claims per claimant and average age of claimants is due to bringing on these employers. It could also be that older patients aren't necessarily sicker but that they just use health care services more, such as for routine screenings and preventive health care." These are hypotheses that Kamala and the data science team can test in subsequent analyses.

Exploratory data analyses are just that—exploratory. They are not designed to yield definitive findings. Rather, they are meant to generate questions and hypotheses that can be more thoroughly explored in subsequent analyses.[20] Now that Kamala has some specific questions in mind, she needs the data science team's help in answering them. "I'd like to understand why older patients tend to have more claims. Is it that they're sicker? Is it that they're more likely to use health care services? Or is there something else at play here?"

"Those are good questions, Kamala," responds Maya. "It sounds like we want to test some hypotheses that may explain the relationship we're seeing between the age of patients and the number of claims they file. From what you said, the main two working hypotheses are that older patients may be sicker than younger patients and/or that older patients may use health care services more than younger patients. Is that right?"

"Yes, that's right." Kamala goes on. "I'm also wondering if this relationship has anything to do with the fact that we recently added some employers to our network that employ older folks. So maybe this relationship is being driven by that handful of employers that we recently added."

"Okay, so we have three questions to answer: (1) Are older patients sicker than younger patients? (2) Do older patients use health care services more than younger patients? (3) Is the relationship between age and number of claims being driven by the handful of recently added employers? Now that we've narrowed down the questions to answer, could you help us clarify some definitions? First, how are we defining 'older' and 'younger' patients?"

"Good question. Let's break up our patients into three age groups: under 40, 40–65, and 65+. That way we can easily distinguish among Medicare-age patients (65+), middle-aged patients, and young patients," Kamala explains.

"That makes sense. We still have some other terms to define. How should we measure who is sicker? Can we look at preexisting conditions for that?" Maya asks.

"Looking at preexisting conditions is one way. We can also look at diagnosis codes to see what conditions folks have been recently diagnosed with," Kamala explains.

"Okay, great. We can measure how sick someone is by looking at the number of preexisting conditions and the diagnosis codes they have."

Kamala is perplexed. "Now that I think about it, this isn't the best measure of how sick someone is because having more diagnoses or conditions doesn't necessarily mean that you are sicker than someone with fewer. For example, someone with pancreatic cancer would certainly be sicker than someone with dandruff and spring allergies, but according to our metric, the person with two conditions would be considered sicker." By clearly stating what metric would be used to measure "sickness," it became clear to Kamala that the proposed definition had limitations.

"I can see how this metric would have limitations. To my knowledge, we don't capture any other data on health status that could be used to measure how sick patients are. What do you think about sticking with our proposed metric but being clear about how we are measuring it and interpreting the results accordingly? If we find the results do not make sense, we can look to import a comorbidity index from another source," Maya proposes. Kamala nods. "That sounds good to me." In the absence of better data, sometimes the best option is to use an imperfect metric while clearly stating definitions, limitations, and interpretations.

"Last question: What do we mean by 'use health care services more'? Isn't use of health care services measured by claims, so anyone who files more claims would use more health care services?"

"Ah, I realized the way I phrased my initial question wasn't clear." Kamala clarifies, "I'm thinking that older patients may make use of routine screening procedures and preventive health care more than younger patients—things like colonoscopies, mammograms, and routine PCP checkups. These are examples of health care utilization that has nothing to do with how sick someone is."

"That's really helpful, so we're interested in utilization of routine screening and preventive health care—and maybe other types of services that are not indicative of severity of a certain condition. For purposes of defining this metric, could we look at patients who receive a procedure code for any service that falls into this category? And do we have a list of procedure codes that we could use to define the relevant services?" Maya asks.

"Yes, I think using procedure codes here makes sense," Kamala agrees. "Let me get back to you on that list. I can work with my team to come up with a list of codes that would cover screening procedures, preventive services, and other services that we'd want to include."

"Thanks. I think we have a clear path forward now. We will get back to you soon with results from our three questions of interest. We will break patients up into the three age groups you proposed, measure health status by counting the number of preexisting conditions and diagnosis codes—noting the limitations of this definition—and measure health care utilization by counting procedure codes for relevant services."

During this productive discussion, Kamala and the data science team aligned on several important points. First, they identified the key hypotheses to test. Kamala explained her thought process to the data science team, which framed her hypotheses as three specific questions. Next they clarified important definitions that will be crucial for conducting the analysis. This included defining age groups, health status, and health service utilization. During this process, they discovered that some of the metrics they will use are imperfect: for example, the health status metric may not be a completely accurate measure of a patient's health, but because they lack more precise data, they will proceed with the proposed definition while noting its limitations. While discussing the question of health care utilization, Kamala had an opportunity to clarify her thinking, and they ultimately decided that Kamala and her team would come up with a list of procedure codes to define the types of services they are interested in. This was a great example of cross-functional collaboration. The data scientists recognized that they needed some structured way to define the services of interest, and they proposed using procedure codes as a means of doing that. They deferred to Kamala to determine the exact procedure codes to use, since she is the clinical expert. Kamala and the data science team combined their clinical and analytical expertise to craft an analysis plan that is computationally feasible and clinically relevant.

In the next section, we will explore how the data science team members answered these questions and how to interpret their findings.

Testing Hypotheses

To answer the question "Are older patients sicker than younger patients?" the data science team decided to use a statistical hypothesis test. A hypothesis test evaluates whether a quantity of interest is meaningfully different from a reference value.[21] Sometimes the reference value is also called the *null hypothesis*. Here are some examples of questions that could be answered with a statistical hypothesis test:

- Are men taller than women? Here the quantity of interest is the difference in height between men and women, and the reference value (null hypothesis) is a difference in height of 0 inches.
- Is manager A better than manager B at hiring employees who stay with the company for at least 1 year? Here the quantity of interest is the difference between managers A and B in the proportions of hired employees who stay with the company for at least 1 year (i.e., "# Hired employees staying > 1Y" / "# Hired employees) and those who do not. The reference value (null hypothesis) is a difference in proportions of 0.
- Is age associated with IQ? Here the quantity of interest is the association of age with IQ, measured by a correlation coefficient. The reference value (null hypothesis) is a correlation coefficient of 0 (no association).

It's important to understand what questions cannot be answered with a statistical hypothesis test: an example is "Why do older patients tend to have more insurance claims?" In general, "Why" questions do not lend themselves to hypothesis tests. Similarly, prediction questions are distinct from hypothesis tests. For example, predicting how many claims a given patient will incur in a year cannot be done through a hypothesis test.

Maya reports the findings from the hypothesis test: "We found that older patients have twenty-two more claims per year on average than younger patients, and we calculated a p-value of 0.003."

Hypothesis tests typically have two outputs: (1) an effect size and (2) a p-value.[22] The effect size is the quantity that we are testing in the hypothesis test. For Kamala's question, the quantity of interest was the difference in average number of claims per year between older and younger patients. The resulting effect size was twenty-two claims per year. In the question "Are men taller than women?" the effect size may be reported as the average difference in height between men and women (e.g., 3 inches). For the question

"Is age associated with IQ?" the effect size may be reported as a correlation coefficient (e.g., $r = 0.3$).

EFFECT SIZES The key question to ask about effect sizes is "How big is this effect?" This is a domain question, not a statistical question, because it involves interpreting the effect size. The data scientists may not know what is considered a big or small effect, but Kamala is able to make sense of it: "I think twenty-two claims is a substantial difference. That could come from several in-person visits, supportive care services, etc. It's big enough that it warrants further investigation."

But effect sizes on their own don't tell the whole story.[23] Effect sizes are nothing more than an average across a population, and as we saw before, averages can be misleading! Remember the group of ten people, one of whom was a megamillionaire? We also have to keep in mind that the effect estimate is a function of our observed data, which may be subject to bias and random chance.

Let's consider an extreme scenario to illustrate how random chance can influence effect estimates. Suppose we're interested in whether men are taller than women in the imaginary town Statsville. It would be infeasible to measure the heights of everyone in Statsville, so we answer this question by measuring everyone who attends the monthly Statsville town hall meeting. For simplicity, let's assume that folks who attend the monthly town hall are representative of the broader Statsville community. That is, we are assuming that this is a random sample of the entire population.

In January, only two people attended the town hall: a 6'2" man and a 5'1" woman. If I calculated an effect size from that data, I would get a difference of 13 inches between men and women. Are men truly 13 inches taller than women in Statsville? Maybe—but probably not. We may be seeing this extreme effect because we've observed data from only two individuals; our sample size is so small that our first participants were a relatively tall man and a relatively short woman due to random chance.

In February, six people attended the town hall: a 6'2" man, a 6'0" man, a 5'6" man, a 5'5" woman, a 5'8" woman, and a 5'10" woman.

If we use that data, our effect size drops to an average difference of 3 inches.

So which effect size is right: the 13 inches or the 3 inches? Neither is definitively right, but we can have more confidence in the estimate of 3 inches because it's based on more data. When we have more data, our effect estimate is more robust to random chance.[24]

Here's another example. Imagine we're given a strange-looking coin and we want to find out whether or not it is fair—that is, whether the chance of flipping heads is 50 percent. Our quantity of interest for this hypothesis test is the percentage of flips where the coin lands on heads, and the reference value is 50 percent (the probability of getting heads for a fair coin).

Suppose we flip the coin once and it lands on heads. Our effect estimate after this flip is 100 percent. Do we conclude that this coin is rigged? Certainly not. Just because it landed on heads this one time doesn't mean that it will land on heads every time. Suppose we flip it again and it lands on heads again. Do we conclude *now* that the chance of flipping heads with the coin is 100 percent? Of course not. It's fairly common to get two heads in a row with fair coins. We need more data to increase our certainty about the estimated probability of flipping heads. The question is "How much does our confidence in our estimate increase with each additional data point?"

The answer to this question lies in the concept of statistical power. The power of a hypothesis test is the probability of correctly rejecting a false null hypothesis (i.e., concluding that there is a significant effect) when the alternative hypothesis is true. In other words, it's the probability of detecting an effect when there is truly an effect.

The power of a hypothesis test is a function of the number of data points, the magnitude of the effect size, and the significance level or p-value threshold (see the next section). For example, increasing the number of data points increases the power of a test because more data means less influence of random chance. Likewise, the larger the hypothesized effect size, the greater the power: if we had a coin that we suspected yielded heads 95 percent of the time, we would need to flip it far fewer times to realize it is biased than we would a coin that we suspected yielded heads 55 percent of the time.

In practice, data scientists use the concept of statistical power to calculate the number of data points needed to conduct a hypothesis test. Given a predetermined power (typically, 80 percent), a predetermined threshold for false discoveries (falsely rejecting the null hypothesis—typically, 5 percent), and a hypothesized effect size, you can calculate the necessary sample size for a hypothesis test.

For example, if we suspected that a biased coin yielded heads 55 percent of the time, we would need to flip it at least 783 times to conclude that the coin was biased (allowing for a 5 percent chance of false discovery and assuming we want 80 percent power). In contrast, if we suspected that the biased coin yielded heads 95 percent of the time, we would need to flip it only 7 times to conclude that the coin was biased.[25] The tricky part with performing sample size calculations based on power is that the true effect size is almost never known a priori. This means that we often have to make educated guesses about the effect size in order to determine an appropriate sample size.

In the real world, collecting data and performing analyses can be expensive, so it's important to conduct a power calculation to make sure that the necessary amount of data to collect is known beforehand to avoid going back and collecting more data.

p-VALUES Recall that every hypothesis test has a reference value, or null hypothesis. If we want to know whether our coin is fair or rigged, our null hypothesis is that the chance of flipping heads is 50 percent. The p-value answers the question "If the null hypothesis is true, what is the probability of observing data that's at least as extreme as what we observed?"[26]

In our coin example, the p-value answers the question "If the coin is fair, what's the probability of getting one heads after one flip?" The probability of getting one heads after one flip with a fair coin is 50 percent, so the p-value is 0.5. Note that this isn't the same as answering the question "What's the probability that the coin is fair?" The p-value is not saying there is a 50 percent chance that the coin is fair; it's saying that *if* the coin was fair, there would be a 50 percent chance of getting the results that we did (one heads after one flip). In other words, we don't have much evidence to suggest that this is a rigged coin.

What if we flipped it again and we got another heads? We can calculate a p-value for this new data set. The p-value answers the question "If the coin is fair, what's the chance of getting two heads in two flips?" The answer is 25 percent, or a p-value of 0.25, which is still pretty likely. In other words, we still don't have much to suggest that this coin is rigged.

What if we flip the coin ten times and get ten heads? The p-value answers the question "If the coin is fair, what's the chance that we get ten heads out of ten flips?" The answer is approximately 0.1 percent, or a p-value of 0.001—a very small number. In other words, if the coin was a fair coin, it is very unlikely that we would've gotten ten heads out of ten flips. Because the p-value is so low, we have strong evidence to believe that this coin is rigged.

Let's come back to Kamala's example. The data science team said that on average older people have twenty-two more claims than younger people and that this effect estimate had a p-value of 0.003. The p-value answers the question "If older people and younger people truly filed the same number of claims, what's the chance that we would observe a data set in which older people have twenty-two more claims than younger people on average?" The p-value suggests that the difference in claims filed between older and younger people is not due to random chance; there may be something inherently different between younger and older people that's driving the observed difference. Thus, we should reject the null hypothesis that older and younger people truly filed the same number of claims.

How do you decide what is a high or a low p-value? For many years, statisticians have used a threshold of 0.05 to label results as statistically significant or insignificant. That is, a p-value less than 0.05 (statistically significant) indicates that there is strong enough evidence to suggest that the null hypothesis is not true. The drawback to this approach is that $p = 0.05$ is an arbitrary threshold.

The key insight is that statistical significance is a spectrum: the lower the p-value, the stronger the evidence to reject the null hypothesis.[27] In some fields, like particle physics, the p-value threshold can be extremely stringent, such as $p < 0.000001$ (less than a one in a million chance that the findings are due to random chance).[28] In other cases, the p-value is not considered critical at all, like when the goal is to develop the most accurate predictions of who is likely to have a large number of claims and there are no restrictions on the model structure or modeling assumptions. In that case, the only goal is prediction accuracy, and the p-values of the input variables do not necessarily play a role.

Interpreting Results

When interpreting results of statistical hypothesis tests, it's important to consider the effect estimate and the p-value together.[29] We can consider four cases, as shown in figure 3.4: (1) large effect size and high p-value (not statistically significant), (2) large effect size and low p-value (statistically significant), (3) small effect size and high p-value, and (4) small effect size and low p-value. While bucketing all possible results into these four groups is oversimplification,

p-value	Effect size		
		Low	High
	Low	Small but statistically significant association between exposure and outcome	Large and statistically significant association between exposure and outcome
	High	Small effect of the exposure on the outcome with weak statistical significance	Large effect of the exposure on the outcome with weak statistical significance

Figure 3.4 Using p-values and effect sizes to interpret the results of a hypothesis test

knowing how to interpret these four cases can help you make sense of the gray areas.

Consider a scenario where the effect size is large and the p-value is high. This is what we saw in the coin example. After one flip of heads, our effect estimate was 100 percent. This is a very large effect size because a coin with a 100 percent probability of heads is an extremely rigged coin. In addition, we found that the p-value for this scenario is 0.5 because if the coin was fair, we'd have a 50 percent chance of observing one heads after one flip. Even though the effect size is large, the p-value is high enough that we have low confidence in the effect estimate. The coin could be extremely rigged, but it could just be that we don't have enough data. In other words, the true effect is uncertain.[30]

Now consider a scenario where the effect estimate is large and the p-value is small. Imagine after ten flips, we get ten heads in a row. In this case, the effect size is very large at 100 percent, and the p-value is small at 0.001. This means we have an extremely rigged coin, and we are highly confident that the coin is truly rigged.[31]

What if we had a small effect estimate and a high p-value? Let's say that after two flips, we got one heads and one tails. Our effect estimate is 50 percent, and the p-value is 0.75 because if the coin was fair, we'd have a 75 percent chance of getting at least one heads every two flips. This is similar to the first scenario, where we simply don't have enough evidence to say whether the effect estimate of 50 percent is accurate or not. It could be, or it could be that we don't have enough data yet.[32]

Lastly, what if the effect estimate is small and the p-value is also small? Imagine we flip a coin 10,000 times and we get 5,200 heads and 4,800 tails. If we had a fair coin, we'd expect the ratio to be closer to 5,000 to 5,000, so we can be pretty sure that this coin is not completely fair (the p-value in this scenario is about 0.00003). But the effect estimate is relatively small because we were saying that instead of a 50 percent chance of heads, this coin gives you a 52 percent chance of heads. This is not a substantial difference, so we would call this a small effect size.[33]

Some statistical hypothesis tests require that the data meet certain assumptions. For example, some statistical tests assume that the data follows a bell curve or normal distribution, with approximately equal numbers above and below the mean.[34] Others may assume that the two groups being compared have equal standard deviations. Note that not all data distributions may meet these assumptions. Remember the distribution of wealth where we had many people around the median and one person at the extreme end who earned a lot more? In scenarios like these, it's important to make sure that the data meets the assumptions of the tests being used.

Armed with this knowledge, we are now ready to interpret the findings of the data science team. Kamala says, "0.003 is a fairly low p-value, and the average difference of twenty-two claims is substantial, so we can be fairly confident that older people do indeed tend to file more claims than younger people. Now the question is 'Why are older people filing more claims than younger people, and what factors make older people more likely to need more claims?'"

These are questions that can be answered using statistical modeling. In the next section, we will see how modeling can help us identify the drivers of certain phenomena.

MODELING Modeling is all about finding relationships between variables. To understand this process better, let's suppose we're interested in the relationship between people's height and weight.

Scatterplots As we've discussed earlier, a scatterplot is a great way to visualize the relationship between two continuous variables.[35] Plotting the association between these two variables, we see a spread of points that slopes upward. If we want to further quantify the relationship between height and weight, we can calculate the correlation coefficient, which we discussed earlier.

Line of Best Fit Another way to quantify this relationship is to ask "For every additional inch in height, how does a person's weight change?" We are looking for an output. We want to be able to make a statement like "For every additional inch in height, a person's weight increases by 3 pounds on average." Alternatively, given someone's height, we want to be able to predict how much they weigh. One way to do this is by fitting a line to the data. By assuming that the relationship between height and weight is linear, we can fit a line through the points of the scatterplot and use the properties of the line to quantify the relationship between height and weight.[36]

The slope of a line can tell us the change in Y for every one unit increase of X.[37] Alternatively, given a value for X, we can calculate a value for Y by using the equation of the line. Remember $Y = mX + b$ from high school algebra? The task becomes determining how to fit a line to this scatterplot. If we were to do this manually, we could take a ruler and draw a straight line through the middle of the scatterplot so that the slope of the line is more or less aligned with the slope of the points. But if we asked five different people to do this exercise, we may get five slightly different lines. How can we do this in a principled way such that for any given scatterplot, there is one precise *line of best fit*?

The approach that mathematicians and statisticians use is to define the line of best fit as the line that minimizes the vertical distances between every point in the plot and the line (technically speaking, the line of best fit minimizes the squared distances for mathematical convenience).[38] It can be shown that for every set of points, there exists a unique line of best fit (figure 3.5). This method can also be applied to study the relationships among more than two variables.[39] For example, let's say we want to understand how a person's weight varies as a function of their height and as a function of their shoe size. Now instead of a two-dimensional plot, we have a three-dimensional plot, where the x-axis is height, the y-axis is shoe size, and the z-axis is weight. And now instead of finding the line of best fit, we're interested in finding the plane of best fit.[40]

Although we can't visualize it, this approach can extend to an infinite number of dimensions. Whether it's four or ten or one hundred variables, we can still use the same mathematical tools to find the n-dimensional "line of best fit" and use the equation of that "line" to quantify the relationships among variables. Similar techniques can also be used to deal with relationships that may not be linear.[41]

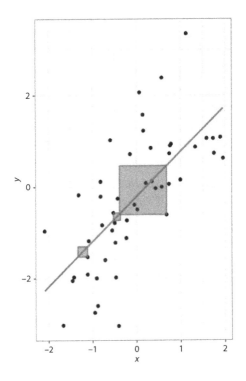

Figure 3.5 Diagram of the sum of squared residuals for the line of best fit. The line represents the line of best fit. Each square represents the squared residual of a given point. The side length of a square is the difference between the point and the line of best fit (residual).

Coming back to our example of height and weight, when we fit a line to a point in this plot of data, we get the equation $Y = 3X - 36$. The slope of this line is 3, meaning that for every increase in X (height in inches), Y (weight) increases by 3. In other words, if a 6' person weighs 180 pounds on average, a 6'1" person will weigh 183 pounds on average. We can also use this equation to predict weight given height: just plug in an adult's height for X, and you'll get the resulting weight by multiplying the height by 3 and subtracting 36. By fitting a line to this plot of data, we can use the equation of the line—specifically, the slope—to quantify the relationship between the X and Y variables. This process is called regression—specifically, linear regression—and the slope of the resulting line is called the regression coefficient.[42] The way to interpret the regression coefficient is as you saw above: a regression coefficient of M indicates an M unit increase in the Y variable for every unit increase in the X variable.

Inference Versus Prediction Two fundamental goals of modeling are inference and prediction.[43] Inference is all about understanding what variables are associated with an outcome of interest and to what extent. The goal of inference is to make statements about trends in a population and therefore can be helpful for gaining insight into a business problem. For example, Kamala wants to know what types of patients tend to submit more claims than others. This is an inference question. At the end, she wants to be able to make a statement like "Patients who have [certain disease] tend to make more claims than patients who don't have [certain disease]" or "Patients who have at least [certain number] dependents tend to make more claims than patients who have fewer than [certain number] dependents." These are statements about associations within the entire patient population. Other examples of inference questions include "What foods are associated with increased risk of developing cancer?" and "What qualities in a teacher are associated with better student test scores?"

Prediction is all about predicting the outcome of interest for a given individual. Here are some examples of prediction questions: "Given a patient, can we predict how many claims they will file in a given year?" "Given a person's diet, can we predict whether or not they will develop cancer?" "Given a teacher's attributes, can we predict the average SAT score of their students?" Before embarking on a modeling task, it's important to clarify whether the goal is inference or prediction. For Kamala, she's not necessarily interested in predicting how many claims a patient will file. Rather, she wants to understand general patterns in claim submissions in order to figure out what subpopulations may require more resources.

Defining an Outcome Every statistical model needs an outcome—the quantity of interest. For Kamala, the outcome is the number of claims submitted by each patient. Defining the outcome is one of the most important, and also most challenging, tasks involved with model building. Misspecifying the outcome can lead to uninterpretable results and poor decision-making down the line.[44] The first consideration when defining an outcome variable is whether the variable is meaningful. Ask yourself "Is this really the variable I'm interested in, or is this a proxy for the true variable of interest?"[45] For example, if we're interested in understanding what drives improvements in student learning, we may select standardized test scores as the outcome variable. This may appear to be a reasonable choice, but it's easy to see that standardized test scores are not necessarily a good indicator of student learning—they might be more indicative of the student's test taking ability, access to preparation materials, and time to study. In this case, test scores are a proxy for our true phenomenon of interest, student learning, an abstract entity that is difficult to measure directly.

In addition to checking for unsuitable proxies, it's important to make sure that the outcome variable definition is clear and correctly specified.[46] For example, let's say you're interested in measuring the effect of a new anticancer drug on improving patient survival. For this question, the outcome variable may be the time from when the patient starts taking a drug to when the patient dies. On the surface, this seems appropriate, but there may be scenarios where this outcome definition is inappropriate. Consider a case where a patient dies in a car accident soon after they start taking the drug. The way we've defined the outcome makes it seem as though the drug didn't work for this patient. Because the outcome definition does not consider how the patient died, we have no way of accounting for the fact that the patient's death had nothing to do with how well the drug worked. Thinking through edge cases or extreme examples like this can help uncover limitations in the definition of the outcome variable.

Another common consideration that arises in modeling is whether to split the outcome variable into two or more categories. Categorization involves combining ranges of continuous values to form groups.[47] Categorizing a variable always leads to loss of information, so in general it should be done only when there are substantial gains in interpretability or when the groups are meaningful. For example, recall how Kamala suggested categorizing the age variable to account for the fact that some patients are Medicare eligible. In this case, grouping ages above 65 is meaningful because that age range represents a specific population. Categorization allows Kamala to make statements about the Medicare-eligible population and the non-Medicare-eligible population. As a counterexample, let's say the data science team wanted to categorize the outcome variable (claims) and define it as either fewer than fifty claims or fifty or more claims submitted per year. This would be an example of categorization with no clear rationale. There is no clear reason why the number fifty makes sense for grouping the outcome variable results, and it's not clear how categorizing the variable results adds any value or interpretability to the analysis.

Independent Variables Maya started formulating a plan for the model. "Our question of interest is why older patients tend to file more claims than younger patients. I suggest we build two models. Both models will determine which variables are associated with the number of claims filed; the first model will focus on younger patients, and the second model will focus on older Medicare Advantage patients. Then we can compare the two models and see which variables contribute differently for younger and older patients."

Kamala was following the proposed approach. "That makes sense. We're building a model for younger patients and another for older patients and then comparing the two. My question is 'How do we pick which variables to include in the model?'"

Independent variables, also known as exposures, features, inputs, or predictors, are the variables for which we are quantifying the association with the outcome. One big question in model building is "Which independent variables should be included in the model?" There are two main approaches to tackling this: a data-driven approach and a hypothesis-driven approach. In the data-driven approach, you can include all variables that you have access to and allow the model to determine which variables are meaningfully associated with the outcome. There are certain statistical techniques that can be used to narrow down a list of the most strongly associated variables from a starting set of many predictors.[48] The advantage of this approach is that it typically requires less thought and planning. It also requires less domain knowledge, since there is no need to determine which variables may be associated with the outcome a priori. The data-driven approach may be better for prediction questions because there are often complex relationships between variables that humans are not good at identifying manually. One disadvantage to this approach is the possibility of false positives: that is, variables that appear to be associated with the outcome but are really just statistical artifacts. In other words, if you test several variables, a few are bound to show up as associated with the outcome just by random chance. The data-driven approach may also yield results that are difficult to interpret.[49]

The hypothesis-driven approach to variable selection addresses some of these limitations. By including only variables that are believed to have an association with the outcome a priori, you minimize the risk of finding spurious associations or surprising results.[50] Models based on hypothesis-driven variable selection are typically more interpretable, but they may have reduced predictive power because they don't include as wide a set of predictor variables. Hypothesis-driven variable selection also requires domain knowledge to recognize which variables may have an association with the outcome.[51]

"There are a lot of ways to determine which variables to include in the model," Maya explained. "A good starting point would be for you and your team to come up with a list of variables that you believe may be associated with the number of claims someone files."

This was an easy ask for Kamala given her familiarity with insurance billing and clinical medicine. "I could give you a list right now! We could look at what diagnoses patients have because certain conditions are associated with more health system encounters. We could also look at how long they've had those conditions and whether they are chronic or acute conditions. The hypothesis there is that people with chronic conditions may have consistently more claims than people without them."

Maya was jotting down Kamala's ideas on the board. "It sounds like diagnoses are a big source of variability. Any other variables we could use?"

Kamala continued. "We should also look at what specific insurance plan they have. Depending on their level of coverage, patients may be more or less likely to seek health care. We should also look at demographics, like place of residence, employment status, number of dependents, etc."

"Nice! This is a great starting point. Let's use these variables to build our initial model, and we'll get back to you once we have some results."

PUTTING IT TOGETHER

A few weeks later Kamala and the data science team reconvened to discuss initial results from the model. David asked Maya to drive the conversation, promising that he would jump in when appropriate. Maya opened with the main finding. "Kamala, thanks again for your list of proposed variables. We're already seeing some strong signals that we want to get your thoughts on. Out of all the variables that you suggested including in the models, the biggest contributor to the number of claims filed per year is the presence of chronic diseases. We also found that the presence of chronic diseases affects claims differently in younger patients versus older patients. In the model for younger patients, the coefficient for this variable was 4.34, which means that—all else constant—patients with chronic diseases file about four more claims per year than patients without chronic diseases. In older patients, the coefficient was 15.17."

Kamala tried to make sense of these results. "The first result is that patients with chronic diseases file more claims—this doesn't surprise me. But the second result is that chronic diseases have less of an effect in younger patients compared to older patients. The natural follow-up question is 'Why do older patients' chronic conditions lead to more claims than younger patients' chronic conditions?' I could think of some reasons off the top of my head—older patients tend to be sicker, for example—but I think it warrants more exploration."

"That's exactly the question we wanted to discuss with you," David responded, smiling. Kamala and the data science team started with a hypothesis and eventually developed a question that could be answered using statistical modeling. By thoughtfully defining an outcome and selecting meaningful independent variables, they were able to generate results that led to thought-provoking discussions about their data and their company.

KEY TOOLS

Important Questions:

- Are there any outliers in the data, and if so, how might they affect our results?
- What assumptions does this hypothesis test make about the data? Are these assumptions valid?
- Is the data normally distributed? If not, how does this affect our analysis and interpretation?
- What other ways could we have set up the hypothesis test to answer the same question?
- Do we have adequate sample size to use this hypothesis test?
- What effect size represents a meaningful effect?
- Did we conduct a power calculation or a sample size calculation before collecting data?
- Are we seeing a significant p-value because we have a large sample size (overpowered) or because there is truly a strong effect?
- Are we seeing a nonsignificant p-value because we have a small sample size (underpowered) or because there is truly no effect?
- Is this a univariable analysis or a multivariable analysis?
- Could there be important confounders at play?
- Is this the right type of outcome variable?

- Did we use an assumption in our statistical test that was not appropriate, such as assuming linearity (Pearson correlation) when we could have used a more robust test (Spearman correlation)?
- Is there a different way we could have done this analysis? For example, could we have used a different model type or different outcome variable specification?
- Does this model make sense for this data?
- How was missing data dealt with? Does imputation/exclusion make sense?

Common Mistakes:

- **Making unrealistic assumptions**: Statistical models are built upon certain assumptions. Making unrealistic or incorrect assumptions about the data or the model (e.g., assuming that the data follows a normal distribution when it doesn't, or assuming independence when variables are dependent) can lead to misleading results.
- **Excluding certain data due to missing information or outliers**: If data is excluded arbitrarily, this could introduce bias into the analysis. Any data exclusion needs to be justified and understood as it may affect the results.
- **Picking the wrong null hypothesis**: The null hypothesis is central to statistical tests. If the wrong null hypothesis is chosen, the conclusions drawn from the test may be incorrect or misleading.
- **Interpreting only the p-value and not the effect size**: A small p-value indicates that the results are statistically significant, but it does not tell you how meaningful or important these results are. The effect size gives you an idea of the magnitude or importance of the effect. Ignoring the effect size can lead to overemphasis on small but statistically significant results.
- **Interpreting only the effect size and not the p-value**: Conversely, while the effect size can give an indication of the magnitude of the effect, it does not provide information on the reliability or repeatability of the results. The p-value provides information on how likely the observed data would occur given the null hypothesis, thus providing a measure of the statistical evidence.
- **Assuming correlation is causation**: Correlation measures the linear relationship between two variables, but it does not imply that changes

in one variable cause changes in the other. Drawing causal conclusions from correlation can be misleading.

- **Not recognizing when confounders may be at play:** A confounder is a variable that influences both the dependent variable and independent variable, causing a spurious association. Ignoring potential confounders can lead to incorrect conclusions about the relationship between the variables of interest.

- **Overfitting (see chapter 5):** Overfitting occurs when a model captures the noise along with the underlying pattern in the data. An overfitted model will perform well on the training data but poorly on new, unseen data, as it fails to generalize. Thus, overfitting can lead to overly optimistic performance estimates of the model.

- **Cherry-picking results:** Selectively choosing positive or significant results while ignoring non-significant ones leads to a biased representation of the analysis.

- **Data dredging/p-hacking:** The practice of performing many statistical tests until a significant result is found is misleading and unethical.

4

MAKING DECISIONS WITH DATA

Kamala walked into her office to find a report sitting on her desk: "New Anti-Cancer Drug Found to Be More Expensive and Less Effective than Older Drug." A group of researchers analyzed a large database of prostate cancer patients, some of whom had received the newly approved drug called ClaroMax and some of whom had received the standard of care therapy that had been used for many years. They did a cost-effectiveness analysis, which looks at how effective the drug was in treating the cancer as well as how expensive the drug was to acquire and administer. They found that the new drug was both more expensive and less effective than the old drug. Kamala saw a Post-it note written in her manager's handwriting on the front page of the report: "Should we remove this new drug from our formulary?" Kamala's company. Stardust Health Insurance, reimburses patients who are on ClaroMax. In light of this new data, her manager wants to know whether the company should continue to reimburse for the drug or stop reimbursing for it, thereby encouraging providers and patients to go with the standard of care therapy.

It's one thing to understand data and collaborate with the data science team. It's another thing entirely to make decisions—sometimes large, impactful business decisions—using data. In this chapter, we will discuss how to make decisions with data and what can go wrong when the underlying data is biased, the presentation of the data is flawed, or the quality of evidence is low. We will also be talking about how to interpret data so as not to fall into common traps that lead to wrong conclusions. We will follow Kamala as she dives into the details of this new study and tries to decide whether the evidence is reliable, whether the data is biased, and, ultimately, whether her company should act on this data by ceasing reimbursement for ClaroMax.

CAUSALITY AND CLONING

Determining causality is one of the main goals of data analysis. Causality refers to the underlying causal relationships between phenomena: X causes Y.[1] We use the language of causality all the time in our daily lives ("An apple a day keeps the doctor away," implying that eating apples causes better health). Nutritional epidemiology studies try to infer causality between food intake and different diseases. Headlines linking wine to better health or Big Macs to cancer routinely grab media attention. Causality can be important in business contexts as well. Meta may be interested in knowing what types of posts cause users to stay on the platform longer. Whole Foods may be interested in determining what placement of products on the shelves leads to increased sales. In an earlier case, Kamala's company was interested in identifying what factors cause patients to use more health care and require larger reimbursements. And today Kamala is interested in figuring out whether ClaroMax truly leads to worse outcomes and higher costs for patients with cancer. She reaches out to David on the data science team to get a crash course in causality.

"David, I need your help in understanding cause and effect. A new study just came out that's claiming a new drug isn't as effective as we thought it was. I need to know whether these conclusions are accurate or not. How can we determine causality from data?"

"Ah, causality! People think that data science is all about making prediction models and doing machine learning—causal inference is an underappreciated field within statistics! I'm happy to give you a primer on causality. We can start with how we infer causality in daily life." David stood up at his whiteboard and started drawing some pictures.

"Suppose I went to a new Mexican restaurant for dinner and ordered nachos and enchiladas. The next day I woke up with severe stomach pains and diarrhea. What caused my stomach issues? Assuming I didn't eat anything else during the day that was out of the ordinary, there's no way to know for sure whether my stomach pain was caused by the nachos, the enchiladas, or the combination of the two. In an imaginary world, one way to figure out which food caused my GI issues would be to clone myself and send my clones back in time. Clone 1 would order the enchiladas, clone 2 would order the nachos, and clone 3 would order both. The next day I could see which of my three clones experienced stomach issues to determine which food was the culprit. If only clones 1 and 3 got sick, the enchiladas were likely the cause. If only clones 2 and 3 got sick, the nachos were the likely cause. If only clone 3 got sick, it was the combination that likely caused my symptoms."

Kamala nodded along. "That makes sense. You can't know which food was the culprit unless you isolate their impacts somehow."[2]

"Exactly!" David pointed his dry-erase marker at Kamala. "This example may be contrived, but the idea of cloning illustrates an important statistical concept in the study of causality. By cloning myself, I am ensuring that the only difference between the three clones is the food that they ordered. In other words, I am controlling for all possible variables so that any observed differences in GI symptoms the next day could be attributed only to the food that the clones ordered. Since the clones are identical in every other way, there could be no other variables other than the food that contributed to their illness."[3]

"Right," Kamala chimed in. "Without cloning, it would be more difficult to determine which food caused your illness."

"Now get ready for a twist," David grinned. "Imagine that instead of cloning myself, I brought two friends to the restaurant with me. Friend 1 ordered the nachos, friend 2 ordered the enchiladas, and

I ordered both. The following day I got sick, but my two friends didn't. In the cloning example, when only clone 3 got sick, we could conclude that it was the combination of nachos and enchiladas that caused the illness. In the absence of cloning, we can't conclude that it was the combination that caused the illness because it's possible that my two friends have traits that make them less susceptible to GI issues than me—it's not a fair comparison. Just because they didn't get sick after ordering only nachos or only enchiladas doesn't mean that I wouldn't have gotten sick! They may have a stronger stomach than me, or they may have eaten at that restaurant before, or they may not have eaten as much as I did, etc. Without accounting for all these possible baseline differences in susceptibility to GI issues, it's difficult to draw causal conclusions."[4]

"Ok, I get that cloning is great, but how can we establish causality in a world where cloning is not possible?" Kamala asked.

David smiled. "Randomization."

THE POWER OF RANDOMIZATION

David erased his drawings of stick people eating Mexican food and started writing. "BioFarm, the manufacturer of ClaroMax, wants to know whether its drug is effective at increasing survival of elderly male patients with prostate cancer. Let's consider how the company could prove a causal relationship between ClaroMax and longer survival. In an imaginary world, BioFarm could use the cloning method. First, it would recruit a representative sample of elderly men with prostate cancer, and then it would clone them, thereby creating two identical groups of patients. BioFarm would give one group ClaroMax and the other group a placebo (a fake drug that has no therapeutic effect) and see which of the two groups survived longer. Because the two cloned groups are identical in every imaginable way, any difference in survival between the groups can be attributed to the drug."[5]

Kamala was following. "That makes sense, just like the restaurant example. They're cloning so that any differences in survival are attributable to the drug and not to any differences in the participants."

David nodded. "Now let's consider how BioFarm could run a similar experiment in the real world, without access to cloning. In real life, such experiments are conducted such that the two groups are designed to be as similar as possible across all important attributes; effectively, the two groups of interest should be as close to 'clones' as possible. Important attributes are those variables that are expected to be related to the outcome of interest. In the example regarding GI issues, important variables to account for included previous exposure to the restaurant's food and the strength of one's stomach. For the ClaroMax experiment, important attributes include variables that may be associated with survival time, such as baseline age, prior medical conditions, and stage of cancer.

"For example, if the elderly men in the group given ClaroMax are on average 70 years old, BioFarm would want the elderly men in the group given the placebo also to be on average 70 years old. In other words, BioFarm wants to 'artificially clone' the treatment group so that it is as similar as possible to the placebo group. That way, any difference in outcomes can be attributed to Claro-Max and to a difference in baseline characteristics. These baseline attributes—like age, gender, race, or class—that may be associated with the outcome of interest as well as the intervention are known as confounders.[6] A confounder is a factor that has a causal relationship with both the outcome and the intervention. The key insight is that when establishing causality, it's not important that the two intervention groups be 100 percent identical across all imaginable variables; rather, they need to be similar enough across the important confounders."

"I see," started Kamala. "So cloning is kind of overkill? Obviously, in a perfect world we'd love to have clones, but if we can make sure that the two groups are similar in terms of important confounders, we can still draw valid causal conclusions."

"Exactly," responded David. "To understand the impact of confounders on establishing causality, imagine that the elderly men in the group that got ClaroMax were on average 70 years old but that the elderly men in the group that got the placebo were on average 80 years old. At the end of the study, if BioFarm found that the ClaroMax group had longer survival than the placebo group, is it appropriate to conclude that ClaroMax was responsible for the increased survival?"

Kamala could answer this one. "No. Because the two groups were not comparable in terms of age, it could be that the baseline difference in age is what led to the difference in survival."

"That's right!" David was proud of his student. "We know that age is an important confounder here; obviously, younger people tend to survive longer than older people. Other important confounders for this study may include comorbidities, baseline severity of cancer, and genetic mutations associated with survival. As long as critical confounders are accounted for, it's not important for the intervention groups to be similar across other attributes."[7]

Kamala interrupted. "Just to make sure I'm following, examples of variables that are not confounders in this example could be things like the length of their toenails, the number of hairs on their head, whether their favorite color is blue, whether they prefer waffles or pancakes, etc. Is that right? Even if 100 percent of the ClaroMax group preferred the color blue and 0 percent of the placebo group preferred the color blue, it is not expected to interfere with our analysis of causality because we have no reason to believe that liking the color blue is associated with longer survival—it's not a confounder."

"You're exactly right," said David. "All those things you listed are not confounders! So to recap, to determine whether or not ClaroMax is effective at improving survival, BioFarm needs to recruit two groups of elderly men who are nearly identical across all important confounders (age, comorbidities, disease severity, etc.). This requirement presents two issues. First, this sounds like a nightmare to coordinate logistically; for every 70-year-old man with stage III cancer and diabetes who gets ClaroMax, BioFarm will need to find someone with very similar traits to put in the placebo group. Second, and more importantly, BioFarm may not be able to measure all the important confounders. Maybe there's a genetic mutation that is strongly associated with shorter life expectancy in cancer patients, but there is no accessible genetic test available to determine who has this mutation. Ideally, the distribution of this genetic mutation should be similar between the two groups, since it is a confounder, but without a way to measure who has the mutation, ensuring an even distribution between the two groups is impossible.

"This is where randomization comes in. Randomizing participants to the two intervention groups will ensure a roughly even distribution across confounders, both those that can be measured and those that cannot. Consider a school where approximately half the children are boys and half the children are girls. Suppose we randomly assign students to group 1 or group 2 by flipping a coin. What is the percentage of boys and girls in group 1?"

Kamala thought for a bit before answering. "Because the starting population was 50 percent boys and 50 percent girls and because we randomly allocated the students to the two groups instead of preferentially assigning groups based on gender, we can expect that the ratio of boys to girls in group 1 is also about 50:50."

"Right." David explained, "The power of randomization is that it allows us to account for both measurable confounders and unmeasurable confounders.[8] When assigning the schoolchildren to two groups, we did not make any special effort to ensure that the gender distribution in the resulting groups was equal—we just flipped a coin! And yet we can expect that the distribution will be more or less equal between the groups with a large enough sample size."

"This would be true for any characteristic: race, height, weight, shoe size, etc., right?" reasoned Kamala. "By randomly assigning the schoolchildren to two groups, we are more confident that whatever distribution of characteristics was present in the overall population will be replicated in the subgroups."

"Exactly," David continued. "Even if the distribution of measurable known confounders is not 100 percent accurate or equal between the two groups, we can be confident that the distribution of unmeasurable or unknown confounders is also more or less equal between the two groups.[9] If BioFarm's group of participants had an average age of around 72, we would expect that two randomly assigned subgroups would also have an average age of 72. That said, we wouldn't be surprised if one group's average age was

71 and the other's 73—this is the nature of randomness. Since age is a confounder, it would be preferable if the age distributions of the two groups were identical (recall cloning!), but often it is sufficient if the distribution of confounders is similar. Perfect concordance is not necessary for causal inference. After all, this is a small price to pay in exchange for knowing that the distribution of confounders, both measurable and unmeasurable, will be roughly equal after randomizing!"

Note that it is possible to deal with small imbalances in measurable confounders between the two groups during data analysis.[10] Randomizing an intervention allows us to draw causal conclusions about the effect of the intervention because randomization tends to preserve the distribution of attributes among the intervention groups. Next we will learn how to apply randomization to conduct many experiments and arrive at causal conclusions.

A/B TESTING

In this section, we will discuss how to use the principles of randomization to answer your own causal questions. We will focus on A/B testing, a framework for designing and executing mini randomized experiments. We'll follow Kamala as she learns about A/B tests from the marketing team, whose job it is to use A/B tests to find the most effective marketing and advertising approaches.

"So there's your mini primer on causality! A great next step would be for you to reach out to Kyra on the marketing team and learn how they use randomization to inform their advertising strategy," David said as he erased his doodles from the whiteboard.

Kamala set up a meeting with Kyra that afternoon. She wasn't sure how learning about marketing would help her interpret this ClaroMax study, but she was enjoying learning about causal inference, so she humored David by taking his suggestion.

"Thanks for meeting, Kyra. I am trying to learn about causality and randomized experiments, and David from the data science team suggested I reach out to you. I'd love to hear about how you use randomization and causal inference in your day-to-day work." Kamala explained why she's interested in learning about randomization and gave Kyra a brief overview of the ClaroMax study.

Kyra was excited to share her insights. "Thank *you* for setting this up, Kamala! I could talk about this stuff for days on end. I didn't have a data science background when I first started here—sounds like you didn't either! But we worked with David and set up processes to embed data science and causal inference into our daily workflows, and, trust me, it has been a game changer. I am happy to walk you through how we use randomized experiments on our team."

Kyra took out a stack of blank paper and started jotting some points down. "The first step in answering a causal question is to define a question! Typically, questions involving causality take the form of 'What is the effect of [intervention] on [outcome]?' The intervention is something that you're interested in testing, and the outcome is whatever quantity you expect the intervention will change. If our marketing team is testing out a new ad, the intervention may be the new advertisement, and the outcome may be the number of incoming client calls. It sounds like for BioFarm, the intervention of interest is the drug ClaroMax and the outcome is survival. For a restaurant chain, the intervention may be reducing the amount of sugar in its desserts, and the outcome may be total dessert sales. As you can see, causal questions can apply to many contexts."

"That seems kind of obvious, doesn't it? Every study has to start with some kind of question," Kamala said. She wasn't sure why Kyra was putting so much emphasis on this.

"You're right. It is obvious, but that doesn't mean it's easy! One common pitfall in defining a question of interest is the use of vague terms. Consider the question 'What is the effect of ClaroMax on patients' health?' Here the outcome is not clearly defined. What constitutes a patient's health? What if the patient experiences painful side effects (negative health outcome) but ends up living longer (positive health outcome)? For a restaurant trying out a new menu, a poorly formed question may look like 'What is the effect of improving our food on client satisfaction?' What does 'improving our food' entail? Is the restaurant going to completely overhaul its menu? Replace the salads with fried foods? Replace the fried foods with salads? Similarly, the outcome is poorly defined. How is client satisfaction being measured? It's important to define interventions and outcomes sufficiently clearly so as to allow for reproducibility."

Kamala nodded. "I see—so crafting the question carefully allows you to be precise about the quantities that you are measuring."

"You got it," said Kyra. "In addition to clear definitions, outcomes must be meaningful. BioFarm could have chosen a number of outcome variables for its ClaroMax study instead of survival time: the percentage of patients who experience adverse side effects, the time until progression of cancer, or the percentage of patients who drop out of the study. There is no single best choice of outcome; it all depends on the question of interest. If the goal is to assess whether ClaroMax is safe, choosing adverse side effects as the outcome may make sense. If the goal is to assess whether ClaroMax extends life, looking at survival time makes sense. The outcome should be concordant with the research question."

"Ok, so define everything clearly—makes sense. Then what?" Kamala was eager to hear about when the rubber meets the road.

Kyra flipped to a clean sheet of paper. "Once the intervention and outcome have been clearly defined, it's time to start designing the study. The next step is to define the study population: Who are the participants that are going to receive the intervention? It's typically useful to define inclusion or exclusion criteria—criteria that describe who will be included or excluded from the study population.[11] For example, if we're running a new ad to target folks who are eligible for one of our Medicare Advantage plans, we'd want to exclude anyone under the age of 60, since those folks wouldn't be eligible for Medicare for at least another 5 years."

Kamala was starting to see the parallels. "That makes sense. In the ClaroMax study, BioFarm excluded patients with highly advanced cancer because their disease had progressed beyond the point at which ClaroMax would have had any therapeutic effect. BioFarm's inclusion criteria included having a diagnosis of prostate cancer and being over the age of 65."

Kyra continued. "Once the inclusion and exclusion criteria are defined, it's important to consider how participants will be recruited. One of the most important considerations is generalizability. To what extent will the recruitment methodology allow you to extend the conclusions of this study beyond this specific population?[12] Let's suppose that BioFarm chooses to recruit participants who are being treated at the top cancer institute in the United States. Can you think of any reasons why this recruitment mechanism may affect the generalizability of the results?"

Kamala thought for a few seconds. "I can think of a few reasons. For one, patients who are treated at this cancer institute may receive a higher level of care than patients who are treated elsewhere in the country. Second, the patients who are treated at this top cancer center may be different from patients treated elsewhere: they may have better insurance coverage, they may be more well-off, they may have more advanced cancer, etc. The recruitment mechanism would cast doubt on whether the results of the study could generalize to patients who are treated elsewhere in the country. Sure, ClaroMax may work if it's administered in the top cancer center in the United States, but what about when it's administered in an underresourced cancer clinic in the rural Midwest? BioFarm should consider recruiting participants from diverse clinical settings to improve the generalizability of its findings."

Kyra was impressed. "You're sounding like a causal inference expert already! Once a recruitment strategy is in place, the next thing to think about is how to operationalize randomization. That is, how will the interventions be randomly allocated to the two groups? For online ads, we have a great software tool that allows us to run randomized experiments. With the click of a button, we can control which ads get deployed to which sites at which times. But it's not always that easy. Sometimes organizational constraints will dictate what randomization schemes are viable. For example, the clinics that BioFarm works with may not have the operational capacity to randomly give ClaroMax to some patients and placebos to others. In this case, BioFarm may consider randomization at the clinic level: certain clinics would give all patients ClaroMax, and other clinics would give all patients a placebo. While this approach may meet organizational constraints, it introduces other complications: namely, BioFarm will need to ensure that roughly equal numbers of patients are allocated to the ClaroMax and placebo groups.

"With a randomization strategy in place, the next important consideration is data collection. How will you ensure that data on the intervention and the outcome is being captured accurately and in a timely manner? Again, we have it easy in the online advertising world. Our computers do all the data collection for us automatically. We know exactly which ads had more people clicking through at any moment in time. I imagine data collection would be more difficult for a clinical trial," Kyra said.

Kamala nodded. "That's right. From what I understand, collecting data from clinical trials can be extremely time consuming. BioFarm would need to work with each clinic to ensure that it has a data collection mechanism in place. Nurses would record the date and time of each administration of the drug, and other coordinators would be in charge of following up with patients to collect data on drug side effects. Finally, the site coordinators would be in charge of tracking documentation of death events among the study participants. All data would be stored on a secure, HIPAA-compliant data server. So many moving pieces to keep track of!"

While conducting a causal analysis can present a lot of nuances, randomization reduces the analytic burden substantially. If randomization is done appropriately and effectively, the data analysis amounts to a simple comparison between the two intervention groups.[13] Once the study is completed, BioFarm can simply compare the survival times for the ClaroMax group and the placebo group using a statistical hypothesis test. The resulting effect-size estimate and p-value can be used to draw causal inferences about the effect of ClaroMax in increasing patient survival. Let's say, for example, that the ClaroMax group ended up with 4 percent increased survival compared to the placebo group, with a p-value of 0.23. This corresponds to an increase in survival time of about 4 percent, which the p-value indicates is not statistically significant. A 4 percent increase in this population amounts to a median increase in survival that is not considered a clinically meaningful improvement in cancer treatment. This would suggest that ClaroMax is not particularly effective in increasing overall survival in this population.

WHEN RANDOMIZATION ISN'T POSSIBLE

In this chapter so far, we've seen how randomized experiments allow us to make causal conclusions about the effect of some intervention on an outcome. But what about scenarios where it's impossible to conduct a randomized experiment due to logistical, ethical, or financial constraints? In this section, we will talk about drawing causal conclusions from nonexperimental data, also known as observational data. We will learn how statistical techniques can be used to simulate randomization, essentially replicating the results and setup of a randomized study but in an observational setting.[14]

"I'm back!" Kamala said as she knocked on David's door. "Kyra so kindly walked me through the process of setting up a randomized experiment. I just wanted to thank you again for all your help!"

David looked up from his laptop. "Oh, I hope you know we're not done with our lesson on causality! We haven't even talked about observational data yet!"

"Observational data?" Kamala was not expecting this.

David chuckled. "We got you so excited about randomization that we forgot to go over what happens when randomization is not possible! As you can imagine, not every question can be answered through an experiment. Are you free to continue where we left off?"

Kamala texted her assistant to clear her calendar for the rest of the afternoon. "Let's get back to it!"

David reclaimed his spot at the whiteboard. "Imagine we were interested in understanding the effect of a specific genetic mutation on a person's chance of having cancer. This is a causal question: 'What is the effect of X on Y?' However, there is no way to run a randomized experiment to answer this question. Another example would be measuring the effect of natural disasters on local economies. Clearly, we can't control natural disasters, so it would be impossible to answer this question through a randomized experiment. Nevertheless, there are analytic tools that we can use to answer questions like these even if it's impossible to conduct an experiment.

"One approach is to look for so-called natural experiments. Natural experiments occur when some intervention is allocated to two groups somewhat randomly, purely due to chance.[15] One famous economics paper looked at the effect of minimum wage increases on unemployment.[16] If we wanted to answer this question through an experiment, we would take a group of people and randomly pay one subgroup minimum wage and pay the other subgroup slightly more than minimum wage. Of course, no one would be likely to volunteer to be paid less than another group of volunteers, but, fortunately, a natural experiment made answering this question relatively easy and this became one of the most famous examples of Difference-in-Differences estimation. In 1992, New Jersey's minimum wage rose from $4.25 to $5.05 per hour. A neighboring state, Pennsylvania, did not increase its minimum wage during this time. Since New Jersey and Pennsylvania are neighboring states, it's reasonable to assume that the people who live immediately on the New Jersey side of the border are more or less similar to the people who live immediately on the Pennsylvania side of the border. In other words, in the region close to the state lines, we can treat whether or not someone lives in New Jersey or Pennsylvania as essentially random. Effectively, one group was randomly assigned to get an increase in minimum wage, whereas the other group was not. This allowed the economists to draw a causal conclusion about the effect of minimum wage increases on employment.

"Policy changes are another example of natural experiments. For example, if you're interested in the impact of a policy on some outcome, you can consider the time before the policy was enacted and the time after the policy was enacted to be separate intervention groups. The assumption here is that the exact time at which the policy was enacted is essentially random. Therefore, we can treat the time before the policy change as the control group and the time after the policy change as the intervention group then analyze the data using an interrupted time series methodology.

"Another creative use of natural experiments involves what's called a regression discontinuity design.[17] A discontinuity is a break along a continuum that indicates a point of inflection. Age cut-offs present a great opportunity to apply regression discontinuity designs. Let's say we're interested in understanding whether having health insurance leads to people spending less time in the hospital. To answer this question, we can use the fact that Americans become eligible for government-sponsored health care through Medicare at age 65. The key insight is that the cutoff of 65 is essentially arbitrary: the government could have very well selected 66 or 64 to be the cutoff. Therefore, we can consider uninsured patients who are just under 65 years old and Medicare patients who are just over 65 years old to be our two pseudo-randomized groups. These patients should be more or less similar across all relevant attributes, so whether or not they have health insurance comes down to the arbitrary decision to use the cutoff of 65 years. The cutoff point of 65 represents a discontinuity. An analysis can compare the rates of hospitalization in the under-65 uninsured group and the over-65 group. Because we established that these two groups of patients should be more or less similar across other attributes, we can attribute any observed differences in hospitalization to having health insurance."

"That all makes sense," Kamala began. "But what about when natural experiments don't occur? Take genetic mutations, for example. Suppose we were interested in the effect of a genetic mutation on cancer outcomes. Genetic mutations are not always random, and there are no natural experiments that allow us to find two randomly assigned groups."

"Ah, that's a great question—statistics to the rescue once again! In this case, all we have is observational data. Perhaps we have data from electronic medical records (EMRs) that contain diagnoses of cancer and whether or not patients have a specific genetic mutation of interest. One statistical technique that can be used in this context to simulate a randomized experiment is called matching.[18] Matching is a way to artificially emulate a randomized experiment by creating two groups of people who are as similar as possible on attributes except the one of interest. In this example, we may find all the patients in our EMR database who have the genetic mutation of interest. We can then apply matching to find patients who do not have the mutation of interest but who are similar to the mutated patients across all relevant traits (possible confounders). Suppose we decide that we want to match on patient sex, race, and comorbidities. Let's say we have a 64-year-old Asian male who is suffering from diabetes and has the mutation of interest. Using a matching algorithm, we can find a 64-year-old Asian male suffering from diabetes who does not have the mutation of interest. In other words, matching is trying to find 'clones' for the patients in the intervention group so that the patients in the control group are as similar as possible."

Naturally, the more characteristics that you want to match for, the harder it will be to find a match. Similarly, searching that requires exact matches is more restrictive than searching that allows some flexibility in the matching.[19] Flexibility involves, for example, allowing a 64-year-old to be matched with a 63-year-old or a 65-year-old. Different matching algorithms exist that allow the user to specify the number of matching variables and the specificity of the matching. One important assumption inherent in matching is that the variables that are selected to match are all there.[20] It's important to know that matching cannot account for unobserved or unmeasurable confounders. Obviously, if there is a confounder at play that cannot be measured, it's impossible to match on it.

SPOTTING BIASES

So far we've discussed the importance of randomized experiments in establishing causality and how we can establish causality through data analysis even when randomization is not possible. But not all data analyses are created equal: analyses that claim to establish causality may be riddled with biases and errors that skew the interpretation of results. In this section, we will go over key pitfalls that arise during study design, data analysis, and data interpretation so that you can spot misleading data science a mile away.

Pitfall	Description
Selection bias	Bias that arises from the nonrandom selection of participants or samples.
Measurement error	Bias that arises from inaccurate or imprecise measurements or data collection methods.
Response bias	Bias that arises when people who respond to a survey are substantially different from those who do not respond.
Reporting bias (publication bias)	Bias that arises from the selective reporting of results or findings that are statistically significant or interesting.
Conditional probability fallacy	Mistaking the probability of A given B with the probability of B given A (e.g. not all rectangles are squares but all squares are rectangles).
Improved detection	Bias that arises from improved diagnostic techniques, leading to an apparent increase in the frequency of a condition or disease.
Absolute vs. percent change	The change in a variable may appear exaggerated when only considering the absolute change or the percent change in isolation.
p-hacking	Bias that arises from the selective reporting or analysis of data to obtain statistically significant results.

Figure 4.1 Summary of biases, fallacies, and other pitfalls in analyzing or interpreting data

We'll start by talking about bias. We've all encountered the concept of bias, whether it's preferential treatment of students by a teacher, discrimination in the workplace, or misrepresentation of reality. While these are examples of bias in interpersonal reaction relationships, bias can also make its way into data and statistics. Here we will talk about biases that show up in data collection, data analysis, and data presentation (figure 4.1). We'll see how these biases can lead to data that is misleading and how being aware of these biases can help you spot fake statistics in real life.

Selection Bias

Kamala clears her schedule for the day as she dives into the results of the ClaroMax study. She needs to spend some time reading the original paper and trying to make sense of the study methods. Her goal is to understand exactly how the researchers arrived at their conclusion so that she can critically evaluate whether it makes sense for her company to act on this new information. She finds the original study paper and starts reading about how they collected their data. It looks like the study was based on a sample of 1,000 patients from five community cancer clinics in Texas. Patients who were receiving one of the two drugs of interest from the centers were eligible for the trial if they were in the late stages of their cancer. She also noticed that 95 percent of the participants in the study was white.

Right away, we can see that the population of the study is very different from the general population—and certainly different from the population of Kamala's patients. Her company insures individuals from mostly Florida and California, and the demographics of these constituents are similar to the populations in those two states. What Kamala has identified here is called selection bias.[21] Selection bias occurs when the group of people selected differs systematically from the population of interest. For Kamala, the population of interest is all cancer patients that her company insures. Kamala asks herself "How similar are the cancer patients in the study to the cancer patients that we cover?"

Her initial read-through suggests that the two populations are different enough that it may affect the interpretation of the results. For example, the study included only people with late-stage cancer. As a doctor, Kamala knows that ClaroMax is also used to treat early-stage cancer. More importantly, her company doesn't insure only patients with late-stage cancer; it insures everyone regardless of the stage of their cancer. "Just because this drug isn't as effective for patients with late-stage cancer doesn't mean that it's not cost effective for patients with early-stage cancer," Kamala reasons. This is an example of how selection bias may affect the interpretation of results.

Measurement Error

Bias can also arise when collecting data. Imagine a study that's trying to measure the average weight of patients at a clinic. Before patients are seen by a physician, they step on a scale, and their weight is recorded. Now suppose the scale that's used to weigh the patients is incorrectly calibrated such that the weight that the scale measures is 8 pounds less than the true weight. We'd call this measurement error or measurement bias, where what is being measured differs from the truth.[22] Specifically, this is an example of systematic measurement error, where the scale consistently measures 8 pounds below the true weight. Consider another example where patients' heights are measured using a freehand tape measure. Getting the tape measure to align with the exact height of patients is tricky, and we'd expect that sometimes this method would slightly overshoot the true height and that other times it would slightly undershoot it. This is an example of random measurement error, where the accuracy varies with each reading in a nonsystematic way.

Nonresponse Bias

Consider a hospital that wants to know how its patients felt about the care they received. The hospital CEO looks at the results of a patient satisfaction survey that the staff had rolled out the previous month. The CEO notices that there are a lot of five-star reviews and also several one-star reviews—but very few ratings in between one and five stars. This is an example of what we'd call nonresponse bias.[23] Nonresponse bias occurs when data is captured only from a specific subset of the population. In this case, the types of people who are most likely to respond are those who loved the experience (and gave five-star reviews) and those who hated the experience (and gave one-star reviews).

Inter- and Intrarater Reliability

Suppose a hospital conducts a survey to measure the level of comfort of its elderly patients. Hospital volunteers are asked to go room to room and rate the patient's comfort on a scale of 1 to 5. Studies where multiple individuals are responsible for data collection may be subject to issues with interrater reliability.[24] Suppose one volunteer consistently rates patient comfort as a 2 out of 5 whenever patients express that they are hungry. This rater feels that not getting enough food is a severe infringement on patients' comfort. In contrast, another hospital volunteer may rate a patient's comfort as 4 out of 5 if hunger is the only complaint. A study like this would have low interrater reliability, or the extent to which two raters arrive at the same conclusion for the same observation. When doing studies where there are multiple people responsible for data collection, it's important to standardize the data collection process as much as possible to ensure high interrater reliability.

Intrarater reliability is also an important consideration.[25] Studies have found that doctors are less accurate at detecting colon cancer after they have just completed many colonoscopies consecutively. It's not surprising that performing multiple procedures in the same day is tiring and impacts diagnostic accuracy. This suggests that the same doctor may come to a different conclusion depending on the time of day they are performing a colonoscopy—an example of poor intrarater reliability.

Reporting Bias

How often do we hear about a plane crash in the news? Typically, we hear about plane crashes a few times a year, and they are usually a big deal. How often do we hear about someone dying of tuberculosis in the news? Practically never. If we took the news as an indicator of reality, we would think that plane crashes are much more common than tuberculosis deaths, when in reality tuberculosis is one of the leading causes of death worldwide (about 4 million deaths per year) and plane crashes result in fewer than 300 deaths per year. This is an example of reporting bias, which occurs when what is reported does not reflect reality.[26]

A particularly insidious form of reporting bias is present in the scientific literature. This is known as publication bias.[27] Publication bias occurs when only certain types of findings are published and other types of findings are not. Typically, studies that show a positive finding, or a finding demonstrating an association between two variables, are more likely to be published than studies that show a negative finding, or a finding demonstrating the lack of an association between two variables. We can see how this may be problematic if we consider studies examining the effect of a new drug. Suppose fifty studies are conducted to test the effect of the new drug in curing disease. In forty of the studies, the drug is found to have no effect on the disease, and in ten studies, the drug is found to have an effect. From this data, we probably would conclude that the drug is not particularly effective. The issue is that scientific journals have traditionally not wanted to publish studies that show the lack of a positive finding. As a result, the forty studies that show no effect are much less likely to be published than the ten studies that do show an effect. In the literature, we may see five studies that show no effect and eight studies that show an effect. This body of evidence is much different than the true body of evidence from the fifty studies.

p-Hacking

There are several biases that can arise during data analysis. One of these is called data dredging bias, or *p*-hacking.[28] *p*-hacking occurs when the analyst fishes for a significant finding by exploring many different statistical associations, even if they are not meaningful. Imagine a research group that wants to find genetic mutations that are associated with cancer. The group has at its disposal a data set with over 10,000 different mutations. The analyst computes the association between each mutation and a cancer diagnosis until they find some significant relationships. The issue is that significance tests based on *p*-values can lead to false positives based on random chance. If you look at enough associations, you're bound to find at least one that yields a significant *p*-value (out of 10,000 associations, we'd expect at least 500 with a *p*-value of < 0.05 purely by chance).

The best way to avoid *p*-hacking is to prespecify analysis plans. Before starting to explore the data, clearly define which variables will be studied and which will not. Prespecifying analysis plans avoids situations where the analyst can modify the analysis plan post hoc if they don't see the results that they desire.

Correlation Versus Causation

A hospital is investigating striking differences in mortality rates across its surgeons, where one doctor consistently has higher mortality rates than the other surgeons. A hospital administrator reviewing the data concludes, "We have to get rid of this guy immediately; he's killing our patients!" Luckily, there was a doctor on the committee who chimed in, "That's not it; he's the best surgeon we've got. That's why we give him all the hardest cases that no one else is prepared to take on. If anyone else tried to do his job, their mortality rates would be several times higher." This is an instance of confusing correlation with causation.[29] The administrator thought that higher mortality rates must be caused by the surgeon's lack of skill when in reality there was a more important variable at play that was not initially considered: the difficulty of the surgical cases.

This phenomenon arises all the time in business settings. Just recently, Kamala was in a committee meeting where an analyst presented results showing that clients of their insurance company who sign up in Michigan tend to stay with the insurance company for almost twice as long as folks in other states. This prompted business efforts to increase recruiting for Michigan. Several months later a review of the data showed that the initial marketing and recruitment efforts didn't actually lead to better client retention. The committee members were confusing correlation with causation. They thought that there was some special quality about Michigan that led to clients being more likely to stay longer with their insurer. In reality, it's not that clients in Michigan stayed with their insurance companies the longest but rather that most of the clients in Michigan were coming from a single employer—an automotive company where employees typically stay for many years without leaving their job. What explains the high retention is not that the clients were from Michigan but that they worked for this specific employer that had particularly high employee-retention rates.

Conditional Probability Fallacy

A mother walks into an emergency room with her son and is screaming "Help! Help! My son has Ebola!" One of the nurses asks the mother why she thinks her son has Ebola. She responds, "He has had a very high fever, and I know that everyone who has Ebola gets a really high fever!" Hopefully you can spot the flaw in the mother's reasoning. Just because everyone who has Ebola has a high fever doesn't mean that everyone who has a high fever has Ebola. This is an example of confusion of the inverse.[30] While this is a very obvious example, there are more insidious examples of confusion of the inverse that are less easy to spot. Implicit bias and racial profiling often stem from confusion of the inverse.

In the wake of 9/11, Muslim Americans faced unprecedented levels of discrimination, partly because the news media portrayed terrorists in a way that emphasized their Muslim identities. In other words, the media portrayed nearly all terrorists as being Muslim. As Americans consumed this narrative, confusion of the inverse took hold, and some folks began to implicitly or explicitly associate all Muslims with terrorism. Confusion of the inverse can also occur when interpreting the results of a diagnostic test. Consider a test for COVID-19 that is designed such that everyone who actually has COVID-19 tests positive. If you take this test and test positive, what is the chance that you actually have COVID-19? If you said 100 percent, you fell into the trap of confusion of the inverse. Just because everyone who actually has COVID-19 gets a positive test result doesn't mean that everyone who gets a positive test result actually has COVID-19.

Absolute Versus Percentage Change

A few months ago an analyst in Kamala's division sent around a report exclaiming that a new advertisement that his team released led to a 30 percent increase in enrollment. This sounds great on the surface, but when Kamala asked what the new rate of enrollment was, the report said that the new ad had increased enrollment from 10 people per 10,000 to 13 people per 10,000. It's true that this was a 30 percent increase, but after looking at the absolute change, it seems much less impressive.[31] The reverse can also be true. If the marketing team's spending on advertising went up by $1 million in 1 year, would you say that's a large increase or a small increase? There's no way to know. In this case, knowing only the absolute change makes it difficult to contextualize. We need to know what the total advertising budget was in order to decide whether this change is large or small. For instance, if we found out that $1 million corresponds to 2 percent of the budget, we may not feel that this is a big change after all.

Improved Detection

A few years earlier Kamala's company saw a dramatic increase in the number of people being diagnosed with breast cancer. This led some folks in her company to suspect that there was some sort of environmental factor that was leading to an increased number of breast cancer cases—perhaps some environmental pollutant or toxic carcinogen. However, they did not see death rates due to breast cancer increase in the following years. How is this possible? The increase in breast cancer diagnoses coincided with a series of new screening measures implemented to increase the rates of mammogram screening across several states. This led to an increase in the number of breast cancer cases that were diagnosed because the mammograms caught cases of early breast cancer that would have otherwise gone undetected. This is a scenario where better detection and higher frequency of data measurement lead to increased rates of diagnosis.[32]

QUALITY OF EVIDENCE

Now that we've discussed biases that arise when collecting data, analyzing data, and interpreting results, let's put these concepts together to assess the quality of a body of evidence. A body of evidence may consist of one or more quantitative analyses or qualitative analyses. Before you make your decision based on this body of evidence, you need to evaluate whether this evidence is actually high-quality or not. In this section, we will talk about questions to ask yourself when evaluating the quality of evidence and about important frameworks to use to determine whether cause and effect can be inferred from a quantitative analysis.

A particularly dangerous error in data interpretation is the myth of the single study. We often see headlines about groundbreaking new scientific discoveries ("New Study Finds That Coffee Is Linked with Cancer!"). It becomes a challenge to interpret these studies, especially when many of them show conflicting results. For example, there are studies touting the health benefits of drinking a glass of wine every day, yet at the same time, we've seen studies linking alcohol consumption to increased rates of cancer and mortality. How do we reconcile these? More importantly, how can we protect ourselves from putting too much weight on the results of a single study? The truth is that a single study, no matter how rigorously conducted, may be subject to biases. Whether that bias is low sample size, measurement error, or improper outcome selection, a single study should ideally not be the end-all and be-all when it comes to decision-making.

For a given question of interest, what is the highest-quality evidence possible that could be generated? Kamala wants to determine whether the new drug ClaroMax is effective in improving outcomes for cancer patients. The highest-quality evidence comes from randomized experiments that have enough patients enrolled to ensure that the statistical results will be meaningful.[33] And what's provides higher-quality evidence than a single randomized experiment? Multiple randomized experiments.[34] In general, multiple randomized experiments that are conducted rigorously and that are free of the biases we talked about earlier provide high-quality evidence. When evaluating the quality of evidence, it can be useful to ask yourself this simple question: "How different is this body of evidence from that of a set of several rigorously conducted, bias-free randomized experiments?"

Of course, no study is ever 100 percent free of bias, but this is a benchmark against which we can measure the quality of evidence that we have access to. In Kamala's case, she has access to only a single study. While this study is indeed a randomized experiment, it wasn't free of biases, and we know that a single study isn't as compelling as several studies.

For questions that cannot be answered through randomized experiments, observational studies are the only option. However, several observational studies can be combined and analyzed as a whole through a technique called meta-analysis.[35] Meta-analysis uses quantitative methods to synthesize the results from many different studies and come up with an overall estimate. Meta-analysis can also be conducted on randomized experiments. Systematic reviews are similar to meta-analysis, but they typically do not include the quantitative synthesis of results.[36] Meta-analysis and systematic review are the best ways to analyze the results across multiple different studies. A group in the UK called Cochrane has put together guidelines for performing meta-analysis and systematic review such that they are rigorous, transparent, and free from bias.[37]

With the number of scientific studies that are published on a daily basis, it's possible to find a scientific publication supporting almost any viewpoint. We see a similar phenomenon with experts that spout advice to the general public. It's possible to find scientists who don't believe in climate change and doctors who don't believe in vaccine efficacy, but it's more important to understand the overall consensus across all experts, not just the opinions of a single expert. Similarly, it's important to consider not just a single study but rather the overall synthesis of evidence across all available studies. This will allow you to get a holistic understanding of the phenomenon in question and will prevent you from being biased by the results of a single study.

CONCLUSION

In this chapter, we've explored causality and study design. Causal questions are inevitable in data-driven fields. As a consumer and customer of data science, it's important to be well versed in using data to answer causal questions. This means knowing when the data at hand is appropriate and sufficient to answer a causal question and when it is not. Using the tools discussed here, you can work with data scientists to design randomized A/B tests, use observational data to answer causal questions, and understand and critique causal analyses that others have completed.

KEY QUESTIONS TO ASK

- Are we interested in determining causality?
- Can we conduct a randomized experiment or A/B test to answer this question?
  - o What are the possible confounding factors, and how can we account for them in our design?
  - o What kind of bias could affect our study, and how can we mitigate it?
  - o How will we determine the sample size needed to have enough power for our study?
- If we can't randomize, how well can we approximate randomization using observational data?
- If we can't randomize, what other methods of causal inference can we consider?
- Is our outcome truly what we're interested in, or is it a proxy?
- How will we operationalize the randomization?
- Is our data infrastructure set up to capture the results of our experiment?
- Are we introducing selection bias with our recruitment protocol?
- How accurately are we measuring our outcome?
- What other biases might be at play here?
  - o How applicable is the evidence to our specific context or problem?
  - o Are the conclusions based on the evidence reasonable, or are there alternative interpretations?
  - o How was the data collected, and were the methods appropriate and sound?
  - o Have we considered the balance of evidence? That is, have we looked at all relevant evidence or just a selection?

o How reproducible are the results, and are the methods transparent and well-documented?

o Does the evidence align with other sources of information or contradict them?

o Are there any conflicts of interest that could affect the interpretation of the evidence?

• Is the evidence we're using to make decisions high-quality?

5

CLUSTERING, SEGMENTING, AND CUTTING THROUGH THE NOISE

S teve's rotation within Shu Financial was now taking him to a new department, Fraud. This is an exciting area of the company staffed with a mix of former police officers, private investigators, phone operators, IT specialists, operations experts, data scientists, and other specialists.

The goal of the Fraud Department is to protect the company from losses as well as ensure Shu Financial customers that their private information is secure. It is usually viewed as an operating center for the company where they seek to minimize fraud losses and ensure the brand's identity. While not a profit center like some other parts of the business, the Fraud Department is considered vital to ensuring the viability of the company, and its employees aim to be "best in class" among their competitors. The department uses a mix of in-house predictive models and industry software to try to identify accounts and specific transactions that are fraudulent.

Identity fraud is a special category of fraud. In these cases, the criminal either commits application fraud, which involves creating a new, fraudulent account by applying for a credit card in someone else's name, or takes over an existing account by changing key account information like the name and address on the account.

Descriptive statistics calculated by the data analysts have shown that most of the company's fraud losses are due to application fraud, a fact that has been consistent for years. The company is very concerned about reducing these losses, as they affect not only Shu Financial's bottom line but also its reputation. The last thing Shu Financial wants is a front-page news story about a fraudulent application that its employees accepted.

The company already has one supervised machine learning model that predicts the probability that an application is fraudulent. This model is a supervised machine learning model because it is trained on a target variable, the indicator of whether or not the application is fraudulent.

A key question that keeps arising is whether there are different types of application fraud or whether application fraud is one homogenous group. Perhaps different criminals who commit application fraud have different ways of getting the false information or target different victims or use the credit cards in different ways once their application is approved.

If there is only one type of application fraud, then it may be reasonable to stick with a single model. On the other hand, if there are a number of different types of application fraud, then it might be advantageous to identify these different types and target them with different predictive models. Steve was brimming with ideas but uncertain as to what steps to take first, so he arranged a meeting with the data science team about his challenge.

DIMENSIONALITY REDUCTION

After hearing the problem description, the lead data scientist, Brett, nodded his head. "Sounds like a classic unsupervised machine learning problem. It is unsupervised in that we don't have a target to predict like the charge-off amount or the probability of fraud. The first thing we would like to do is find a good way to visualize the customer data. This will help us see if there are obvious groupings of fraudulent applications. Again, we are not trying to predict the probability of fraud but rather trying to see if there are patterns that can be detected among the frauds. Unsupervised machine learning not only is useful for finding subpopulations but also is a very good tool for conducting exploratory data analysis in general, where we can find patterns in the data that we currently aren't aware of or don't use."[1]

Steve understood the goal, but the actual steps seemed unclear. "There are so many variables for each application: variables on the application itself, comparisons to other applications in that zip code, information from the credit report, the transactions on the account, and the online and telephone activity. How can you possibly graph all of those variables and make any sense? Are you going to make hundreds of scatterplots?"

Brett explained, "Unsupervised machine learning will quickly surpass anything you would do on an Excel spreadsheet. You are right; there are huge numbers of possible variables, and we will need to be clever about doing the data exploration. Luckily, there is a great method called principal components analysis that can help us make sense of situations where there are a lot of features.[2] We'll do that as the first step."

Principal components analysis is called a *dimensionality-reduction method*, since it tries to reduce the number of dimensions that a user would consider in the analysis. Here, "dimension" refers to a variable, or a column in a dataset; dimensionality reduction is the process of reducing the number of columns in a dataset while retaining the important signals. Essentially, it maps the original data set into a new data set that has the same information as the original data set but that looks at the data through a different lens, a transformed lens. The goal is to reduce the number of dimensions as much as possible while not discarding a lot of information.[3] Clearly, this is a balancing act where the customer needs to understand what is being gained and what is being lost.

It is important to note that principal components analysis is not the only algorithm for dimensionality reduction, but it is probably the most popular. Its popularity stems from the fact that it is extremely effective, is fairly intuitive, can be performed quickly, and has been around for over one hundred years.[4] There is a wealth of multidimensional scaling algorithms that can be used instead of principal components. Another popular method, t-SNE, is often used when it is difficult to separate clusters using linear assumptions like those in principal components analysis.[5]

Principal components analysis works best on continuous variables like age and credit score and can also help with ordinal variables like level of education.[6] It also works best when using variables that have a lot of variance and provides little information when using variables that lack variance. For example, if 95 percent of the customers finished high school, then separating out the customers into two groups, those who did finish high school and those who didn't, is not very useful. On the other hand, if you have an ordinal variable that represents whether the customer did not finish high school, finished high school but not college, finished college but not graduate school, finished graduate school, and so on, then it is a much more informative variable. Categorical variables like region of the country and sex are not as useful in principal components analysis.[7]

The first step is to eliminate the variables that have limited incremental information. This is considered a preprocessing step in that it is about cleaning the data before implementing the principal components analysis. Variables that have little variance as well as variables that are highly correlated with other variables provide little incremental information and so are usually dropped from the analysis. By eliminating unnecessary variables, the algorithms can converge more quickly to a solution, and that solution can be more readily interpreted.[8]

The second step is to standardize the inputs. Instead of variables like age being on a years scale and amount purchased in the first month being on a dollars scale, the variables are adjusted so that they are on the same scale.[9] A simple scaling would be to standardize the values to the normal distribution with a mean of 0 and a standard deviation of 1. This is often called normalizing. To normalize the customer's age, the mean age is subtracted from the customer's age, and then the difference is divided by the standard deviation. When this is done for all customers, the average value of the age is 0, and the standard deviation is now 1. Another simple standardization is a range standardization where the minimum value is set to 0, the maximum value is set to 1, and then all values in between are proportional. Other standardizations include midrange standardization, interquartile range standardization, and mean standardization. In some cases, normalizing is not the optimal method for standardizing, but this is something that a data scientist can explore by testing different standardizations to see which produces the best principal components and clusters.[10] In practice, many statistical software programs do this standardization as a routine step in the data processing,

The next steps involve computing the first principal component. This calculation identifies what combination of the standardized input variables explains the most information in the entire data set. This combination is the sum of different weights that have been multiplied by the standardized input variables. The second principal component is computed by looking at the remaining information that is not explained by the first principal component and then finding what combination of input variables explains this remaining information. The first and second principal components are perpendicular, meaning that there is no correlation between these two components.[11] Each additional component is perpendicular to the previous components. The process of adding components continues until there are as many components as there are input variables.

Brett proceeded to clarify. "Once we develop the principal components, we can look at how much information is explained by the first few components.[12] If, for example, the first two explain 80 percent of the variance in the original data set, then we can focus on just those first two for our data visualization. This is similar to the process used for image compression. There we start with an image that is a large set of red, blue, and yellow values. We map it to a new space, like we just did with the principal components. We then retain only the most critical information to produce a jpeg file."

"I see the analogy with image compression, but I don't understand exactly what these components mean in principal components analysis? I understand exactly what the customer's age is, but I have no idea how to interpret what the first, second, or third component is representing," countered Steve.

"This is where we need to use your business insight. Each component has coefficients corresponding to each variable. By interpreting the size and direction of the coefficients, we can try to interpret what each component represents. This first component has very large positive coefficients for the credit risk score and the amount spent in the first few transactions, and most of the other coefficients are close to 0. How would you interpret this group?"

Steve responded, "Easy—these are fraudulent applications where the criminal targeted someone with good credit, and then as soon as they got our credit card, they made a big purchase immediately. The fraudster did their research in advance to select a good target, such as someone with a high FICO score, and then wants to steal as much as they can quickly before we can figure out that the application is fraudulent."

Steve and Brett worked side by side to examine the amount of variance explained by the different components and agreed that they would focus initially on the first three components, since that explained the majority of the variance in the data. They characterized these first few components based on the variables that had the largest positive and negative coefficients so they could quickly interpret what the components meant. This characterization also would help later with the interpretation of any clusters they might see in the graphs. These clusters are groupings of fraudulent accounts where those in the group are similar for these first three principal components and those in different clusters are dissimilar for these first three principal components. This partnership between the business unit, which provides domain-specific knowledge, and the data science team is critical. The business unit helps provide insight that can illustrate the interpretation of not only the principal components but also the clusters themselves. The stronger this partnership, the more useful the final product. When this partnership is weak, often the data science products do not meet the business needs, resulting in wasted time and money.

By reducing the data set from a large set of features about the accounts to just these three principal components, they have achieved dimensionality reduction—having fewer dimensions to work with will make the problem much easier to understand analytically and lead to faster solutions. A key in performing this dimensionality reduction is to be certain you don't discard too much critical information that you will want in the analysis.[13]

The second component had large positive coefficients related to how often the customer checked the account online in the first few days after receiving the card and how many gas station purchases they made in the first few days. Steve understood that these were criminals who wanted to make sure that the card was still active and that they wanted to do anonymous transactions like testing the card at a gas station. This group was cautious as to how they used the card, avoiding interacting in a store or in front of people.

A series of scatterplots helped the team quickly identify a few clusters within the fraudulent applications. The first component, the good credit scores where the criminal immediately tried committing large frauds, was actually composed of three groups, based on the speed and types of transactions the fraudsters attempted. They called these different groups the bold, the hesitant, and those "riding the fence."

Now that the different groups of fraudulent applications had been identified, the data science team planned to build separate models to target the different clusters. The team also planned to try using the principal components themselves as inputs to the model to see if this was more effective than using the features themselves. This use of the components themselves in the predictive model is a common technique that often produces strong models with a minimal number of features. In order to produce the principal components, the team still needs to use the preprocessed variables.

The data science team planned to run the general fraudulent application model as well to make sure that cases weren't slipping through their defenses. For each model, the team would provide reason codes to the fraud investigators so they would understand why the account was being flagged by the system as well what specific style of application fraud the models thought was most likely. This information helps streamline the investigators' work and leads to further operational improvements.

With a predictive model, we can look at the accuracy of the prediction to decide if the model is sufficiently good. With unsupervised machine learning, we don't have a target variable we are trying to predict. This means we can't state how "good" the model performed. Rather, we need to see how well the output of the model can be described and used in a practical sense. If the features in clusters are not very different, then it is difficult to describe what the clusters represent. This happens when the clusters are not well separated. Contrarily, if the clusters are describing very different populations, then the clusters will be well separated, and there will be features that are very different for the different clusters.[14]

Cluster profiling refers to the process of generating unique descriptions for each cluster using the input variables. The profiles are usually generated by looking at the average characteristics in each cluster and labeling each cluster based on a few variables that are the most extreme (large or small) in that specific cluster. When the number of clusters is relatively small, then this profiling is best done collaboratively by the data science team and the client—in this case, Steve and experts in the Fraud Department are the clients. When the number of clusters is very large, a manual process of labeling clusters is not feasible, and an automatic labeling process based on the input variable values is more practical.[15] When the data science team members explore different clustering algorithms, distance metrics, standardizations, and other parameters, they can track not only the number of clusters identified and the percentage of the population in each cluster but also the cluster descriptions. This will help indicate if some methods are better at identifying subpopulations that are more hidden from other methods. The characteristics used to profile the clusters could include information about the target population's demographics like age, sex, and location; the transactions of the fraud, like at gas stations or ATMs; and other information about patterns in online transactions.

Often subject-matter experts will be called in to review the clusters to assess whether they make sense and are readily distinguishable. In Steve's case, he can ask members of the Fraud Department to review the cluster analysis and give their opinions on whether these clusters are really distinguishable and represent subpopulations in the real world. That consultation also opens up the conversation around how they can use these clusters to improve their investigations.

If too many clusters are identified, then the information may not be useful. This increased information about the clusters can clearly help the investigators, but it is possible to exceed the capacity of the team. If the modeling identified fifty different clusters, then the investigators might find the information to be excessive. Perhaps they can't consider fifty different protocols, so they may begin to ignore the modeling output. This would be a major opportunity loss for the organization that should be avoided.

A consequence of this operational limitation is that Steve should discuss with the operational teams that will be using the modeling results exactly how they plan to use the model output and what their capacity limitations are. They might be able to quickly develop streamlined processes for five different types of application fraud and let the rest fall into the "Other" bucket. If so, then the modeling should align to the operational capacity while opening up the conversation regarding whether there is value in working toward a point where more clusters could be handled operationally.

This type of data exploration can also be very helpful in developing new features that can be used to improve predictive models. The data science team could examine the details of the first few principal components to see if they represent features that are not already explicitly in the predictive model. If they are not already included, the team can create new features that capture this important information.

CLUSTERING METHODS

Unsupervised machine learning is broader than clustering, but this is one of its most common applications. As you saw in the application fraud example, all of the cases were fraud. They were not trying to predict fraud, since the answer would have been "yes" every time. Rather, the team members were trying to understand if they

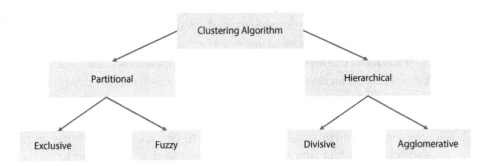

Figure 5.1 Example taxonomy of clustering

could group the cases in a way that brings together similar frauds and separates out dissimilar frauds.

There is a wealth of different algorithms used for clustering, including Gaussian mixed models, expectation-maximization models, latent Dirichlet allocation methods, and fuzzy clustering algorithms. As a customer, however, you don't need to try to learn the complete taxonomy of algorithms. Rather, it is useful to have a clear understanding of some of the most popular methods (figure 5.1) and then ask the data science team members to explain which methods they used and why.

What are the main types of clustering algorithms? One way to think about clustering algorithms is in terms of whether the customers are assigned to only one group or whether they can belong to multiple clusters. Exclusive clusters are simple to understand—customers belong to one and only one cluster. Other algorithms allow customers to be shared across multiple clusters, and at the most extreme are fuzzy clusters, where the customer has a certain probability of belonging to every cluster. From Steve's point of view, it is worthwhile to ask the data science team whether the clustering is exclusive or not. If not, then there should be a reason why the team chose a more complicated way of clustering.

Another way to think about clustering algorithms is in terms of whether they are hierarchical. This refers to the idea that the smallest clusters belong to larger clusters that belong to even larger clusters. Hierarchical clustering is common for some algorithms and allows the user to quickly understand how the decision on the number of clusters impacts the way the clusters are characterized. Hierarchical clusters are easy to visualize, since the clusters can look like branches of trees. If the user decides that they would prefer to use more or fewer clusters, then they can simply go higher or lower in the hierarchy.[16]

The opposite of hierarchical clustering is partitional clustering.[17] As with the question of exclusivity (from the customer point of view), the decision to use a hierarchical or a partitioning algorithm is not critical, but it is helpful to understand why the data science team made the particular decision. Sometimes there are good data-driven or operations-driven reasons why one algorithm is chosen. Other times the decision may be driven more by the simplicity of or familiarity with one algorithm over another.

Across nearly all of the clustering methods, the general approach is similar. The features are standardized so that they have similar dimensions, a step described earlier for the principal components analysis. There is often a step where the dimensionality is then reduced. This can be done by performing a principal components analysis, selecting features with a minimal amount of variance and dropping features that are very highly correlated with other features, or by using another dimensionality-reducing method. This preprocessing of the data results in a more streamlined data set that can then be explored with one or more clustering algorithms.[18]

After the clustering is performed, the clusters are characterized, usually by describing the features that have the largest positive and negative values in each cluster. The clusters are also described in terms of size. A cluster that includes half of the customers is quite different operationally from one that includes only 1 percent of the customers. These clusters can be handled differently—either by making separate predictive models for the different clusters or by treating them differently operationally.

As Brett explained to Steve, "Let's start with one of the most popular of the partitioning-based methods, K-means clustering.[19]

K-means starts with the team fixing the number of clusters, K, at a specific value—say, three. We would select three observations to be the centers of the three different clusters, where it is best if these three are very far from each other. These three starting points become three clusters by assigning the closest observations to each seed. To determine which observation is closest, we need to decide how we measure distance. The simplest way to do this is the Euclidean distance. When all of the observations have been assigned to one of these three clusters based on their distance to the starting point, the center of the cluster (called the centroid) is computed, and that becomes the new starting point for the three clusters. We then repeat this process over and over. Pretty soon the algorithm settles down to consistently drawing the same clusters, and then we know we are done with that value of K."

Steve smiled and said, "But, Brett, I have no idea how many clusters there are. That's one of the questions I wanted your help to answer. I was told that operationally we can handle between one and about ten clusters before the investigative team will throw in the towel on this fraud application segmentation. Also, how do I know how good these clusters are in separating out the fraudsters?"

Brett's response was simple yet perfect. "We will let the data tell us how many clusters are optimal by testing the entire range from one to ten. So we don't really walk in knowing how many clusters work best; rather, we test all possible values of K. Our algorithm works by trying to find the clusters that explain the most variance in the data. There are a lot of ways to look at the data later to decide which value of K worked best . . . the joke we have on the team is that when we use twelve different algorithms to select the best K, we hate it when we get twelve different answers."

K-means clustering is popular because it is a very fast, simple method that is intuitive. Additionally, K-means clustering has the advantage of scaling up linearly with the number of observations, meaning it can be used readily on large data sets. One issue is that it can obtain results that are suboptimal—for example, finding less than perfect clusters—and can be heavily influenced by the starting points. That is why the algorithm usually explores a number of different possible starting points before settling on a final set of clusters, and the customer (in this case, Steve) needs to be involved in the evaluation of the clustering algorithm's results. A variation of K-means that is popular is fuzzy K-means, where customers can belong to more than one cluster.[20] The probability of belonging to a cluster is simply based on the distance from the centroid of the cluster. This is intuitive in that the closer the customer is to a cluster, the higher the probability that they belong to that cluster, while the farther away from the cluster, the lower the probability.

Another category of clustering algorithms that are popular and intuitive is the hierarchical algorithms. A good way to think about hierarchical algorithms is to remember the stacking Russian dolls, where one fits inside another that fits inside another. From Steve's point of view, this means that he can quickly see how different clusters combine at a higher level or split up at a lower level. If Steve can use only use five or six clusters, then the data science team can show him which clusters are being combined to get him to that number of clusters as well as what each of those clusters represents.

Hierarchical clusters can be created in one of two directions. Agglomerative algorithms work bottom-up.[21] You start by letting each customer be their own cluster, where the distances between the clusters are the same as the distances between the customers. You then find the closest (most similar) customers and merge them to form a new cluster, so there is now one less cluster than before. You repeat computing the distances between the new cluster and the other clusters. Whichever clusters are the closest are then merged, so there is again one less cluster, and the process repeats and repeats until every customer belongs to one single cluster. So which number of clusters should you use? Different algorithms provide recommendations by generally looking at how much additional variance in the data is explained by using an additional cluster and then stopping when the additional clusters are not very helpful.

The decision of how the distances are computed impacts the shape of the clusters.[22] For example, if you use the closest distance between any two elements in the clusters, you may merge different clusters than if you use the average distance between all of the elements. Alternatively, you could use the distance between the farthest elements in the clusters as the criterion for merging. How you choose to measure distance and link clusters has major ramifications for the clusters developed, so you should ask the data science team to explain which criteria were used and why.

Divisive clustering works top-down and is the opposite of agglomerative clustering.[23] It starts with all of the customers belonging to one single cluster. These customers are split into separate clusters and are then split again into new clusters. This process continues until each cluster is made up of one and only one customer. Because it is a hierarchical method, each cluster fits inside another at a different level, meaning the team can quickly understand what happens to the cluster size and characteristics when they go from four clusters to six to ten clusters.

Steve's head was swirling a bit, so he called Brett. "As a customer, do I really care whether the algorithm was divisive or agglomerative?" Brett immediately replied, "No, the more important questions for you are what the resulting clusters represent and how they are used. That said, if your data science team members can't tell you what algorithm they used and why they selected it, then this should raise a lot of red flags about their methods and capabilities."

Hierarchical clustering models are popular because they are intuitive, they perform well, and the results can be easily communicated. That said, they do have some downsides. Hierarchical models struggle with large data sets because the processing time scales with the square or more of the number of observations. As with other clustering methods, there are many different ways to measure the clustering performance, so you can't easily say that one solution is the best clustering answer.[24]

In some situations, there is some partial labeling of data. For example, there are different types of fraud, including fraudulent applications, account takeovers (where the legitimate account holder applied for the card but then a fraudster took control of the account), card thefts, illegal use of lost cards, and skimming (where a second card is made using the data from the first card). If the members of Steve's team have already tagged some of the cases they have investigated, then the data science team can look to see if the clusters correspond to known fraud types. This helps interpret the clusters and also could be used as a way to test which clustering techniques are more accurate at distinguishing different types of fraud. Since there is a target involved in this type of analysis, there is a large family of supervised machine learning algorithms that can also be used to address this question. These will be discussed in later chapters.

USING CLUSTERS

Once a cluster analysis has been completed, it can be used not only to interpret the past but also to help understand new situations. Let's see how things worked out for Steve in his fraudulent application example.

Brett began the project debrief. "Here's the rundown of the clustering project. We started by doing a principal components analysis, which showed us that there was definitely going to be some separation between the different fraudulent applications, though it was unclear exactly how many clusters to use. We selected the three top principal components, which accounted for 90 percent of the variance, and then began our cluster analysis. The components were all standardized, where some initial exploration showed us that range standardization worked best. We used K-means clustering to test a range between two to ten different clusters. The final number of clusters was set at six, though we could have made pretty good arguments for any number between four and seven. Once we had our final number of clusters, we reviewed the average input values of each cluster and named them."

Steve nodded his head. "Yes, I remember all of these steps. Of course, my manager is going to want to know what value we got out of doing this clustering. She is very focused on making sure I can answer the question 'So how does this translate into Shu Financial stopping fraud losses?'"

Brett smiled. "Yes, many times she has interrupted me with that sharp question. But we are prepared to answer it. There are a few ways we used this cluster analysis to help the company. The first is that we used to have only one model to predict the probability of application fraud. The cluster analysis helped us to develop other behavioral-based predictive models that target some of the specific features of the different clusters. These separate models are far more accurate at predicting fraud than our single model was, so our fraud detection rate is now much higher, meaning we can prevent more fraud losses and lower our operating expenses, since investigators' time is better targeted."

Steve interrupted. "So the unsupervised machine learning actually helped us build new supervised machine learning models to help detect fraudsters more quickly."

Brett continued. "Yes, in fact this happens often. Unsupervised machine learning and supervised machine learning often are partners in solving real-world problems. In addition to the new models, we use the cluster analysis directly by scoring each application and assigning it to a cluster. We send the information about which cluster the application belongs to over to the investigators along with some of the application's distinguishing features. These features serve as reason codes that inform the investigators as to what makes an application unusual and worthy of attention. This cluster and reason code information helps the investigative unit where the employees have divided themselves into different teams to focus more efficiently on different clusters."

"This means that our cluster analysis helped us not only gain insight into our data but also create new models and improve the operational efficiency of our units."

KEY QUESTIONS

Clustering Concepts:

- Do I have a reason to believe that there are subpopulations of interest (clusters), or do I think this is one homogeneous group?

- If I did determine that there were clusters, can I use that information operationally?
- Is there a limit to how many clusters I can use in my operation so as to improve performance?
- What factors do we normally use to segment populations, and how do these compare with the factors identified in the modeling?

Dimensionality Reduction:

- Which method did you use for dimensionality reduction, and why did you choose that method?
- How much variance is explained by the different components? Can we reduce our focus to just a few components, or do we lose too much information?
- How do we interpret the components? What do we think the first, second, and third components represent?

Clustering Algorithm:

- Is the clustering exclusive? If not, then why did you decide to use that algorithm?
- Which clustering algorithm was used?
- What metric was used for the distance and the linkage between clusters? Why were those criteria used?

6

BUILDING YOUR FIRST MODEL

"**K**amala," Annie said, "we need to do something about these prior authorizations. We are just not making the right decisions. Costs are going up, and it doesn't look like patient outcomes are improving either."

Prior authorization is the process in which an insurance company requires a physician to get clearance for reimbursement from the insurer before providing a service or performing a procedure. The patient's physician submits evidence attesting to the justification for the service, and an employee at the insurer reviews the evidence to determine whether the service meets the company's criteria for reimbursement. Insurers use prior authorizations to ensure that they reimburse for services that are medically necessary and to control costs by adding a bit more friction to the system for physicians and patients.[1]

Annie was talking about the recent spike in costs for patients getting spine surgery for back pain. Spine surgery is expensive, so insurers like Stardust Health want to make sure that when the company pays for surgery, it is the right treatment for the patient's condition.

"I hear you," Kamala tried to console her. "We need a way to make better decisions as to which surgeries to approve and which to deny. Right now we have too many false positives and false negatives—there are patients who need surgery who aren't getting it, and patients who don't need surgery who are getting it! It's clearly leading to higher costs, and we've seen that often the patients who get surgery end up having complications or continued back pain.[2] Physicians advocate hard for surgery when they submit their authorizations, but it's sometimes tough for them to see what a patient's life may look like after an unsuccessful surgery."

Annie nodded. "I think this is something that David and the data science team can help us out with. Instead of having humans manually review which cases to approve and which to deny, let's consider adopting a strategy where we empower our human decision-makers with data."

Kamala set up a meeting with the data science team to hash out a plan. She explained the context of rising costs and poor decision-making, "We're seeing that our reviewers are finding it difficult to determine whether a patient would benefit from a nonsurgical treatment option for their back pain. Some combination of physical therapy and pain medication might be better for many patients. The biggest issue is that our reviewers have trouble deciding if a patient would do well on nonsurgical treatment, so they end up approving the surgery."

SCOPING

David, the senior data scientist on the team, had been listening carefully. "It sounds like this is a difficult decision for the reviewers. Do you see this as an issue related to reviewer training, or would this be a difficult decision even for the most highly skilled reviewer?" David wanted to make sure that before building a data-driven solution, they were exploring all possible alternatives.

Kamala responded. "Even the most highly skilled reviewer would have trouble with this because what we're asking them to do is predict the future. We're asking them to consider whether a specific patient would do well with nonsurgical management of their back pain and, if so, to deny the surgery. Right now we do see cases where the patient's request for surgery was denied and they ended up doing quite well with nonsurgical management. But there are also many folks who get denied surgery and end up having continued or worsening back pain. It's hard for us to predict who will fall in which bucket."

"Predicting counterfactuals, huh? Yeah, humans aren't always great at that. Imagine we helped you build a model that could say 'This patient has a 90 percent chance of success on nonsurgical treatment.' Would that help the reviewers make a decision?" David asked.

Kamala's eyes widened. "If we had a model that could accurately determine who would do well on nonsurgical treatment, it would be of huge value. Not only would it save our reviewers time, but also it would help bring down costs and save patients from unnecessarily going under the knife." Kamala's mind was already racing with possibilities for how her team could use such a model. "What are the next steps to get started on this model?"

"Well, first, we need to scope out the problem statement in great detail. Can you organize a meeting with all the key stakeholders? During that meeting, we will flesh out exactly what we are trying to predict and align on our approach." David spoke slowly to allow Kamala to take notes. "The data science team members can build the model, but we need to make sure we're using the right data for the question your team has in mind. We also need to align on how the model will be used and who will be using it."

TO EXPLAIN OR PREDICT?

On the clinical side, the main stakeholders included Kamala and Jenna, head of prior authorization. From the data science team, there were David and Maya, a data scientist.

David started out by giving a brief description of prediction from a data standpoint. "Prediction is a fundamental data science task. Essentially, it involves feeding some input data to a model and predicting some outcome. This outcome can be continuous, like predicting the amount of money someone will spend, or categorical, like predicting whether someone will live or die."[3]

Kamala smiled. "David, this isn't the first time you've built a model for us. Remember the model your team built to help us understand which patients had higher costs? You're treating this like it's a totally different exercise, but haven't we done this before?"

David understood Kamala's perspective. "You're right. We have built models before, but not all models are equal! The key difference lies in our reasons for building the models. In the model we built to quantify patient costs, we were interested in finding specific variables that led to higher cost. We wanted to explain which phenomena led to higher costs so your team could act on them. To put it simply, we wanted to *explain* why certain patients had higher costs. Now we don't necessarily care about *explaining* why someone would be a good candidate for nonsurgical management. We want to *predict* as accurately as possible who would benefit from a nonsurgical approach. It's a subtle distinction, but depending on whether our goal is explanation or prediction, our approach to building the model will be substantially different."[4]

DEFINING OUTCOMES

David stood up at the whiteboard. "The first thing we need to do is define the outcome. The outcome is the quantity that we want to predict. You guys mentioned that it would be helpful if we could predict a patient's chance of success on a nonsurgical treatment plan. How do we define success?"

Kamala started. "Let's throw out some options. One clear choice is whether or not they overcome their back pain. That would be the clearest definition of success, right?"

"Yes, it's obviously important, but it's hard to measure," Maya explained. "How would we know if a patient overcame their back pain or not? Remember that we're limited in terms of what data we have access to: our main data source is patients' insurance claims."[5]

Kamala nodded. "That's a good point. Insurance claims tell us only what health care resources they used. We can't really know what the patient is feeling just from their insurance claims."

Jenna piped up, "What if we looked at catastrophic events, like being hospitalized or dying of complications? Hospitalizations are bad for the patient and expensive for us, so if we can determine who is likely to have a hospitalization without surgery, that would be very useful information for us."

"I agree hospitalizations and deaths are something we want to avoid, but they don't tell the whole story," Kamala chimed in. "Someone could not be hospitalized but still be using a lot of health care resources. What if we look at health care utilization?[6] Once a patient starts on a nonsurgical treatment, will they end up using a ton of resources or not? If a patient who really needs surgery doesn't get surgery, they may end up using more pain medications and physical therapy than normal."

Jenna agreed. "That sounds like a good outcome to me. If we can predict what a patient's health care utilization will be if they don't get surgery, we can show that some patients who don't get the surgery will still have low health care utilization, suggesting that their back pain may be well managed without surgery. Separately, we could build another model to predict the chance of a catastrophic event, like dying of complications from the spine surgery. The health care utilization model will be the primary model, but if we see that someone's predicted risk of death is too high, that would take precedence."

David was scribbling furiously on the whiteboard. "Do we need to specify what kind of health care utilization we're measuring? For example, let's say someone gets diagnosed with cancer around the same time their back pain starts acting up. We wouldn't want to count their chemo regimen costs when calculating their utilization for this model, right?"

Jenna and Kamala nodded in agreement. "I think we should look only at utilization related to back pain, like medications, injections, and physical therapy," Jenna suggested.

"That makes a lot of sense," said Kamala. "We should restrict the definition of our outcome to home in on exactly what we want to measure." Kamala was beginning to understand the importance of specific outcome definitions. "Speaking of restricting the definition, should we look at health care expenditure in a specific time frame? Maybe something like 1 year after they first submit the prior authorization for the surgery?"

Jenna had some thoughts from her experience reviewing authorization proposals. "I don't think 1 year is long enough. Let's look at 3 years after to be safe. When folks resubmit an authorization request for a previously denied surgery for back pain, the time frame is often greater than 1 year after the previous request."

David chimed in, "It would be great if we could make accurate predictions three years into the future, but the reality is, the further in the future you want to predict, the harder it is to make accurate predictions. I suggest we try out a range of prediction windows, ranging from one month to one year, and see how the model accuracy changes as we increase the length of the prediction window." The others nodded in agreement.

David synthesized the discussion up to this point. "Alright, it sounds like health care utilization makes sense as an outcome. Just to play devil's advocate, if we use this as the outcome for our model, are there cases where the model's conclusions may be misleading?"

"I can think of at least one case," Jenna responded. "We're basically saying that if a patient has lower predicted health care utilization, it means their back pain is well managed. But some patients may be less likely to seek health care for their back pain compared to others. For example, patients who live far away from health centers may be less likely to seek health care than patients who live close to health centers.[7] Just because the model predicts that someone has lower utilization doesn't mean that their back pain is well managed."

Kamala's eyes widened as she thought about Jenna's argument. "David, what Jenna's saying makes sense. It sounds like using this outcome may introduce some bias into the model. Is there some way we can address that?"

"It's a good point. No model is perfect, and we certainly don't want to be systematically overpredicting or underpredicting for a certain group of patients. We can do some analyses to check if certain groups of people tend to have lower or higher health care expenditure on average, and we can keep a close eye on this issue when we test out the model,"[8] David said, trying to reassure them.

"This point about edge cases is making me wonder," Jenna started. "If we're looking at people's health care expenditure 1 year after their authorization request, are we assuming that they will be alive for that year? Some of our older patients die soon after they submit a request. How would the model deal with those cases?"

Maya responded, "It's a good point, Jenna. The reason we set the time window for measuring expenditure is so that we're getting comparable amounts of data for all patients. Obviously, if someone dies one month after making a request, they're going to have less expenditure. Before we decide how to deal with those cases, I'd want to look into how often someone dies within a year of making a request. If it's a common occurrence, we may need to make some changes[9] because the model would consider those folks to have lower expenditure and may systematically underpredict. One change we could consider is setting a maximum age for using this model. For example, maybe we run the model only for patients who are 60 or younger—in other words, folks who are not as likely to die in a year."

FEATURES: THE BACKBONE OF ALL MODELS

"So we've aligned on an outcome and a population of interest. What else do we need to build this model?" Jenna asked.

David explained, "Probably the biggest determinant of model success is the features. The features are the variables that we will use to predict our outcome."[10]

Kamala wondered out loud, "Where do we get this data from? Can we use any source of data that we want?"

"That's a good question," David responded. "We want to consider what data we will have at our disposal at the time we want to run the prediction model. We want to run the model on a patient at the time of the prior authorization, and while we may have data on patients after their prior authorization, we want to ignore that data when we build the model because we wouldn't have access to it if we were running the model in real time."

"Ok, so it sounds like there are some temporal restrictions on what data the model can take in. We want to use only data that was collected before the prior authorization because that's the data we will have access to when we actually apply this model." Kamala was having fun thinking about these technical considerations. "What about types of data? Can the model make sense of any type of data, or are we restricted there too?"

Maya, who will be in charge of building the model, responded to Kamala. "The type of model we're using will take in tabular data—think spreadsheet. If we can put our data into a spreadsheet format, then we can use it in our model."[11]

Jenna looked worried. "So does that preclude things like text data? Oftentimes the prior authorization write-up will include a note from the patient's clinician. That note can contain a lot of valuable information that may help us decide whether the patient will respond well to a nonsurgical option. But that note is written in sentences—not really suitable for a spreadsheet."[12]

David didn't look worried. "This is where we can leverage feature engineering. Feature engineering is the process by which we create variables to feed into our model from other data sources.[13] Even though the model wouldn't be able to understand the clinician's notes in raw format, we can use feature engineering techniques from the field of natural language processing to help us convert that free text into a table of numbers. The details aren't important, but the point is that we can take a block of text and turn it into a table of numbers that the model can understand."

"That's great—so we're not wasting that information!" Jenna let out a sign of relief. "Sometimes the prior authorization application also contains scanned PDF documents of lab results. Would it be possible to include those types of data in the model?"

"Theoretically yes." David was less enthusiastic now. "We can use a method called optical character recognition to extract numerical and text data from the PDFs—basically turning scanned PDFs into machine-readable format.[14] Keep in mind that extracting features from images and text data can be time intensive but is continuing to get easier with the release of new software and increased data availability. We should make sure that we've exhausted all our existing tabular data before we spend too much time fiddling with scanned PDF images."

Every data science team has its strengths and weaknesses. Stardust Health Insurance's data science team does not deal with image data on a regular basis, so building out the infrastructure to ingest and handle scanned PDFs would be a substantial lift. It's important to define what is in scope versus out of scope for feature engineering. Otherwise, you run the risk of spending too much time creating features, which can be a long and expensive process, especially if new data infrastructure needs to be built.

"We have access to a lot of claims data that is stored as data tables," David continued. "I mention that just because the fact that something is already in tabular format doesn't mean that we're done. It's often possible to extract even more features from data that's already in tabular format."

Kamala looked intrigued. "What would be an example of that?"

"Well, for instance, we may know from our insurance claims whenever a patient is hospitalized," David suggested. "Using that data, we can create a feature that counts the total number of times a patient was hospitalized in the 1 year before the prior authorization submission."

"I see. So we'd essentially be aggregating the claims data that we have in different ways to create patient-level metrics," reasoned Kamala.

Maya nodded. "Exactly. Aggregating is a great way to approach feature engineering.[15] We can do this with total number of hospital visits, total number of medications prescribed, average number of claims per month, and much more. Another great approach is to create rate-of-change features. For example, we can find the percentage by which their prescription drug use increased in the 6 months before the prior authorization submission. These are all features that we can create using our existing tabular data and that may help us in predicting our outcome.

Kamala was starting to make sense of all the possibilities that feature engineering afforded. "I see. So these aggregate measure and rate-of-change metrics can all be calculated using our existing claims data. If we combine all these features with the features that we create from transforming the text data and the PDFs, we could have a lot of features for our model to use. Is there a specific number of features we need to have?" Kamala asked.

"There's no set rule. What we're trying to find are the most highly predictive features. If we could wave a magic wand and find a single feature that perfectly predicts health care utilization for nonsurgical treatment, we could call it a day. But because we don't know a priori which features are good predictors, it's in our best interest to come up with as many candidate predictors as possible." David's explanation made sense to those in the group, and now they were more interested in the mechanics of the model.

"How will the model be able to sort through all of these? Will it just use all of them at the same time?" Jenna wondered.

Maya responded, "Each model is a little different, but fundamentally the goal of a model is to identify statistical relationships between variables. If we create five hundred features, the model is going to look through each one to find the ones that have the strongest relationship with our outcome of interest."

Jenna jumped in. "Naive question, but is it possible to have too many features, so that the model gets confused?"

"It's a good question!" Maya always got excited when the nontechnical folks participated in technical discussions. "In general, the more data points you have per feature, the better. The reason is that the model needs some data points to learn whether or not a feature is important. If the data points–to–features ratio is too low, the model won't be able to learn well which features are most important. So if you start out with too many features, you'll need to use some method of feature selection to narrow down the number of features that ultimately get passed into the model. A rough rule of thumb is to have at least ten data points per predictor, and there are more sophisticated ways to calculate the number of data points you need depending on how many predictors you have and the nature of the outcome variable."

FEATURE SELECTION

Feature selection—how to identify which features to include in your model—is an important challenge that must be addressed in any predictive modeling. If you put a large number of irrelevant variables into your model, you won't improve the model prediction, but you are likely to end up adding more noise, resulting in worse predictions.

Regardless of what data-driven methods you use for feature selection, it is important to have some domain knowledge. Domain knowledge is a crucial component of feature selection that supports data-driven approaches. If you are building models to predict mortality, then you should have some understanding of what variables have been shown to be predictive of mortality in other data sets or models. Doing literature searches and talking with experts are important to ensure you are not missing major features and to identify when you are getting counterintuitive results.

The most basic data-driven method for variable selection involves the use of filtering methods. For example, some common filters select variables that have a high correlation with the outcome variable. The distribution of the feature itself can also be used, since extremely rare features or ones with minimal variance are not likely to be strongly predictive. These filtering methods are fast and crude (often a bit too crude). But if you have 100,000 possible features, it can be helpful to quickly bring this down to a more manageable number. One limitation of these methods is that they may exclude features that are less predictive on their own but that may be predictive when combined with other features.[16]

More-advanced methods for feature selection, called wrappers, have been used for decades.[17] Wrappers such as forward selection, backward selection, and stepwise selection all seek to reduce the features by examining how useful each feature is in the model's performance. Forward selection means the model adds the most important variable, then adds the next most important variable, and continues until there are no more significant variables to add. Backward selection works the opposite way. You start with all of the variables in the model and then remove the least predictive variable. You continue to remove variables until only the significant variables are left in the model. Stepwise selection is a more complicated variation of forward selection, where, after each variable is added, the model looks to see if any of the other variables that were already in the model should be dropped. The nice thing about using an automated method is that you can reduce the number of features very quickly, but there are several downsides, including overfitting, exclusion of important variables, and instability. Because of the suboptimal results of wrappers, data scientists often prefer to use embedded approaches for feature selection.

Embedded approaches automatically include variable selection as part of the model's optimization algorithm. Classification and regression tree (CART) modeling (and its variations of random forests and gradient-boosted machine learning [GBML]) can be considered an embedded method in that the variable selection occurs automatically as part of the development of the model.[18] Features that have a variable importance of 0 are not used in any of the trees.

Another embedded method is the least absolute shrinkage and selection operator (LASSO). This is a variation of regression where the algorithm minimizes the sum of the squares of the residuals plus the sum of the absolute values of the regression coefficients.[19] This can be distinguished from least squares regression, which minimizes the sum of the squares of the residuals. In implementing the LASSO algorithm, features are automatically dropped as the algorithm optimizes its results. Similarly, ridge regression minimizes the sum of the squares of the residuals plus the sum of the squares of the regression coefficients. By adding a constraint to ridge regression, the process of dropping features becomes embedded in the model development process.[20]

In summary, while there is a multitude of different supervised machine learning methods, each method has its own situations to

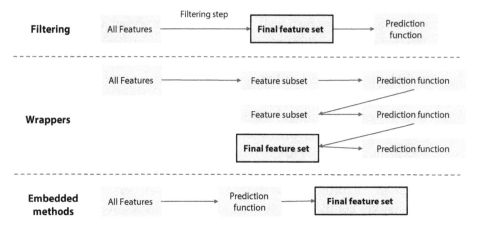

Figure 6.1 Variable selection methods: filtering, wrappers, and embedded methods

which it is particularly well suited (figure 6.1). Rather than looking for a single solution, it is best to have the data science team explore a few different solutions and test which one model works best on naive data sets.

MODEL TRAINING AND TESTING

Kamala was enjoying this foray into predictive modeling. "David, you and your team have done a great job explaining all these details. I never thought I'd be interested in getting into the weeds of modeling! I'd love to learn more about how the model 'learns.' And once we develop it, how are we going to make sure that it works well?"

"The simple answer is that we're going to train the model and then test it," David explained. "Training and testing are technical terms, but they mean pretty much what they sound like. Training the model involves feeding it some data and allowing it to learn the patterns in the training data. Testing involves showing previously unseen data to the model and allowing it to make predictions based on what it has learned from the training data. Then we evaluate how well the model performed on the testing data—hence, the name *test*.[21]

"It almost sounds like the model is a child who's trying to learn new things," Jenna reasoned.

"Conceptually, it's really similar. As children, we learn patterns based on things we've encountered, and then we apply those learnings to new situations. Imagine you were teaching a little kid how to distinguish between cats and dogs. After you showed them a few pictures of cats and a few pictures of dogs, they'd learn pretty naturally that dogs tend to be bigger, have floppier ears, have shorter tails, etc. Then if you showed them a new picture and asked them to identify whether it was a dog or a cat, they'd probably do a pretty good job."

"But, David, that's humans we're talking about. We subconsciously pick up characteristics that we observe and synthesize them. How does a model do the same thing?"

"We use our eyes and ears and powers of observation to learn: a model does this using statistical associations and correlations. Just as a human learns that cats often have long tails and short ears and agile figures, a cat-versus-dog image classification model would identify statistical patterns: animals with long tails are cats 80 percent of the time, or animals with big ears are dogs 70 percent of the time, etc. In our case, we're hoping the model will be able to identify patterns that would be difficult for us to identify. For example, maybe our model will figure out that patients older than 55 with no prior history of back pain tend to use relatively little health care when managed nonsurgically."

Kamala was realizing there's a lot of nuance in how the model works. "This is all pretty high level. Can you explain in a little more detail what's going on under the hood? I'm not a math whiz, but I'd like to understand what exactly the model is doing to 'identify statistical patterns.'"

David uncapped his dry-erase marker. "The easiest way to understand what the model is doing is to think of fitting a trend line to a scatterplot. I'm sure many of you have made scatterplots in Excel and fit a trend line before! A trend line is actually a basic type of prediction model—a linear prediction model.[22] Once you fit a line to a set of points, you can use the equation of the line to calculate or 'predict' the y variable given a value of the x variable. Remember the equation of a line from algebra: $Y = mX + b$? Here m is the slope of the line, and b is the y-intercept. These are the numbers that Excel figures out for you automatically in order to plot the lines. Under the hood, Excel is doing a bit of linear algebra to figure out the optimal values of m and b in order to find the line of best fit. Once you know m and b, you can plug in a value for X (input) and get a predicted Y (outcome). Remember our discussion of model training and testing? 'Training' the model involves doing some math to figure out the optimal values of m and b—all the various parameters that together optimize the 'fit' of the model."

"So, to put it simply," Kamala said hesitantly, "the model uses the training data to find the 'line of best fit.'"

"Exactly. The only difference is that with a scatterplot, you have one X variable and one Y variable. Usually, good prediction models have more than one predictor variable. If we had fifty predictor variables in our model, for example, the model would be finding the fifty-dimensional 'line of best fit' instead of the two-dimensional line of best fit. It's impossible to visualize what a line would look like in that many dimensions, but as long as you can understand the concept in two dimensions, you can understand it in fifty dimensions," David said reassuringly.

Kamala had made a lot of scatterplots with trend lines in her day. She couldn't totally wrap her head around more than three dimensions, but she understood the concept of feeding a model data and allowing it to find the values of parameters that optimize the fit. "What happens if you ask the model to predict a data point that is really different from what it has seen before? How will it perform? Basically, I'm asking about a situation where you ask the kid to identify pictures of cats and dogs and then all of a sudden you show them a picture of a hippo. Won't they be confused?"

David was impressed by Kamala's questions. "You're right. That would be a scenario where the training data was not representative of all the possible situations that may arise in real life. In a case like this, it would be hard to predict how well the model would perform. It wouldn't be surprising if it performed poorly."

Kamala was encouraged to hear that her question was well-founded. "How can we protect against that issue? We want our model to be as robust as possible."

"We can do our best to ensure that our training data is as representative as possible so that our model has the chance to learn the patterns from a diverse array of cases," David responded. "Another option is to filter out data points that look dissimilar from our training data and avoid making predictions on them: basically, we're saying 'Hey, this picture doesn't look like a cat or a dog, so we're not even going to try to make a guess.'"

Jenna chimed in with her own idea. "Why not just include all the data we have access to in the training set? Wouldn't that be building the most robust model possible?"

Maya responded. "In order to test the performance of the model, we need to leave some data aside. The idea is that we train the model and then we test it on some new data that the model has never seen before. There's a tradeoff in deciding how much data to use for training and how much to use for testing. The more data you use for training, the better the model will perform on the training set, but the harder it is to quantify the performance of the model on an unseen test set with high certainty. A rough rule of thumb is to use 20 to 40 percent of the available data for testing and the rest for training but with huge data sets the amount reserved for testing could be 1 percent or less. If you want to be more precise, you can calculate the amount of data you need in your test set based on the level of certainty you want in evaluating the performance of the model."

Depending on the size and variability of the data set, the amount of data held out for testing can vary. In a huge data set, just 1 percent of the total data may be sufficient to use as a representative test set.[23]

"Going back to my question about showing the model new data," Kamala said, "how different can the new data be? Eventually, we want to be able to use this model on our new patients—patients that we don't have data on now. Will the model be able to handle these new patients?"

She smiled as she continued her train of thought. "During my medical training, we thought by the end of medical school that we had seen it all. Then I spent a summer volunteering in India and was shocked to see how little of what I learned in medical school was relevant. I literally encountered patients with conditions that I had never seen before in the United States. Sure, you still had your flu and your diabetes, but I had no idea how to deal with conditions like leprosy and drug-resistant tuberculosis, and I needed to go back to the books and get more training . . . you just don't see those types of things here in the United States anymore."

"Building machine learning models sounds pretty similar to getting trained as a doctor, Kamala!" David joked. "A case of the flu in the United States is going to be pretty similar to a case of the flu in India. But what threw you off were the diseases in India that rarely show up in U.S. populations! Those were the conditions for which you had to be retrained! To answer whether our model will be able to handle new patients, we need to think about how the new patients may differ from our current population.

"For example, if we're bringing on a group of new employees from a car dealership, I would think that our model would generalize well. I have no reason to suspect that those employees are different from our current patient network in a meaningful way with regard to health care utilization for back pain. On the other hand, if we're bringing on members of a coal miners' union, it may be a different story. Coal miners may be more likely to experience back pain than the overall population due to the nature of their work, and because they are more likely to live in rural areas, coal miners may have different rates of health care utilization compared to other professions. Also, they may be dealing with other health issues that could impact their use of health care services. For a case like this, we may want to do some targeted testing to make sure our model generalizes to that specific population, and we may even need to retrain our model if we see that it's performing poorly on that subgroup." David's example landed with the group.

Kamala still had more questions for the team. "What happens if we test our model and we find it's not working well? Can we go back and retrain the model?"

"I'm glad you asked this," Maya said, looking like she had been anticipating this question. "Let's say we do the modeling using the training data, and we test it out on the testing data, and we see that the performance isn't great. Then we go back into the training data and tweak the model a little bit, make some changes to our features. Finally, we try it on the test data again and find that it's working much better. The problem is that in machine learning, this is considered cheating."

David picked up where Maya left off. "It reminds me of my son, who recently had a big exam at school. After several days of studying, he finally took a practice test and got a C. He realized he needed to study harder, so he studied for a few more days and then retook the same practice test—this time he got an A. What my son didn't understand is that just because he did well on that practice test doesn't mean he's going to do well on the real test. Since he had already seen the practice test before, he knew exactly how to change his studying to help him pass that practice test the second time around. But if he were given a completely new test, I'm not confident that he would get an A."

Maya nodded. "It's exactly the same issue here with model building. When we see our performance on the test set and we go back and make modifications to the model training and apply it again to the test set, we run the risk of overfitting the model to the testing data.[24] That is, we've optimized the model to perform really well on our testing data, and in doing so, we run the risk of having designed a model that doesn't work well on other data sets."

On cue, Kamala chimed in with the key question: "So how can we continuously improve our model, evaluate its performance, and continue making improvements without overfitting—or cheating?"

David was back up at the whiteboard. "One common approach that people take is to split the data into three groups: a training set, a validation set, and a testing set.[25] After training your model on the training set, you can see how it's doing with the validation set. If the performance on the validation set isn't great, you can go back and make adjustments and then check it again on the validation set—and repeat this process as many times as you need. Then, once you think the model is in good shape, you can try it out on the test set."

Just as David was about to continue, Kamala chimed in, "I don't get it. Isn't this the same as just having a training set and a test set essentially? If you go back and forth between the training set and the validation set, won't you just end up overfitting to the validation set?"

David smiled. "You're exactly right, and this is why more and more folks are moving away from the validation set approach. Instead, it's recommended to do something called cross-validation.[26] Here's how it works: The setup is to split your data into a training set and a testing set. Next you split up your training data into equally sized bins or folds. Usually, we take ten folds. Then you repeat the training and validation process once for each fold. For example, first, you would take fold 1 and treat it as your validation set; then you would take the other nine folds and treat them as your training set. You train your model on the nine folds and test it on the first fold. Then you store the predictions that your model made on the first fold for later evaluation. Next you repeat the same process, treating fold 2 as your validation set. You train the model on the remaining nine folds and test it on fold 2. Then you store these predictions for later evaluation. At the end of the day, you will have generated predictions for ten mini validation sets, each of which was predicted by models trained on slightly different training sets. The reason cross-validation works so well is that you're not dependent on a single validation set to test your model, so it's less likely that you will overfit."

Jenna tried her best to think of an analogy to make sense of all this. "So if having a single training and validation set is like studying for an exam and then taking a practice test, cross validation is like . . . ?"

Maya helped her out. "Cross-validation is like getting ten people to study for a little bit and then answer a few questions on a practice test. This way they can determine whether their study approach is good or not."

"And by repeating the process on ten similar but slightly different data sets, there's a lower chance that you overfit to the training data set," David chimed in.

MODEL TUNING

"So cross-validation is a way for us to see whether our model is working well. What if we see that our model is not working well? What kinds of changes can we make to improve the performance of the model?" Kamala asked.

"If the performance of the model isn't as high as you want, there are three main levers that we can pull to try to improve the performance. The first and most powerful lever is changing the data that the model is using. We can do this by adding more features to the model or by transforming the features that we've already included. The reason this is the most powerful lever is that by introducing new features, we are giving the model access to more information to incorporate into generating a prediction.[27]

"Another lever we can pull is changing the type of model or the type of feature selection.[28] If we see that a regression model isn't working well, we can try a decision tree, for example. We can also try using a penalized regression model that performs feature selection automatically during the modeling process.

"The other lever I want to mention is tuning the hyperparameters.[29] A hyperparameter is like a setting knob on a model." David enjoyed explaining technical concepts in a way that nontechnical people could understand. "Going back to our studying analogy, a hyperparameter for our studying approach may be the amount of time you spend reading a page in a textbook. In a textbook that has lots of images and little text, you may want to spend less time per page, but in a textbook that has lots of dense text, you may need to spend several minutes per page in order to get the most out of your studying. In a sense, the time spent reading a single page of a textbook is a hyperparameter that we can tune to optimize our studying for the specific content that we're studying. Similarly, different models have different knobs or hyperparameters that need to be tuned such that they are at the optimal setting for the data at hand."

In practice, any combination of these three levers may be used to improve model performance. Depending on what data is accessible, it may not be feasible to add more features to the model, so the data scientist must rely on hyperparameter tuning and model selection in order to improve the quality of predictions. In general, model tuning should always be done during cross-validation to prevent overfitting.

MEASURING MODEL PERFORMANCE

Kamala was eating up every bit of David's explanation. "So we perform cross-validation, and we see how well our model is working. If it's not working as well as we want, we can add more data, change the hyperparameters, or even change the type of model that we use. Then we can do cross-validation again and see if the performance of the model has improved. Now my question is 'How do we decide when the model is performing well enough?' Alternatively, 'How do we decide when there's not much more that we can do to improve the performance of the model?'"

David responded, "Deciding how well we want the model to perform is entirely dependent on how the model is going to be used. For our model, I would throw that question back to you: 'How accurate does our model need to be for it to be useful to the prior authorization reviewers?' If you can help us answer that, we can let you know whether the model is meeting that bar. To your second point, there's no hard-and-fast rule to decide when to throw in the towel. Typically, the easiest improvements to make are tuning hyperparameters and trying a different model architecture. Sometimes adding features can be easy, but other times it can be very time consuming. Maybe we will get to a point where the only way to improve the performance of the model is by extracting features from the scanned PDF documents submitted by the patients' physicians. Even if those features are highly predictive, there is a cost associated with going through those scanned documents and extracting the relevant information in a machine-readable format. If we get to that point, we need to discuss the trade-offs between the cost of extracting those features and the potential improvements to the model."

Jenna chimed in, "We've been talking a lot about the performance of the model and whether the model will perform as well as we need it to. Mathematically, how do we quantify the performance of a model?"

"I'm glad you asked!" Maya was excited to see her colleagues interested in the math behind modeling. "Picking the right metric to quantify the performance of a model requires a lot of careful consideration. There are an infinite number of possible performance metrics, each with its own quirks. In our model, we're predicting health care expenditure measured in dollars. One commonsense way to evaluate the performance of a model is to look at the predicted expenditure of our model and compare it to the actual expenditure. One way to do this is to take the absolute value of the difference between the predicted and the actual expenditures. If the patient actually spent $3,000 and the model predicted $4,000, the absolute value of the difference is $1,000. If we calculate this for every patient in our data set and take the average, we get what's called the mean absolute error. The mean absolute error is a very interpretable metric to evaluate model performance: it gives us a single number such that we can say 'On average, our model is off by $X.'

"One limitation of mean absolute error[30] is that large errors and small errors are treated the same—that is, an error of $200 is penalized twice as much as an error of $100. A similar metric is called the mean squared error. Whereas the mean absolute error is the absolute value of the difference between the predicted and the actual values, the mean squared error is the square of the difference between the predicted and the actual values. By squaring the difference, the larger discrepancies are penalized more than the smaller discrepancies. For example, if the error is $100, the squared error is $10,000, and if the error is $200, the squared error is $40,000. As you can see, even though the error was twice as large, the squared error was four times as large. When building a model in which large errors are particularly undesirable, using mean squared error may be an appropriate choice."

MODEL PERFORMANCE FOR BINARY OUTCOMES

Performance metrics also exist for models where the outcome is binary or categorical. Imagine a model intended to predict whether a patient will be hospitalized or not. There are many types of models that can be used to predict a binary outcome, such as logistic regression, probit regression, random forest, and support vector machines. Many of these models will return a probability between 0 and 1: for example, "This patient has a 60 percent probability of being hospitalized." For this type of model, we want to know how well the predicted probabilities correspond to the actual outcome. For example, for patients who will be hospitalized, a high-performing model will return probabilities close to 1. For patients who will not be hospitalized, a high-performing model will return probabilities close to 0. A common performance metric used to evaluate probability prediction models is called the Brier score. The Brier score is just a mean squared error used to compare the predicted probability to the true outcome (0 or 1). Similar to mean squared error, the Brier score does not have a clear interpretation: it's difficult to interpret what a Brier score of 0.23 means, for example. However, the Brier score can be used to compare the performance of two models: the model with the lower Brier score is better.

Another important metric to evaluate probability prediction models is calibration. A model that is well calibrated is one where the predicted probabilities behave like true probabilities.[31] The way to check the calibration of predictor probabilities is by comparing the predicted probability to the frequency of the outcome within a certain group of data points. For example, if you looked at all the data points where a well-calibrated model outputs a predicted probability of 30 percent, you would expect that 30 percent of those patients would actually be hospitalized. Imagine that the model predicted a probability of hospitalization of 40 percent for one hundred patients. If the model was well calibrated, we would see that approximately forty out of those one hundred patients were actually hospitalized. This would suggest that the output of a model represents a true probability.

In many cases, building a probability prediction model is not enough: the desired output may be a binary "yes" or "no," not a probability. In this case, we need a way to turn the predicted probability into a binary "yes" or "no." The most common way to do this is by thresholding. Thresholding involves picking a probability threshold and designating all predicted probabilities above that threshold as a "yes" and all product probabilities below the threshold as a "no." For example, if we pick a threshold of 0.43, anyone with a predicted probability of hospitalization above 0.43 will be labeled "yes," and anyone below will be labeled "no."

Many model builders fall into the trap of arbitrarily picking 0.5 as their probability threshold. Upon first glance, 0.5 may seem like a logical decision. A 50 percent threshold represents equal probabilities for "yes" and "no," so it makes sense that you would lean toward "yes" if your probability is greater than 50 percent and similarly toward "no" if your probability is less than 50 percent. There are two pitfalls with this approach. The first is that it assumes that your model is well calibrated. In other words, it assumes that whatever probability the model returns represents a true probability. Unless the model is well calibrated, this assumption may not hold.

Second, even if the model is well calibrated, picking a threshold of 50 percent implicitly assumes that false negatives are equally desirable as false positives. There are many situations where this may not be optimal because in the real world false positives may be worse than false negatives, or vice versa. Imagine a model that predicts who needs surgery in the next 24 hours. Anyone the model identifies as needing surgery will be prioritized for evaluation by a surgeon, and anyone the model does not identify will not be evaluated by a surgeon. In this scenario, a false positive would be a patient who is unnecessarily flagged for evaluation by a surgeon. A false negative would be a patient who is not flagged for evaluation but should be. If this model is being used by doctors to decide who to evaluate and who not to evaluate, the doctors would likely prefer to have a false positive compared to a false negative. The "cost," or undesirability, of a false positive is merely the cost of doing a surgical evaluation, but the cost of a false negative is potentially delaying treatment for someone who needs urgent surgical care, which could lead to poor patient outcomes and an increase in downstream costs. For this model, using a probability threshold of 0.5 would not make sense. Instead, a threshold closer to 0 would more accurately reflect the preference for false positives over false negatives.[32]

The important insight to keep in mind when building classification models is that the data scientist cannot be the one to decide whether false positives or false negatives are more costly. That can be determined only by the person using the model. The data science customer should communicate to the data science team the relative costs of false positives and false negatives.

Once a threshold is selected, the performance of the resulting classifier can be measured. There are four important numbers (figure 6.2) from which key performance metrics can be calculated: true positives, true negatives, false positives, and false negatives.[33] Sensitivity, also known as the true positive rate, is defined as the number of true positives divided by the number of true positives plus the number of false negatives. In other words, sensitivity is the percentage of all positives your model will identify. Specificity is the percentage of all negatives your model will identify. It's also called the true negative rate and is defined as the number of

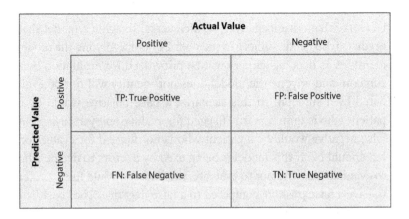

Figure 6.2 Confusion matrix

true negatives divided by the number of true negatives plus the number of false positives. When the model is used in real life and it returns a prediction of "positive," the model users want to know the probability that it is a true positive. This probability is the positive predictive value, defined as the number of true positives divided by the number of true positives plus the number of false positives. Similarly, if the model returns "negative" and you want to know the chance that it is a true negative, you would calculate the negative predictive value, which is the number of true negatives divided by the number of true negatives plus the number of false negatives.[34]

NEXT STEPS

"I'm excited to put this model to the test," said Kamala, smiling. "How long will it take for your team to create the features, do the training and cross-validation, make improvements, and test the model?"

"We'll need at least a couple of weeks, but we'll touch base with feedback in the interim," David said, nodding to Maya.

"Looking forward to it!"

KEY QUESTIONS

Questions to Ask When Building Prediction Models:

- Population:
  - What population will we be applying the model to?
  - Is this the same population that we're training the model on?
- Outcome variable
  - What are the limitations of choosing this outcome?
  - In what scenarios may our outcome variable lead to incorrect or misleading results?
  - How could our outcome variable be more meaningful?
  - Is the outcome variable really what we want to measure, or is it a proxy?

- Feature selection:
  - What features do we think will be the most predictive?
  - What steps did the data science team take to perform feature selection and how do the results align with our domain knowledge?
  - Were any feature importance techniques such as statistical tests or feature ranking algorithms used for feature selection?
  - Did you consider any feature engineering techniques, such as creating interaction terms or transforming variables, to improve the predictive power of the selected features?
- Training:
  - What machine learning algorithms or models did you use for training? Why did you choose these particular models?
  - Did you split the dataset into separate training and validation sets? How did you decide on the split ratio?
  - How did you handle class imbalance, if present, during model training? Did you use any techniques such as oversampling, undersampling, or class weights?
  - What strategies did you implement to avoid overfitting? Did you use regularization techniques, cross-validation, or early stopping?
  - Can you describe the hyperparameter tuning process? How did you determine the optimal hyperparameter values for the chosen models?
- Model performance:
  - What performance metric is most appropriate for our use case?
  - What evaluation metrics did you use to assess the performance of the trained models?
  - How did you perform model evaluation on the validation or test set? Did you employ techniques such as k-fold cross-validation or holdout validation?
  - What was the performance of the model on different evaluation metrics? Can you provide a summary or comparison of the results?
  - Did you consider any ensemble techniques, such as model averaging or stacking, to improve the overall model performance?
  - How did you validate the generalizability of the model? Were there any concerns about overfitting to the specific dataset, and if so, how did you address them?

7

TOOLS FOR MACHINE LEARNING

Kamala knocked on David's door to tell him some good news. "David, I'm really happy with how our model is working out. Our prior authorization reviewers are able to make more-accurate decisions in a shorter amount of time, and we're even seeing that costs are coming down while improving patient outcomes!"

"That's great news, Kamala! I sense a 'but' coming . . ."

Kamala chuckled. "We really like the model, but we think it can be even better. Before, I am ashamed to admit, nearly half of our prior authorization calls led to unfavorable outcomes: either the folks who got surgery ended up facing complications and didn't have their back pain resolved, or the folks who didn't get surgery ended up using a lot of health care resources to manage their ongoing back pain and didn't improve with a nonsurgical treatment. Now our initial analysis shows that the proportion of incorrect decisions has dropped from 50 percent to about 30 percent. That's a great improvement, so I wanted to ask you if there's a way we can get even better performance. In an ideal world, close to 0 percent of our prior authorization decisions would be incorrect. Is this something that we could achieve?"

"Well, we're probably never going to get to 0 percent. There will always be a few patients who won't do well with surgery or with nonsurgical treatment. Whether that group is 30 percent or

10 percent or 2 percent I don't know, but what you're asking is if we can optimize the model even more to improve its performance." Kamala nodded, so David continued. "It's true that we built a straightforward linear model with a limited number of features. That's generally our approach because we don't like to invest too many resources in building a sophisticated model if we don't know whether a simple one will work or not. Also, building a simple model can help us understand the data better and can form the foundation for a complex model. In this case, it sounds like our simple model is working fairly well. Let me see what we can do—I'll have a discussion with my team and get back to you soon."

In data science, it's always best to start simple and evaluate how much room there is for improvement. In exploratory data analysis, it's best to start with descriptive tables and scatterplots. In machine learning, it's best to start with a simple model. If a simple model isn't able to work well, chances are that a complex model won't do much better. Also, there may be added costs to building out complex models.

A few weeks later David set up a meeting with Kamala to discuss the plan for improving the model. "In our weekly data team meeting, I brought up your request and asked if anyone on the team had ideas for improving the performance of the model. I got way too many proposals: people want to try all sorts of things, and they were really excited to hear that the initial model was working well. So instead of picking one approach and going for it, I decided to organize a hackathon within the data team. Members of the data science team will form teams and come up with the approach they think is best for improving the performance of this model. I'll give them 3 days to see what they can come up with. At the end, they'll each present their findings, and we can then make a decision on which approach we want to pursue. I also have a little trick up my sleeve, but I'll tell you more about that toward the end of the hackathon."

Kamala could sense the excitement in David's voice. "So you're saying that the entire data science team is going to be focused on improving our model and in just 3 days I'm going to be presented with a bunch of high-performing options? That's an offer I can't refuse!"

EXAMINING RESIDUALS

"I'd like to welcome you all to the inaugural Stardust Health Insurance data science team hackathon!" David was having fun as the emcee of the event. "Our teams have been hard at work to optimize our model to predict health care expenditure for patients with back pain who receive nonsurgical treatment. Before we get started, let's recap the current state of our model.

"The outcome for this model was predicted back pain–related health care expenditure in the 1 year following the request for prior authorization. In terms of features, we had access to patients' demographic data, including their place of employment and type of employment, zip code, age, sex, race, ethnicity, and information about dependents. We also had access to their medical claims, which include almost every encounter they had with the health care system that came through our insurance. We also had access to their prior authorization report, which includes medical documents prepared by their physician. In terms of model architecture, we used good old linear regression.

"After training our current model using ten-fold cross-validation, we ran it on a test data set that the model had never seen before. On average, the absolute difference between the model's predicted health care expenditure and the true health care expenditure was $12,000 for the 1 year following the prior authorization request. The actual differences ranged from $50 to $50,000. The top features that linear regression selected were prior history of back pain, prior medication usage, and age. Those on the prior authorization team have been using this model for the past several months with success: they are seeing reduced health care expenditure as a result of their prior authorization decisions, and initial analyses show improvements in patient outcomes as well. Although the model was designed to predict expenditures for 2 years, these initial results are promising, and now we want to see how well we can improve the performance of this model.

"The first team we will be hearing from didn't actually change the model architecture: the team members used linear regression, but they did some clever analysis to figure out how to improve the model. I'll hand it over to them!"

The team lead walked to the front of the room and flashed their slides on the screen. "Thanks for the introduction, David. The performance of the original model was good, but we felt that there was still more that could be done within the confines of linear regression. We decided to do a deep dive into what types of patients the model performs well on and what types of patients it doesn't perform as well on. To do this, we examined the residuals."

A residual is the difference between the true value of the outcome and what the model predicted.[1] The smaller the residuals, the better the prediction. In all forms of predictive modeling, residuals are your friends. Patterns in the residuals point to ways to improve the model. Are the residuals bigger for smaller predictions than for larger predictions? Consider transforming the outcome variable by taking its logarithm and then modeling the transformed variable instead. For example, seasonal patterns in the residuals, such as large positive residuals in the summer, may suggest you need to add some features to the model that vary by the time of year.[2]

The team lead continued. "What we found was that some patients have very small residuals: the model was able to correctly predict their health care expenditure over one year to within $2,000. But for other patients, the model performed very poorly: on average, the model was off by over $25,000. We ran some descriptive statistics to see whether those groups of patients were different in any meaningful way. What we found is that the patients with higher residuals tend to have jobs that involve more manual labor—for example, farming or mining or construction. This tells us that our model isn't good at incorporating information specific to a patient's job. So instead of changing the model architecture, we decided to add more features regarding a patient's job. We took this information from the patient's intake documents, where they talk about how sedentary their job is and whether there are any occupational hazards associated with the job. When we added in these new features, we saw that the residuals for the previously poor-performing group dropped from $25,000 to $15,000. In other words, we were able to improve the performance of our model for that group of patients by about 40 percent. Overall, we were able to bring down the average residual from $12,000 to $9,000—all by just adding a few well-selected features!"

INTERACTION TERMS AND TRANSFORMATIONS

David took the mic and welcomed the next team. "The next team also stuck with linear regression but took a clever approach to feature engineering."

The team lead took to the stage. "Thanks for the intro, David. We also felt that the biggest limitation of our model was the features. It doesn't matter if you use linear regression, random forest, or a neural network; if your features aren't good, your predictions won't be good. That said, we're limited by the types of data we have access to. So we decided to engineer new features using the ones that we already had. Specifically, we calculated all two-way interaction terms for the features in our set, which dramatically increased the number of features we had access to."

One of the simplest approaches to automated feature engineering is calculating interaction terms.[3] An interaction term represents the relationship between two main terms. For example, patient age and patient sex may be included in the original health care expenditure model as main effects. In linear regression, the model will output a value (coefficient) that represents the change in the outcome for every unit increase in one of the main effect variables—change in health care expenditure for each additional year of age, for instance. But what if the relationship between health care spending and age depends on sex? This would mean that as patients get older, the change in how much they spend depends on whether they are a man or a woman. We can add an interaction term by including the product of age * sex as a new feature in our model. This interaction term allows for different slopes for the relationship between expenditure and age for men versus women.

"That's right, folks," another member of the team explained, "by including all possible two-way interaction terms, we gave our model access to relationships between variables that we hadn't considered including in the original model. Not only that—we also performed transformations on variables that appeared to have a nonlinear relationship with health care expenditure. Depending on the relationship, we performed a square transformation, a square root transformation, or a log transformation."

A linear relationship means that as the feature doubles, the contribution to the outcome doubles. If the model has a linear term for age, then as age doubles, the contribution that the age feature adds to health care expenditure doubles. If you have a reason to believe that the relationship between a variable and the outcome is nonlinear, adding a polynomial (like the square of age = age * age) or taking the log or square root might improve model fitting.[4] A general rule of thumb is that you should always include the lower-order terms. If you are including age * age in your model, then you should also include age.[5] A basic question you can ask the data science team members is whether they included polynomial terms in the regression model.

The team lead summed up the results. "When we added in these new features, we were able to bring down the average residual from $12,000 to $8,000. It's amazing what a little automated feature engineering can do!"

WEIGHTING AND OUTLIERS

Kamala was enjoying hearing about the different approaches the teams took. "I had no idea you could get so much improvement just by messing with the features of the model!"

"Features are the backbone of every model!" David was smiling. "But this next team didn't touch the features. Instead, its members used special techniques to make the model more robust."

The team lead took the stage. "Instead of thinking about how we could improve the features, we took a critical look at the data we were using to train the model. One thing we noticed was that we were using data on prior authorizations from the past 5 years to train the model. This sounds reasonable at first, but we remembered that we changed our procedures about 2 years ago to make it easier for Medicare Advantage patients to submit prior authorizations. As we know, Medicare Advantage patients are typically 65 or older; this means that starting 2 years ago, the demographic of patients who were requesting prior authorizations suddenly skewed older, since it became easier for these patients to make submissions."

Kamala was nodding in agreement. "That's an astute observation. But what effect would this have on the model?"

The team lead continued. "Our training data includes data from the past 5 years—3 years' worth of data before the policy change and 2 years' worth of data afterward. We suspected that the 2 years' worth of data after the policy change was more relevant, since that data would be more representative of the current demographic of patients who are submitting prior authorization requests."

"So you were concerned that the training data from before the policy change would skew toward younger patients and throw off the results of the model?" Kamala asked.

"Exactly," said the team lead. "At the same time, 3 years' worth of data is a lot of data, and we didn't want to just throw it all out. So we used a weighted regression to weight the recent data more heavily than the older data when fitting our model."

Weighted regression can also be used when training data is not collected in a representative way. For example, let's say that in the training data, 70 percent of the patients were men when, in the real world, men make up only about 50 percent of patients. This means that the training data has more men than a random sample. In statistical terms, we would say that men are *overrepresented* in the sample. It's important to consider whether the model is built on a representative sample—either a random sample or the entire population. If not, a weighted regression may be appropriate.

"That's a really clever solution. Instead of throwing out potentially valuable data, you just weight it less." Kamala was taking in every detail of the presentation.

"We noticed something else when we were digging into the data," added the team lead. "There were a handful of patients who had outsized health care expenditure—orders of magnitude greater than the vast majority of other patients. We'd call these folks outliers—people who incurred hundreds of thousands of dollars of back pain–related spending over 3 years. Our original model used least squares linear regression, which means it's trying to minimize the squared residuals. This is problematic, however, because least squares is affected by outliers more than by nonoutliers, so our model was getting thrown off by those heavy spenders."

Kamala asked for more clarification. "Sorry, can you explain why squaring residuals is problematic?"

David jumped in. "Think of it this way, 4 is the double of 2, but 4 squared is not the double of 2 squared—it's quadruple. This means that in our model a residual of 4 is not considered twice as bad as a residual of 2—it's considered four times as bad! As a result, our model is going to change its predictions to minimize the error for those outliers, and in the process, we might get worse predictions for the nonoutliers."

The simple arithmetic examples always helped Kamala make sense of larger concepts. "I see. So we need a way for the model to not be overly influenced by the outliers."

"You got it," the team lead responded, "and we have just the tool for that. Instead of using least squares linear regression, we used least absolute deviation."

One of the most basic methods to handle outliers is a technique called least absolute deviation, where, instead of squaring the residuals (the way least squares regression modeling works), the absolute value of the residuals is taken.[6] Another popular method for developing robust regression estimates is quantile regression. Quantile regression focuses on identifying the median or any other specific quantile of interest.[7] Medians (and other quantiles) are robust to outliers, meaning that if you add or remove a few customers who spend more than $25,000 a month from your data set, the quantile regression coefficients will not change much.

A good way to think about this robust method is by considering the difference between the mean and the median when you have outliers. Imagine computing the average wealth of a group of 100 people. You compute both the mean and the median wealth. The value comes out to about $50,000 for both metrics. Now 4 people now walk into the room: Bill Gates, Jeff Bezos, and two unnamed people who have zero wealth. The mean wealth of this new group of 104 people is roughly $1 billion, but the median remains the same, $50,000. Quantile regression helps you focus on that median without being influenced by the outliers, while least squares regression would be severely impacted by the outliers.

The team lead flashed the team's money slide on the screen. "As you can see, the combination of weighted regression and least absolute deviation helped us bring the average residual down from $12,000 to $8,500."

K-NEAREST NEIGHBORS

"This next team moved away from linear regression and tried out a different model architecture," said David, as he stepped down from the stage.

The team lead picked up the mic. "One characteristic of linear regression is that it uses all the data points in the data set to make a prediction. This can be good in some cases, but we felt that for something like health care expenditure, you may not want the model to make a prediction based on all the patients in the data set. We thought it might be better to use an approach where the prediction is based on only the handful of data points that are most similar to the patient in question—in this case, the patient requesting prior authorization. Therefore, we used a K-nearest neighbor regression model."

K-nearest neighbor (K-NN) modeling is a different approach to predictive modeling. It can predict categorical or continuous outcomes by using only local information instead of using the entire data set to create coefficients for all observations. The concept is intuitive in that you are trying to make predictions by looking at what happened to similar observations.[8]

The first step of the modeling process is to choose the parameter K, which represents the number of observations the model will use to make a prediction. For example, if K = 20, the model will look at the 20 data points that are most similar to the data point it is making a prediction from.[9] The next step is to determine how to define *similar*. The most common approach is to calculate the Euclidean distance between data points: this amounts to adding the squares of the distance in each dimension (for text variables, Hamming distance is often used).[10]

The team lead went on. "We determined through cross-validation that the optimal value for K was 100. Simply put, our model makes predictions for new patients by averaging the expenditures of the 100 most similar patients in the data set." For categorical outcomes, K-NN finds the K observations that are closest to the data point and assigns the predicted value to the class with the most votes.

The size of K needs to be explored by your data science team. Small values of K yield noisy results; large values of K are more computationally expensive and less "local," in that they use data points that are not necessarily so close. A quick rule of thumb is to use a value of K that equals the square root of the number of observations in your training data set.[11]

Rather than just taking the average value of the closest K neighbors, you can add a distance weighting. This distance weighting results in the closest observations having the most weight in the prediction and the farthest having the least weight. When K is large, weighting the observations by distance is definitely helpful.[12]

Another consideration is what features you should include in K-NN. You want to use only features that are relevant in predicting the outcome of interest. Often there must be some filtering of input variables to first remove the ones that aren't predictive. The features then need to be normalized so each feature has about the same range. If you don't normalize the features, then those that have a much larger range will dominate the distance computation, and other features with smaller ranges won't contribute much to the modeling.

The team lead concluded, "One of the advantages of K-NN is that it can make predictions for nonlinear relationships because it makes no assumptions about linearity.[13] We were able to reduce the average residuals from $12,000 to $10,000. It's not a huge improvement, but our team's guess is that K-NN performed better on the patients who were harder for linear regression to predict."

NAIVE BAYES

The next team to present its model approach was introduced by David. "Moving on to the next team, these folks used a different type of model called Naive Bayes. Let's hear what they have to say."

The team lead took the stage and explained, "Naive Bayes is a probabilistic machine learning model that is commonly used in classification problems. The idea is to use Bayes' theorem, which is a mathematical formula for calculating conditional probabilities, to predict the probability of an event occurring given certain evidence or features. Since Naive Bayes is a classifier, instead of predicting the exact dollar amount of health expenditure, our team predicted whether or not health expenditure would exceed $20,000 in the given year—a binary outcome."

Naive Bayes is based on the assumption that each feature is independent of all other features in the data set—hence, the *naive* in its name. This assumption allows the model to estimate the likelihood of each feature independently and then multiply them together to obtain the probability of a specific class. Naive Bayes is a simple and fast algorithm that can work well with small data sets and high-dimensional feature spaces.

The team lead continued. "One of the advantages of Naive Bayes is that it requires a small amount of training data to estimate the parameters necessary for classification. It also works well with high-dimensional data, making it a popular choice for text classification problems. However, it may not work well with features that are highly correlated, since the assumption of independence may not hold."

The training process for Naive Bayes involves estimating the prior probability of each class and the conditional probability of each feature given the class. Once these probabilities are estimated, they can be used to classify new data points. To classify a new data point, the model calculates the posterior probability of each class given the features of the data point using Bayes' theorem. The class with the highest posterior probability is the predicted class.

Overall, Naive Bayes is a powerful and efficient algorithm that can be used for classification problems with high-dimensional feature spaces. However, the assumption of independence may not hold in some cases, and the algorithm may not work well with highly correlated features.

"We achieved an area under the curve of 0.72 on our test set, which we think is pretty good, considering the simplicity of the algorithm and the small amount of data we had to work with," the team lead concluded.

DECISION TREES

The next team lead took to the stage. "Similar to the last group, we wanted to account for possible nonlinear relationships between variables. We also wanted the output of the model to correspond to easily interpretable patient profiles. A regression tree model was the perfect choice for our goals."

Classification and regression tree (CART) modeling consists of dividing the population into smaller subpopulations and then making predictions on those smaller subpopulations.[14] It is a clever algorithm for dividing the population that is cyclical, meaning the algorithm repeats itself over and over. CART modeling starts with the entire population in the *root node*. It searches for the best variable and value of that variable for separating the low- and high-outcome groups. Once the root node is split into two or more branches, the algorithm repeats again on each of those branches.

After each split, the algorithm repeats over and over until it reaches a *stopping rule*.[15]

For example, assume we're building a regression tree that splits the population into two groups for each node. To predict health care expenditure, the algorithm would find the best variable and value of that variable to separate out the high- and low-cost patients. Once this first split is done, there are now two groups, the low- and the high-cost patients. The algorithm is then applied to each of these two groups to again find the best variable and value of that variable to split each of these groups into two more groups, so there are now four groups. The algorithm will stop when there are not enough customers in each group to split again or when it reaches some other stopping rule. When the CART model is completed, the entire population will be assigned to one and only one group, called a leaf, and the characteristics of each leaf can be easily read. For example, the highest-cost leaf may be male patients over 65 years old who live in the Northeast, and the lowest-cost leaf may be female patients under 18 who live in the South. A prediction for a new patient would be made by identifying what leaf the customer belongs to and assigning the average value of that leaf to that customer.

CART modeling has several advantages. First, the data scientist does not have to make assumptions about the features and their supposed relationship with the outcome; only the splitting and stopping rules need to be defined for the tree to be produced.[16] Second, CART models can be used to predict binomial variables, categorical variables, and continuous variables, and they are not as sensitive to outliers as other regression methods are. Tree-based models can also be built with missing data, while the other regression models often struggle with missing data.[17] Third, CART models can easily represent nonlinear relationships and interaction terms without the need for the modeler to specify them in the model itself. Lastly, CART modeling is easily interpretable in that it produces subpopulations of high and low values based on a set of if/then statements, allowing you easily to look at the rules and ask if they make sense.[18]

Despite these advantages, CART modeling has limitations. For instance, a small change in the data sample (for example, the addition or deletion of rows) could result in a very different CART model. This is different from other models, like linear and logistic regression models, which will generally produce similar regression coefficients with a small change in the data sample. CART models are also limited in the way they measure the contribution of variables to the outcome. Whereas a least squares regression model produces a coefficient that represents the change in the outcome for every unit increase in the predictor variable, a CART model does not produce such coefficients.[19] Instead, partial dependence plots and variable importance scores can be used to measure the impact of features. Partial dependence plots are graphs that show the relationship between features and outcomes while holding all other variables constant. Variable importance metrics are another way to measure the impact of a predictor on the outcome. They are usually calculated by making small perturbations in the variable of interest and seeing how the resulting prediction changes.[20]

CART models can be cleverly combined to develop more-complicated models that often have more predictive power. One variation of this is called a random forest. As you would expect from a forest, the random forest is a collection of classification and regression trees. So what about that word *random*? There are two different places where randomness comes into play. First, a large number of random samples of the data are created, and then a separate CART model is created for each sample. The more CART models there are in the forest, the longer the processing time will be, and the more the model prediction will generally improve (though this improvement will level off after a certain number of trees). Your data science team can easily test how many trees to have in the forest (it is rare to see more than a few hundred trees in a forest). The second application of randomness is when only certain input variables are randomly allowed to be used at a specific node.[21] As with the CART model, reviewing the variable importance and partial dependence plots will help you understand which inputs are driving the results and what the general relationship is between the features and the outcome variable, while the most critical question is "How does the model perform on a naive data set?"

The team lead summarized the results. "Our tree-based model didn't reduce the average residual by much: we went from $12,000 to $11,000. But we discovered we could develop this tree-based model much more quickly than we did the original model because the data did not require much preprocessing. Since tree-based models can handle missing values and variables of very different scales, it's relatively quick to train a model once you have the data collected."

BOOSTING, BAGGING, AND ENSEMBLING

David clapped for the last team and went back up on stage. "Now that we've heard from all our teams, I want to present a surprise that the data team leaders have been working on since the end of the hackathon. We've all heard the old saying 'Two heads are better than one.' But have you heard the more recent saying 'Two machine learning models are better than one'?" The audience laughed.

"After all the teams submitted their models, we had a secret team working in the background to combine all the models using ensembling methods. For the machine learning newbies in the audience, ensembling methods are techniques for combining the predictions of several models into a single, more accurate, more robust prediction.[22] Our team applied these techniques to all the models that were submitted to generate an ensemble model that outperformed each of the models individually."

One of the most common ensembling methods is stacking. In model stacking, different models are first created, and those models are then used as input variables to a new model, which is used to make the final prediction.[23] The first models are known as level 1 models, and these level 1 model predictions serve as inputs to the level 2 model. Stacked models can be thought of as a method to weight different models to produce a final result. A very common model-stacking approach involves the inclusion of commercial or external models as level 1 models that act as one or more of the inputs to the level 2 model. If you are focused on risk modeling, FICO can be a good level 1 model. For mortality modeling, the Charlson Comorbidity Index is a common level 1 model. The level 2 model, also called the stacked model, can outperform each of the individual models by more heavily weighting the level 1 models where they perform best and giving those models less weight where they perform poorly.

A special case of ensembling is called *bootstrap aggregation*, or bagging for short. Bootstrapping refers to making several data sets from the original data set by resampling observations. For example, from a starting data set of 1,000 observations, you may create ten bootstrapped data sets, each containing 1,000 observations resampled from the original 1,000. A model is fit to each of the bootstrapped data sets, and the resulting predictions are aggregated. It has been shown that bagging can improve prediction accuracy and help avoid overfitting.[24]

Another technique commonly used to improve the performance of machine learning models is gradient boosted machine learning, also known as GBML.[25] The word *boosted* is critical here. Boosting involves having models learn by giving the misclassified observations more weight in the next iteration of the training as well as by potentially giving more weight to the more accurate trees. This boosting process means that as the algorithm repeats itself, it will improve on the observations that are more difficult to predict while not sacrificing too much on the ones that are easier to predict. There are many boosting algorithms; two of the most commonly used are Adaboost and Arcboost.[26]

David continued. "The models that we included in our ensemble were the original linear regression model, the K-NN model, and the regression tree model. We gave each model access to all the features that were engineered by the different teams, and we applied bagging and boosting to the regression tree model to improve its performance. Finally, we developed a stacked model, which combined the predictions from the three level 1 models using a level 2 linear regression model. Our stacked ensemble vastly outperformed each of the individual models: we were able to decrease the average residual from $12,000 to $5,000!"

Kamala was floored. How could the stacked model be that much better? "David, I'm wondering how the stacked model performed so well. Before the ensembling, the best model was one of the linear regression models that had an average residual of $8,500. All the other models had residuals higher than that. How is it that adding a model with residuals over $10,000 to a model with residuals at $8,500 leads to a model with residuals at $5,000?"

"That's the beauty of ensembling." David smiled. "Imagine you're on a trivia game show with a partner. Your partner is a quiz bowl whiz. They know just about everything—except they've never had a penchant for pop music, so they're completely useless when it comes to any question relating to music. You, on the other hand, know absolutely nothing about geography, sports, science, or history. But you're a huge music and movies fan, so any question on pop music that comes your way is a piece of cake. Individually, your partner would perform way better than you. They may get 90 percent of all questions right if you assume the remaining 10 percent are about music. You, on the other hand, would do terribly on your own. You'd be lucky to get 15 percent if you assume those are the questions about music and movies. Now what if we put you two together on the same team? You can complement your partner's knowledge on music and movies, and they can carry the team for all the remaining questions. Individually, it's unlikely either of you would get 100 percent, but together you have a real shot at a perfect score."

This made sense to Kamala. "It's like forming a committee. The different backgrounds of the committee members complement each other, and, collectively, they're able to make a better decision than they would individually."

"Exactly. Two models are better than one!"

KEY QUESTIONS

- What can we learn from examining the residuals of this model? Did you identify any patterns in the residuals?
- Does the relationship between the feature and the outcome align with intuition?
- Can we include polynomial terms or interaction terms as features?

- Based on our knowledge of the data itself, are there specific interaction terms that we expect to see?
- Which features should be transformed before being used for modeling?
- Does the data contain outliers that need to be dealt with? If so, how will those outliers be treated?
- Would it make sense to weight certain observations in this data set? If so, what weightings would be appropriate to explore?
- Would a K-nearest neighbor approach be superior to a parametric regression approach in this scenario?
- Should we try out metalearning methods like boosting, bagging, and ensembling? What are the potential benefits and risks involved in these explorations?

8

PULLING IT TOGETHER

Following Steve's success in the Fraud Department, he was promoted and transferred to a newly created division. Shu Financial was embarking on a new business venture, a consumer real estate business. The basic plan was straightforward: Shu Financial would buy used homes, renovate them, and then rent them. The business should make money by renting the homes and potentially by selling them if they appreciated enough in value.

Steve was thrilled at the promotion and the opportunity to tackle this new business's challenges. He would need to lead model building in a new area, gaining business-specific knowledge about real estate while also using many different methodologies that he hadn't previously used in his other rotations.

The senior vice president of real estate, Charissa, quickly debriefed him. "Our situation is a bit different from Fraud. We are a new business, so we need to first figure out some basics about the business, while those other divisions where you worked had been operating for many years."

Steve nodded his head. He was excited about working in an area with more "blue sky" after his previous rotations had put him in some well-defined projects. "What do you suggest I do as a first step?"

Charissa smiled, as she liked Steve's approach of asking for guidance. She then responded, "This is what I like to refer to as a 'pulling it together' opportunity. This work will force you to leverage your past knowledge as well as build new skills in order to succeed. Your best friend here is going to be Jerry. He runs the operations for our division. His hybrid skill set makes him a very rapidly rising star here at Shu Financial. In fact, in a few more years he will probably be my boss instead of the other way around. His background is in business development, but he also picked up a master's in data science. He's still taking online classes in advanced statistics, Python, PowerBI, and Tableau. The two of you are going to be a team. Work closely with him to develop the data science strategy for the Real Estate Division. Focus on the most critical items. We need to be profitable quickly while flagging all of the nice-to-haves for future work."

Steve's first meeting with Jerry was a 30-minute whirlwind of facts and references. Jerry gave him a list of background materials to read along with the plan that they would meet for 1 hour every other day to help Steve get up to speed quickly on machine learning applications in real estate.[1]

Jerry also chatted briefly about artificial intelligence (AI) and deep learning. His take-home message was simple: get the job done, and don't get caught up in buzz words. In his own words, "AI is a very general idea: having the computer do tasks that are usually done by humans because they used to require human intelligence. Generative AI, which is capable of generating text, images, or other media in response to prompts is really going to be a game-changer. Right now, we are using property managers to set the rental prices, but we are pretty confident we can do it better using algorithms.[2] For businesspeople like us, we are less concerned about understanding the details of the algorithms that are used and more concerned about solving the problems. As you already know, machine learning automatically learns from past data without programming explicit rules. The goal of AI is to make a smart computer system like humans to solve complex problems."

"What about deep learning? Should we be using it here?" asked Steve

Jerry responded, "Deep learning is all the rage these days . . . but remember to solve problems—don't run to buzzwords. Deep learning involves neural networks with many layers of processing. The different layers often serve different functions like identifying edges in an image or, at the output level, making a prediction. You may find neural networks used in some applications, or you may find other methods are more appropriate. Do your reading, and then come back with some suggestions."

"What about autoencoding? Anything I should know about it?"

"Autoencoding is a very clever application of neural networks where the input is the same as the output."

Steve scratched his head. "Why would we ever want to build a model where the input is the same as the output?"

Jerry smiled. "Yes, it is a little counterintuitive at first. With autoencoders, we are trying to understand how to compress the data so we have fewer features. Think of it as a sandwich with the original features as the input and output layers and a much smaller layer in the middle. That inner layer is a compression that can be used for modeling itself or for gaining insight into what the important pieces of information are in the original feature set. Image compression is one possible application of autoencoding: the goal is to represent the essential components of the original image in a lower-complexity space by removing unnecessary or noisy features. My advice: let's keep talking more about modeling and see what the right tool for the problem is—and not just what the tool you read about this week is."

Meeting number two was a much deeper discussion, as Jerry led off by explaining the business's key challenges. "We have a financial model that is pivotal for our business. It was adopted from our other lines of business but basically computes the return on investment given key inputs such as the purchase price of the house, the future rental price of the house, the occupancy rate, the delinquency rate, the cost of the renovations, and a few other variables. The main variable that drives the model is the future rental price. Many of the other inputs have a limit to their variability or can be dealt with using good models we already have in place. After all, we are great at predicting credit risk and utilization."

"So how are we currently estimating the future rental price?" asked Steve.

Jerry replied, "Today we are purchasing an off-the-shelf solution. There are companies that specialize in this work. The problem is that their models are very expensive and not very accurate. I could lose my shirt if I simply used some of the models out there and trusted that they were accurate."

"Got it. So let's build our own," Steve suggested. "I worked closely with the data science team in Fraud and in my other rotations to build some great supervised machine learning models that are currently in production."

"Gee, now why didn't I think of that?" Jerry replied with a smile. "Your main task is to help build models to predict rental prices. We tried doing some basic model building before, but the performance was poor. Maybe we didn't explore enough diverse data sources, or maybe we didn't think creatively enough about the modeling method."

Steve recognized that his suggestion was a bit obvious. Reflecting on his readings, he countered with "We know this is a new business—one where we have very little in-house data that is relevant. While we have strong cross-learnings from other lines of business, where we fall flat is in not having a lot of relevant in-house data for the rental price model. In terms of outside data, there are some potential data sources we should test. First, there are the real estate listings themselves. They provide the basics on the size of the home, year built, number of bedrooms, number of bathrooms, and location."

Jerry pushed Steve in this area. "Remember that the data is the basic step. No data, no model. What other information is available that we could use?"

Steve was ready with some ideas. "Besides the listing itself, there is neighborhood-level information available from third-party vendors. They aggregate information about the neighborhood's safety, level of education, employment, and other critical factors for future renters and homeowners. We can pay for a license to access this data, and it gets updated on a monthly basis. Of course, there are also government data sources that we can leverage for free, published annually at the zip code, city, and state levels. While it would be nicer if this was at a smaller level of resolution, like the city block, we do get information at the census tract level."

"The problem with the census data," cautioned Jerry, "is that it is not updated as frequently as we would like. Those data sources will help give us a mediocre model like some of those commercial models that are so bad that relying on them would cause my business to tank. Any other data sources you can think of?"

Steve continued. "Two other sources that I am very excited about that are mostly ignored by other modeling teams are the detailed home description found in the advertisement and the photos posted by the seller's agent. The home description is a text field that often has critical information about the home that is mostly ignored. We could use natural language processing, or NLP, to extract additional features and descriptions about the home and put in it our model. The photos can be processed through an AI algorithm to develop features related to the home such as its level of maintenance, the quality of the roof, recent renovations, or deteriorating conditions."

"Lots of good ideas there, but let's make sure we focus on our core competencies," Jerry advised. "If we are Google, then NLP is business critical, and they go very deep in that area. Uber is similar with geospatial analysis and Tesla with computer vision. Expertise in those areas is business critical. Find the right level of depth by learning the basics so we can get value."

Steve nodded his head. "Got it. Any other advice?"

Jerry continued. "Start with NLP, but be careful. Lots of people here at Shu Financial know the phrase NLP, but few seem to understand that it's is a lot more than just doing a simple text search. You will need to do some self-study on that and then come back to the data science team with a very precise request and a set of requirements. Luckily we now can use GPT to help extract useful information from written text without the major effort it would have taken years ago. As a first pass, the team will simply give you a list showing how many times each phrase you identified was used . . . and, believe me, that isn't going to be very useful. As for AI, you are entering uncharted territory, so learn as much as you can, and let's see what can be delivered. You will work closely with the data science team and update me on a weekly basis in terms of the progress. When we have something definitive to show off, we can arrange a chat with our boss, Charissa."

With those words of encouragement, Steve was off to the races. Step number one on this journey would be natural language processing. He knew Jerry was right that the acronym NLP is thrown around all the time, but few seem to really understand what exactly it is and how it may be used. His first goal was to better understand NLP and then discuss with the data science team what could and couldn't be done in that area given the data sources, technical limitations, and capacity constraints.

Charissa was able to use her influence as a senior vice president to get Brett temporarily assigned to work with Steve so they could continue working as a tightly knit team that combines their business and data science knowledge.

Jerry and Steve lined up their project management tools and decided to focus as a first phase on the development of data sources and features. Their logic was simple: Jerry had already done an extensive exploration of the competitive landscape of vendors selling rental price models that they could use. Once they had a good data set, they were very comfortable building the models themselves.

For the data sources, the search began with a blue sky session. This session was facilitated by Steve, who prepared everyone with a discussion guide that summarized what he knew about rental price modeling from his background research, such as the features that have been identified by other researchers and companies as being important, the vendors that already produce rental price models and their descriptions of these models, and the data sources that have been used by others. He then laid out some key questions that he wanted the participants to discuss. These key questions included what features might influence a rental price and what some potential data sources are. Participants at the blue sky session included not only Jerry and Brett but also two former property managers who were familiar with the operations of renting properties and could lend their real-world insight. The people with operations insight turned out to be the most helpful, as they brought up suggestions that had not been considered. One insight was that people who view properties often post their reactions to the viewings on a few websites. Analysis of their reviews could help identify positive or negative sentiments. The distribution of these sentiments and their relationship with other features could serve as inputs in the rental price model. Additionally, the property managers noted that real estate brokers often have key words they use that signal issues with a property. Any "sun-drenched" residence that is "intimate" and "quaint" may turn out to be an old, tiny, dark place depending on the broker. And a "handyman's special", "fixer upper" or "bring your architech" definitely signaled that major work was going to be needed while "just renovated" indicated the opposite. This extra information got Steve and Brett excited that NLP, computer vision, and network analysis could help their model outperform those of the commercial vendors.

Steve realized that he needed to become more familiar with these concepts in order to help drive the business forward while remembering that his goal was not to become a subject-matter expert but rather to be able to ask good questions and make good decisions.

NATURAL LANGUAGE PROCESSING

Natural language processing is a very popular application of AI. It focuses on understanding and analyzing the language that people speak and write. The inputs to NLP are written or spoken communications rather than structured, tabular data that has been crafted by a data analyst. The range of what can be used as inputs for NLP is quite broad. Similarly, the applications are far-reaching. They can include speech recognition that takes spoken words and converts them to text, automatic language translation where text in one language is translated to another language, intelligent searching of databases and the internet, spam filters, sentiment analysis, and chatbots that try to solve customers' problems.[3]

Because the number of NLP applications is so vast, the number of methods can be overwhelming. A way to approach understanding

NLP is to begin with some basic concepts through the example of applying sentiment analysis to feedback provided by people who viewed a rental property.

The first step is that the data usually undergoes some form of a cleaning process.[4] The cleaning process depends on the problem being solved. In some cases, you will want to remove symbols like $, but if you are working on a problem with multiple currencies, then that $ is critically important. In some cases, punctuation like ? or ! is highly relevant and needs to be retained, while in other cases this will be dropped. Another important consideration is the relevance of capital letters. If the capitalization isn't relevant, then a common data preprocessing step involves shifting all of the text to lowercase. This step allows the analysis to not get confused among Cozy, COZY, cozy, coZy, and other variations of capitalization of the same word.[5]

A good question to ask the members of the data science team is "What specific steps did you take in the data cleaning and preprocessing?" This can help you not only understand what they did but also flag concerns if they mistakenly removed critical information that will be relevant to your problem.

A follow-up step often involves tokenization.[6] This converts the sentence, paragraph, or document into individual words, called tokens. Imagine the sentence "You are a terrific reader who understands everything in this book" being tokenized. The output would be a list of the different words in the sentence (*you, are, a, . . .*). This list is going to be useful later in the NLP analysis.

The tokens can represent all of the distinct words in the document, but often this list will include a lot of words with little distinguishing value. After all, the words *the, of, is,* and *a* will likely be some of the most common words in many documents. These words, known as stop words,[7] usually have little value in a predictive analysis and could add noise. A standard step in NLP is to remove these stop words, but since there is no standard list of stop words, this removal should be reviewed with the business unit.

Another key step involves stemming.[8] This reduces each word to its stem (or root). For example, words like *walk, walking,* and *walked* all have the same stem—*walk*. Removing the endings allows the analysis to focus on the key point of the word *walk* without treating those other words (*walked, walking*) as separate ideas. This is particularly useful when you are trying to see how often an idea is mentioned in a review. Lemmatization is similar to stemming, but it has the constraint that the stem must be a word. For example, the stem of *sharing* and *shared* is *shar*, while the lemma would be a word, *share*.

A commonly used step is to search not only for word frequencies but also for N-grams.[9] *Pretty* means attractive, and *ugly* is the opposite. Both are N-grams of length 1, or unigrams. But when Brett announces that his first model is "pretty ugly," it is a bigram (N = 2) that means the model is rather poor. Trigrams are three-word sequences such as "this clearly demonstrates." N-grams preserve the order of the words, which is critically important, since the phrase "ugly pretty" doesn't mean anything to a native speaker, but the reverse order, "pretty ugly," does. NLP analysis of N-grams looks to identify the most frequently used N-grams. By using longer N-grams, such as those with five or more words, a computer can often mimic human writing by automatic text generation. This can be handy in creating chatbots that mimic human writing.[10] It is also critical in sentence completion when you are typing on your phone or laptop and it offers you a suggestion of how to complete your sentence, which is often very accurate.

Steve was excited to share his knowledge of NLP with Brett but was soon redirected to the world of text data vectorizing. As Brett explained, "This is how we can convert text information into numbers that we can use for analysis: for example, by developing a bag of words to identify how similar two reviews are based on the words that appear."

Bag-of-words analysis is a method that can examine a pair of documents and create a list of the words used in the two sources.[11] It then measures how often the same word appears in both documents. Two very similar sentences will have a lot of overlap in words, while two sentences that are quite different will not. Another simple analysis performed with a bag of words is to look at the term frequency, which is just the probability that a random word in the document matches the word you are looking at. If the review has fifty words in it and mentions "cozy" three times, then "cozy" has a term frequency of 6 percent, which is really quite high! This term frequency is often used in combination with another metric, the inverse document frequency, which measures whether a term is common or rare in a set of documents.[12] It is computed by a function of the ratio of the total number of documents in the corpus to the number of those documents containing the term. Multiplying the term frequency by the inverse document frequency produces a new metric that reflects how important a specific word is with respect to a given document in a collection of documents.

Going back to our "cozy" example, a document that used the word *cozy* a lot would have a high term frequency. If only a small percentage of the documents used the word *cozy*, then the inverse document frequency would also be high, resulting in a product that would be high. This means that the word *cozy* is specially used in that review as compared with other reviews. Contrast *cozy* with a common word like *the*. *The* has a very high term frequency in most documents but would have an extremely low inverse document frequency, resulting in a product of the two that is low.

Another commonly used NLP tool is word2vec.[13] This algorithm is often used to help identify how similar two words or sentences are, based on their usage. Additionally, word2vec can be used to suggest words for sentence completion. The idea behind word2vec is described in the name itself. This algorithm creates a vector for each word and then can compare how similar the vectors are for two different words. In Steve's application for real estate, the team might want to start by using a pretrained word2vec algorithm that may not be specific to real estate. If the pretrained algorithm has poor performance, then the team could explore developing a customized application by training the algorithm on real estate text.

Armed with this background information about NLP, Steve debriefed with Brett and Jerry. They agreed that bag-of-words analysis would be helpful as part of the modeling. It would help identify terms that characterize different property descriptions. Those terms could then be used as features in the modeling itself.

Steve asked, "Do you think we can use sentiment analysis as part of rental price estimation?"[14] The conclusion was that they could try applying sentiment analysis on the property description but that it may not show much information. Brokers would not use negative words or phrases to describe their property. On the other hand, comments and postings about the property on social media sites would definitely reflect a range of opinions. With that plan in mind, they brought the sentiment analysis component into the project scope. Since there was some evidence for its use in the literature, the first step would be to see if it could be valuable in the analysis.[15] Later steps would involve identifying the frequency with which they would need to obtain the latest text feeds, score sentiment, and then incorporate that information into the model. The logic of using sentiment analysis was that if properties are consistently described as positive, neutral, or negative, then those sentiments could provide additional useful information to the rental model prediction.

Steve already understood the basics of NLP but needed to better understand sentiment analysis. Sentiment analysis uses text as an input to figure out whether a person had a positive, negative, or neutral reaction.[16] Brands often scrape information off the web to understand how customers feel about their products, locations, programs, and policies. They can also use sentiment analysis to prioritize communication into buckets of urgency.

Many prepackaged modules already exist in Python and R that ingest text data and output. The simplest approaches are rules based. After performing the data cleaning, stemming, and tokenization described above, one looks at the distribution of words and phrases. A sentiment score is assigned based on whether those commonly used words and phrases are positive or negative. Of course, there are some additional rules applied so that the analysis distinguishes between "the house has nice kitchen cabinets" and "the house doesn't have nice kitchen cabinets." With a rules-based approach, the phrase lists and their corresponding positive or negative associations must be maintained and updated. In particular, there may be specific phrases that have different connotations in real estate than they do outside of real estate.

The machine learning approach to sentiment analysis is usually considered a supervised machine learning problem. The output variable is often categorical, such as positive, negative, or neutral. It may also be numerical, such as scoring on a scale of −10 to 10, where −10 is extremely negative, 0 neutral, and 10 extremely positive. The text goes through preprocessing similar to that used in the rules-based approach, and often a bag of words is created. This bag of words is then input to the supervised machine learning model using the same methods described previously. The training set relies on using some text already scored by a human for its sentiment for the model to learn. New text can be scored using the final algorithm.[17]

Jerry was not terribly wrong when he said that many people claim to be doing NLP but are really just doing text searching. That is, they are creating long lists of phrases and then doing a simple search of the document to see if the phrase exists and to count the number of times it appears. How can you determine whether or not the team is doing a full NLP analysis? By asking detailed questions about what exactly the team is doing and why. There is a wide range of complexity in NLP models. The simplest are nothing more than the type of text searching that Jerry had dismissed as not being very helpful. The more complicated incorporate phrases and groups of words into applications like sentiment analysis or advanced searches. The most advanced models, such as deep learning NLP, use models that have been trained on enormous corpuses of text, such as the models developed by data science teams at major companies like Google and Facebook.

NLP is a rapidly changing area of data science. Large language models (LLMs) such as GPT, LLaMA and PaLM2 have radically changed the world of NLP. These models fall under the category of generative AI because of their ability to generate human-like text. Intuitively, they work by generating the most likely token or phrase to come next. Just as you might fill in the blank of "I'm going to the store to buy some ____" with a word like "milk", LLMs leverage their vast training corpus to understand the probabilistic relationships between words, allowing them to predict or generate the most likely sequence of words that follow a prompt. Using simple prompt engineering, users can now perform effective sentiment analysis, extracting mean from large sets of text and other NLP tasks with minimal effort. The most effective way to use LLMs is to combine them with high quality, domain-specific datasets. Data is the most valuable asset, not any specific model. With advances in open source models, practically anyone can deploy a large language model, but only you have access to your organization's proprietary data. An out-of-the-box LLM is like a new graduate hire—a semi-competent generalist. To be truly effective, they need to be trained on the specific competencies required to succeed at your company—they need to become a specialist. Likewise, the best way to optimize the performance of an LLM is to train it or fine tune it on your company's data. While these tools are extremely powerful, approach with caution. LLMs are known to hallucinate, can be expensive to deploy, and may be susceptible to cyber attacks. Work closely with your security team before exposing your data to an LLM.

GEOSPATIAL ANALYSIS

In reviewing the data available, a key item that kept coming up was the use of geospatial information. Jerry's advice on this was clear: let Brett be your guide, since he has already done some geospatial analysis in the Fraud Department.

Brett led off with his usual confidence. "People make it seem like geospatial analysis is some foreign language compared to other data analytics, but it is really just one more area that can be explored. Basically, you are using location information as part of the modeling where that location information can be gathered from various sources. Often the challenge is getting things linked together given the different location systems used, but, luckily, there are geographic coordinates and some useful tools for connecting different systems."

Steve followed up with a question. "What data sources do we have that include geospatial information that can be used, and what is our experience in analyzing this type of data?"

Brett responded immediately. "In terms of data sources, we have a lot. Every property comes with information about its location in terms of latitude and longitude. This allows us to estimate both the distance and the travel time to other locations. We also have government data that provides information about income, family size, population density, and other demographics. This information can be provided for the nation or by state, county, zip code, census block, census block group, census tract, and even metropolitan statistical area, which is really just a fancy phrase for the nearly four hundred cities or groups of cities the Census uses to combine populations.[18]

"We also have vendors who sell data on quality of life, school quality, safety, consumer spending, business trends, social media trends, and other statistics at the zip code level. So for each home, we can add this information into our model."

"But these are very different levels of geographic resolution. Exact latitude and longitude is much more precise than the over 11 million census blocks or the roughly 41,000 zip codes in the United States. Which variables should we use?"

Brett replied, "We need to consider how frequently the data is updated as well as what level of spatial resolution makes sense. Data at the state level is clearly way too broad. The zip code level or even smaller makes sense. That said, we also need to consider how often the data is collected. Some of this data is updated only every 5 or 10 years. Those variables may not be as helpful in determining the factors driving the rental prices, but we can explore the features to see which ones are providing value . . . letting the data help inform us about which features are and aren't important in predicting rental price."

The process Brett described simplifies many of the geospatial calculations. If we are aware of the relationships between the entities, such as the latitude and longitude of the different census tracts and zip codes, we can use the location of the house to get information about other geographically encoded information.[19] This becomes an exercise in linking across data sets and then assigning the value of the features to the correct zip code, census tract, or other identifier for that house.

Knowing the specific location of the rental properties also enables other computations. A common approach is to do a spatial smoothing by computing the average rental price within a fixed distance from the property of interest.[20] In its simplest form, this would take the average of the rental prices within X miles of the rental property and use that as another feature in the model. This is an extremely simple way to do a weighted average. The properties within X all are weighted the same, while properties that are more than X miles away have a weighting of 0 in a weighted average. Weighting can be made more sophisticated by using a weight that scales inversely with the distance so that properties that are closest to the one of interest have the highest weights and those that are farthest have the lowest weights.[21] The scale can be linear, where properties that are twice as far have half the weight, or nonlinear, where properties that are twice the distance have much less than half the weight. The choice of weightings as a function of distance is critical and should be explored systematically.

A more advanced approach to geospatial analytics involves using the latitude and longitude data from the rental property and then analyzing the distance between that location and other points of interest.[22] Which points of interest? That depends on what is being modeled. In the case of the rental price modeling, the distance to transportation hubs such as subway stops can be a critical feature. The distances to shopping malls, parks, and other points of interest are potentially strong features. This is a simple analysis that looks at the distance between points. Other geographic information system (GIS) analysis can be more advanced. For example, one can examine the travel time between the rental property and the nearest transportation hub. This is more complicated than computing the distance, as it involves other considerations such as the route, average speed on the road, and road quality. There are algorithms that compute this given two locations, the same functionality that you find on your smartphone.[23]

Geographically encoded information allows the user to explore other concepts like density and how that changes in different locations. Going back to our real estate example, we may have education, safety, or even rental price data at a census block or zip code level. But we also have rental price information at the exact location of the property. We could examine the density of low- and high-rental-price properties by developing maps of the average rental price across a smoothed area of our choosing. We could use a wide smoothing, such as a 3-mile smoothing, and then compare that map to one with a much smaller smoothing. Using the smaller smoothing window, we will see far more variance in the rental price mapping and possibly some pockets where there are very expensive streets next to much cheaper streets. If that is the case, then we would want to focus on a smaller radius when performing our geospatial smoothing. As with other smoothing algorithms, the narrower the smoothing, the smaller the sample size and the greater the variability in the smoothed value.

One of the most common applications of geospatial data is for data visualization, creating maps that display the distribution of key variables as a function of location. These maps can often tell a story that other data visualizations can't, such as how similar the values of nearby properties are.

In order to develop these maps, geospatial data is required. There are two main types of geospatial data, vector data[24] and raster data.[25] Vector data represents features such as properties, cities, roads, and parks. It contains points (properties), lines (roads), and polygons (parks and cities). Think of this vector data as the information used to draw the outlines of the map, including the borders between properties and the locations of interesting places.

Raster data is gridded or pixelated data. Think of this as a matrix where the rows and columns represent the longitude and latitude. The cells in the matrix represent the values that can be analyzed or plotted.[26] When we look at a weather map, the raster data used to make the map is the cells in the matrix containing information about the temperatures. A map of social media data could show Instagram trends as a function of the location of the person posting.

There are GIS capabilities and many real-world examples of applications in Python, R,[27] and other software packages, but it is worthwhile to note that many use ArcGIS,[28] a commercial GIS software, or its free version, QGIS.[29]

With the various internal and external databases linked with the available geospatial data, the analytic file that would be used for the modeling is taking shape. From the GIS work, they will use not only the average price within a 2-mile radius but also the travel time to public transportation and major shopping areas. The NLP algorithms have succeeded at extracting a number of keywords and bigrams that will serve as potential features. Time for Steve to revisit the question of computer vision and how it could be used in the rental price modeling.[30]

COMPUTER VISION

Computer vision (CV) is a field of AI that enables computers to extract useful information from digital images, videos, and other visual inputs.[31] CV analyzes these inputs to determine what objects are in view, where those objects are located, how the different objects can be distinguished, how far away the objects are, whether the objects are moving, and whether there is something wrong in an image. Focusing on the subset of inputs that are static images such as photos, CV relies on a large set of tagged images. This tagging identifies items that are critical to the application. In our real estate case, the tagging could include not only identification of the roof or chimney of a house but also the condition of the roof or chimney. Within the house, this tagging could reflect the type and quality of the ceiling, bathroom furnishings, kitchen appliances, cabinets, and other details that would often not appear on the real estate listing description but that would influence the price.

CV is a specialized area within data science where the commercially available solutions often appear as black boxes. We are going to dig a bit deeper into the details of CV algorithms so that the customer has a better understanding of what is likely to be happening inside that black box.

A common algorithm for CV is the convolutional neural network (CNN). CNNs are known for having many different layers of processing that occur in sequence, with different processing layers serving different functions. The layers receive input from other layers, perform a computation like a nonlinear weighting, and then output to a different layer.[32]

The input to a CNN in a CV example is the image, a set of pixel levels where each pixel level has a specific location in the image. If it is a black-and-white image, then the pixels are numbers on a gray scale ranging from bright white to dark black. Often these black-and-white pixel values range from 0 to 255. For a color image, there are three sets of pixel information, one for red, one for green, and one for blue, where the red, green, and blue values can all range from 0 to 255.[33]

The early layers of processing involve extracting features such as the brightness, edges, and direction of shading. In a CNN, the data scientist does not prespecify what features the layer examines. Rather, the neural network will learn these features on its own as part of the training process. The mapping from the input layer to the feature maps results in what are called the convolution layers—hence, the name convolutional neural network.[34] These early rounds of feature identification are combined to create feature maps. These feature maps are then combined to eventually create translation invariant identifications. This means that the mappings are identified regardless of where they are placed on the image. Other invariances, such as rotational invariance, are developed so the orientation of the roof or countertop is not important in detecting the object in the image. Translational and rotational invariances are critical in CV, since you can't rely on the images having the object of interest in the same position or same orientation.[35]

The CNN's final layer is an output layer that can produce an estimate of the probability of what is contained in the image, whether that be marble countertops or laminate ones, newly tiled roofs or peeling rooftops in immediate need of repair, or other critical features.

While CNNs are popular in analyzing static images, recurrent neural networks (RNNs) are commonly used with video content.[36] RNNs are different from many other neural networks in that they include loops that link back to earlier layers of analysis. Specifically, they save the output of specific layers and feed this output back to the input. This feedback step is then used to predict the output of the layer. RNNs were developed to address specific limitations in other types of models that struggle with data that is changing over time. Because RNNs examine a series of information over time, they are used for a variety of applications that involve time-varying information. These include the extraction of information about what changes are occurring in videos, the captioning of videos, time series prediction (forecasting), and NLP. For Steve's real estate application, CNNs are sufficient to extract key information about the property from static images. The exploration of videos does not have substantially more information, so they do not implement RNNs.

For the real estate application, Steve needs to first understand the existing data sources that could provide outdoor and indoor images. The first source is the real estate postings themselves; other sources include tagged social media images, such as those on Twitter, Facebook, Instagram, and LinkedIn, as well as other publicly available images. There are services that can be hired to go to a property and take additional photos. This service is expensive, and it isn't obvious that it would add value to the model.

After understanding the potential sources, Steve needed to better understand what possible internal and external features could be extracted from images. A literature search would help provide some information, as would a discussion with the operational leads and data science team. The basic questions they would be discussing are "What information can be obtained from this new data source and technique that cannot be obtained in another way?" and "What other data sources can be used?" and "Are there better ways to obtain this information?"

The output of the CV analysis includes a set of probabilities. These probabilities can relate to outdoor items, such as the need for roof work or chimney repairs, and to indoor items, such as the details of the kitchen, bathrooms, floor quality, or ceilings. Wall-to-wall carpeting from the 1970s should get identified easily, but the type of material used for the countertops is a far more difficult question to address with CV. Many of the values will be blank because either there are no images or the images do not contain the information needed. A set of summary statistics about the completeness of the images would illuminate how many properties have images, how many have images showing different parts of the inside and outside of the property, and how many properties have images that provide meaningful information about the property details. The information from the CV analysis becomes features that are added to the data set that is being used to develop the rental price model.

With these pieces in hand, Steve scheduled a discussion with Jerry and Brett to review progress.

NETWORK ANALYSIS

Jerry smiled as Steve provided his overall plan of the analysis, including database development, data sourcing, and applications of NLP, CV, and geospatial analysis. He nodded while saying "Sounds like you have the basics down. Just curious, Brett, if you have offered any of what you claim is special sauce that will make our efforts better than anything we can buy off the shelf?"

Brett immediately replied, "As a matter of fact, if we can leverage the real estate brokers' network, we can apply network analysis. This would let us identify the overall structure of the brokerage system, including the key connectors and their linkages."

Jerry looked puzzled for the first time since Steve had known him. "Why should we care about a network of brokers? How is this network going to help us build better models for predicting rental prices?"

"Social networks display the connections between individuals as well as groups of people," Brett answered. "My idea is that the network will have agents who are well connected and those who are not. The well-connected ones are probably able to draw more people to their showings. More showings could mean higher rental prices, so the level of connection of the brokers could help predict rental prices. Also, we can examine the accuracy of the property descriptions, the use of specific adjectives, and the overestimation of features and link them back to the agents who posted them."

Jerry responded with suspicion. "It seems like quite a stretch. But some part of data science involves incurring some risk in exploring methods and data sources. After all, if we knew the answer before we started, then we wouldn't call it science. Let's get clarity on how much time and money it will cost us to explore network analysis, and then we can decide if it is worth pursuing. Just curious—has anyone published anything about applying network analysis to rental price or home price prediction before?"

Steve nodded his head. "I did an online search and checked the academic journals. There are a few references."[37]

Jerry continued. "Well, then let's stay on the leading edge but not be on the bleeding edge here. Figure out how much money and time we should spend on exploring network analysis, and then stick to it. If Brett is right and it really is a special sauce that will make us stand out, then great. If not, then at least we cut our losses and chalk it up to research expenses."

With that guidance in mind, Brett paid to access the application programming interface (API) of Agentster, a social media network for real estate agents. It serves as the Facebook, LinkedIn, and Twitter of real estate.

In general, a social network consists of nodes (sometimes called actors or vertices) connected using a relation, also called a tie, link, arc, or edge.[38] The nodes can be individuals, groups, or teams. In the case of Agentster, the nodes are the brokers. The relations reflect how those different nodes are connected. This basic idea of a network is even reflected in how the data is structured. Network data always consists of at least two data sets. The first data set is a nodelist, where the nodes are the units of observation. In our case, it identifies all of the brokers in the network. The second data set defines how those nodes are connected. It can take different forms, but common ones include the adjacency matrix (also called a network matrix) and the edgelist. In an adjacency matrix, the columns and rows are the nodes, and the cells of the matrix define the relations.[39] An edgelist provides a list of all of the relations between different nodes. In an edgelist, all pairs of nodes that have relations are listed along with the type of relation. An edgelist can be readily converted into an adjacency matrix, and an adjacency matrix can be converted to an edgelist.

The simplest adjacency matrix or edgelist consists of only binary data: that is, a set of 0s and 1s that show if someone is or is not connected.[40] Binary data does not convey the strength of the connection but rather only whether or not a connection exists. A more complicated data set would have values that are scaled to reflect the strength of the connection. Those with no connection would still have 0s, but other connections could fall within a range based on the strength of the relationship, either as an ordinal value (weak, medium, or strong) or as a continuous value (such as a range between 0 and 10). Valued networks provide a lot more information than binary networks but are far more work to collect and analyze. Our agent network is a binary network in that it indicates only whether or not two agents are connected and nothing about the strength of the connection.

Some networks are directed, while others are undirected. With directed networks, the connections don't necessarily go both ways. These are asymmetric relationships.[41] Twitter and Instagram users know that you can follow someone who doesn't follow you. That means the relationship is directed. You can imagine this relationship as a set of arrows where many of the arrows point in only one direction. The sender, also called the source, is where the information comes from, and the arrow points at the receiver (or target). If you have a directed network, you can describe which nodes have the most inbound connections (what data scientists call the node's *in-degree*) versus outbound connections (the node's *out-degree*). The brokerage network is undirected, meaning the number of in-degrees is equal to the number of out-degrees. This makes the analysis a bit simpler, since direction is not a consideration.

This undirected network can be compared with directed networks. Think of the difference between Twitter, a directed network, and Facebook, an undirected network. With Facebook, when you connect to someone as a friend, then they have connected to you as well. This is an undirected network.[42] This can be imagined as an arrow with two points, connecting in both directions. Of course, all friendships are not symmetrical in the real or the virtual world. Even if it is an undirected network, the strength of the connection in one direction may be stronger than the connection in the opposite direction. Think of this as a situation where two people are connected and one side gets far more responses than the other side when a message is sent.

Steve decided to check in with Brett to see if he could get some more tutoring on network analysis. Brett was happy to share some of his knowledge. "There are a few basic principles that seem to hold in most networks. Individuals are more likely to be connected to those who are similar than to random individuals. This is referred to as homophily."[43]

Steve interjected, "Brokers who work in similar regions or with similar types of homes are more likely to be connected than brokers who work in entirely different geographic or business spaces."

Brett nodded his head. "Exactly. There is also the idea of triadic closure or, more simply put, the transitive rule. This says that friends of friends are more likely to be friends than people who are not connected through a mutual friend.[44] You can think of this in your own social media network, where Facebook recommends people you might want to connect with on Facebook based on a number of factors, including a very basic one, people who are already connected to many of your friends."

"In our case, if Betty the broker and Billy the broker are both connected to Buddy the broker, then there is a higher than random chance that Betty and Billy are also connected," Steve suggested.

Brett smiled. "Strange choice of fictitious names there, but, yes, you got it right. Lastly, there is the idea of cliques within networks.[45] Think of that clique from high school or B-school: the people who spent a lot of time together, often with only limited interactions outside of their group. The same idea translates over to network analysis, where the frequency and density of cliques can be examined as a way to describe how different brokers, friends, or other components of a network interact."

Steve was concerned that he was about to dip into a theoretical exercise with Brett. "Can we step back from the network concepts to focus on only the most critical aspects of network analysis as they relate to our modeling work? It seems like there are a lot of network-level metrics that could be very helpful in describing the network as well as some individual-level metrics that could help us understand the key connectors. Should we just focus on the individual-level metrics and see if they are helpful in the model?"

Brett disagreed. "You don't want to just blindly dive into individual-level metrics without understanding the basics of the network you are analyzing. A few metrics will get you very far. At the network level, there are dense networks where a large percentage of the possible connections actually exist, and there are diffuse networks where many people have only a small number of connections. The maximum possible density is 100 percent, where everyone is connected to everyone else, while the minimum would be 0 percent, where no one is connected to anyone . . . though 0 density networks are not seen in corporate settings."[46]

"Here's my translation," offered Steve. "The Real Estate Division management team here at Shu Financial is a dense network in that nearly everyone works with other team members and Charissa holds weekly division-wide meetings. The Fraud Department was a loose network, where there was far less interaction across the management team, and with only monthly meetings, many rarely spoke with each other."

Brett continued. "Another useful network metric is the average path length.[47] This is the average number of edges along the shortest paths to connect all possible pairs of network nodes. Networks with short path lengths are easier to manage, since you can go from one broker to another with fewer steps than with a long path length. A similar concept is the width of a network. This represents the longest path from one node to another; networks with small widths are easier to navigate than networks with large widths, where it takes a lot of steps to get from one node to another."

Steve understood that identifying the key influencers was the top priority for the analytics. "My concern is that we need to make sure we show value from this analysis. The most direct application is to identify key influencers in our brokerage network and then see whether using those measures of individual node importance is predictive of rent pricing. Can we discuss possible influence metrics?"

"A very simple metric is to count the number of inbound and outbound connections or, in the case of our undirected brokers' network, to just count the number of connections for each broker. This gives an indication of connectivity," responded Brett.[48]

"Perfect. Let's do that and see if it works," instructed Steve.

"The problem with this metric is that it doesn't distinguish the quality of the connection," cautioned Brett. "Imagine a person has a huge set of Facebook friends, but those friends are not connected to many other people. When that person posts an image and their friends like it, the image may not go viral because these friends are not well connected. Contrast that to someone connected to the same number of friends but these friends are very well connected. A popular image has a much better chance of going viral due to the added network strength of the poster's friends' friends. Eigenvector centrality, also known as the eigencentrality or prestige score, is a commonly used metric that distinguishes the quality of the connections.[49] This measures the influence of a node in a network by examining not just the number of connections but also the number of connections those connections have. In particular, a broker who is connected to ten other brokers who are not connected to anyone else has a much lower eigencentrality than a broker who is connected to ten other brokers who are each connected to five more. It's sort of a simple version of Google's PageRank. Of course, there are other network centrality measures that you could learn about if you were really interested."

"Is this necessary?" asked Steve. "Seems like a lot more work."

Brett responded, "There is almost no incremental time or effort. It is a pretty easy computation given that we already have the data set prepped to analyze the connectivity. It is important to keep in mind that there are packages that do this type of work very quickly that have been validated and used by many people already . . . so you don't need to build this yourself. With that in mind, another measure of node importance is the closeness centrality. This measures how close a node is to all other nodes, where high closeness scores have the shortest distances to all other nodes. This is a metric that helps detect nodes that can spread information quickly through the network, while nodes with low closeness scores would have a more difficult time spreading information. Again, minimal effort is needed to compute this once you have the data set prepped."

The next day Steve reviewed his notes with Jerry and Brett. Brett was keen to explore all possible network-related analytics, as he had just finished an online Python course dedicated to the topic and wanted to put some theory into practice. Jerry was much more interested in getting a quick assessment of whether the effort will yield value or whether they should stick with the information they already have to build the rental price model. He turned to Steve and said, "You've been doing some research on network analysis. What are the basics we should examine this week to decide if it is worth digging further?"

Steve cleared his throat. He was expecting Brett to answer this question. After a few seconds, he blurted out, "So far we have learned that the network is a binary, undirected network. There are no measures of the strength of the connections—only that two brokers are connected. The simplicity of this structure should help us do our analysis quickly. Since we can access the edgelist from the API, the first thing I would like to compute is the network density. From that, we will have a sense for whether this is a diffuse or a dense network."

He looked around the room and saw nodding heads, so he continued. "From there, my priority is on identifying a measure of the broker's influence. My logic is that brokers who are more influential amongst their peers are probably able to also bring more people to view properties. Properties with more showings are more likely to obtain higher rents than those that are viewed by few people. I think we can easily capture the basic measures of broker influence and test each one in the rental price model to see if any of them add value. Specifically, I suggest we compute the number of connections, the eigencentrality, and the closeness centrality for each broker and then determine if any of these three measures of influence has incremental impact after using all of the other data sources."

Jerry inquired, "Why are we looking at the network analysis inputs as the last possible source rather than the first?"

Steve responded immediately. "A few considerations, but mostly time and money. We already have all of the other data elements in place. Most of these data sources are free or have already been purchased at discount prices, since they are used in other parts of the company. Access to this broker database's API is not cheap, and the Real Estate Division will be incurring the full expense, since no other department uses it. Since we would need to constantly update the brokerage influence data, there would be a substantial recurrent expense. I need to understand the costs of acquiring the data as well as the costs associated with updating it and cleaning it so it is usable. Of course, we are assuming that the data is of a high enough quality that it is usable . . . an assumption that is not always correct. Just because someone provides data doesn't mean it is high-quality data. We really don't want to find ourselves in a situation where we paid a lot of money for a database and then discover that the data is so dirty, with missing data or incorrectly entered information, that it is of little or no value."

PULLING IT TOGETHER

Brett headed off to do the analysis. When they regrouped in a week, the results were unambiguous. They did not find incremental value from using the brokerage network data in the model. In particular, while Steve was correct that the network contained some brokers who were very connected and some who were fairly isolated, the measures of brokerage connection did not add value to the rental price model. During their meeting with Charissa, they reviewed the model's performance and its different data sources.

Charissa was pleased with the results. The in-house model had a reported accuracy that was slightly better than that of the commercial vendor's model and at a fraction of the price. The addition of the GIS, computer vision, and NLP information clearly made a difference in the model performance, as they could measure the improvement in accuracy as each set of variables was introduced. As for the network analysis, Charissa summed it up perfectly. "It didn't add value in this case, but it can certainly help in other situations. We didn't know going into the network analysis if the broker information was going to be useful, so we tested . . . after all, data science is a science. Key for me is that you figured out how to test this idea and come up with a conclusion without risking a lot of time or money. By the way, we just decided to license an automated machine learning tool. Steve, this means you can do some of the modeling yourself without becoming a Python guru like Brett."

Steve responded, "Happy to learn more . . . I am already doing a little programming myself. Just basic querying for now."

Charissa smiled, looked at everyone, and then announced, "Great job team—promotions for everyone!"

Steve jumped up. "That's amazing. I can't believe I am getting promoted so quickly." His huge smile slowly left his face as he noticed everyone looking at him puzzled.

Jerry shook his head. "Steve, that's how Charissa likes to announce that the meeting is over. But, seriously, you did a good job in learning the basics, asking good questions, and driving to an answer."

KEY QUESTIONS

NLP:

- What specific steps did you take in the data cleaning and preprocessing?
- Did you remove stop words? If so, can we quickly review the stop words that were removed to make sure none are relevant to the business?
- Is sentiment analysis appropriate for this problem?

- With what frequency will the text undergo sentiment analysis?
- Did you use Generative AI? If so, were you using an open source app or an API to do your prompt engineering?
- If you used a large language model, what security measures did you take to ensure that the data fed into the model will be safeguarded?

Geospatial Analysis:

- What data sources do we have that include geospatial information that we can use?
- How frequently are the different geospatial data points updated, and what update frequency is needed for the project?
- Can we use some form of spatial smoothing to obtain estimates of the average rental value in the area?
- What radius should we use for spatial smoothing?
- How did we weigh the closest properties versus the farthest properties?
- Did we test the weighting algorithm?
- Did we examine whether the distance to points of interest was a significant feature?
- Which points of interest were examined?

New Data Sources:

- What information can be obtained from this new data source and technique that cannot be obtained in another way?
- What other data sources can be used?
- How much will it cost to access this data both initially and as an ongoing expenses?

Computer Vision:

- Are there simpler or better ways to obtain this information than using computer vision?
- How complete is the coverage of the images (what percentage of the items have image data)?
- What specific information can and cannot be obtained from these images?

Network Analysis:

- Regarding the network itself, is it a binary network or a valued network?
- What metrics were used to describe the network itself? Is this considered a dense or a distributed network?
- What information about the network is actionable as compared to information about the network that simply informs us about its structure and characteristics?
- What metrics were used to identify who the key connectors are? Why were those metrics chosen?

9

ETHICS

Kamala walked into her office on Monday morning and took out her laptop. She opened up her email and found a calendar invitation from the executive team titled "Urgent: Data Ethics." She knew exactly what this was about. Over the weekend, it was reported that one of their biggest competitors had implemented a discriminatory actuarial model that led to higher premium increases for Black patients living in low-income areas. Incidentally, this was discovered when a hacker broke into the company's data systems and accessed the details of its algorithm. The competitor was facing severe backlash from the public, not to mention potential legal consequences.

As data becomes more and more ingrained in the business models of corporations, serious consideration needs to be given to data ethics. In this chapter, we will talk about considerations for ensuring that data is collected, stored, and used with integrity so as to minimize harm. The ubiquity of data means that more and more people can use data to make decisions and generate insights, even though accurately interpreting data is a science and a skill that requires training and practice. Those who are not properly trained can make decisions based on false evidence or draw misleading conclusions that skew the decisions of others.

"You all know why we're here," the CEO started. "We need a plan to ensure that what happened to our competitor does not happen here. I will not condone any use of data that exacerbates or creates undue harm to our patients. Kamala and David, I'd like you to work together to develop a comprehensive data ethics strategy. David, your team is closest to the data. If there's anything wrong with the way we handle our data, your team ought to know about it. Kamala, your team uses data to make decisions, sometimes decisions that affect thousands of patients. We need a strategy that governs everything from how we store data to how we analyze it to how we use it make decisions. If we don't figure this out now, we are doing ourselves and our patients a disservice. I'd like to see something within the next couple of days."

Walking out of the meeting, Kamala found herself yet again in a scenario where she needed to get up to speed on technical topics in a short amount of time. "David, I know how my team uses data to make decisions, and I know the impact that our decisions have on our patients. But I don't know the first thing about data ethics as it relates to data storage and use."

"This will certainly be a collaborative process," said David, nodding. "We need to work together to make sure that the systems we set up within the data science team are effective and appropriate for the way that your team uses our data. Let's get together this afternoon and start brainstorming our strategy."

DATA SCIENCE CODE OF ETHICS

As Kamala and David walked out of the meeting, Kamala was reminded of her early medical career. "I remember during the first week of medical school we had our white coat ceremony, where we marked the start of our medical education by receiving the quintessential white coat and reciting an oath that affirmed our commitment to the values of medicine. Our oath drew from the Hippocratic oath—you may have heard the phrase "do no harm"—and included a broader set of values that we should aspire to as doctors, like delivering patient-centered care, combating inequities, and making ethically sound decisions. So, I was wondering, is there a similar pledge of values or ethics for data scientists?"

David replied, "Over the last few years, we've seen enough examples of data being misused that people have proposed a set of ethical principles for all data scientists to follow. Many groups have created their own codes or checklists of ethics. Actually, the National Academies of Sciences, Engineering, and Medicine released a data science oath, adapted from the Hippocratic oath. Reading that data science oath, it's clear that there are some direct parallels to medicine:

- I will not be ashamed to say, "I know not," nor will I fail to call in my colleagues when the skills of another are needed for solving a problem.
- I will respect the privacy of my data subjects, for their data are not disclosed to me that the world may know, so I will tread with care in matters of privacy and security. . . .
- I will remember that my data are not just numbers without meaning or context, but represent real people and situations, and that my work may lead to unintended societal consequences, such as inequality, poverty, and disparities due to algorithmic bias.[1]

"Other groups have developed their own codes of ethics. Datapractices.org has released a set of twelve data principles, ranging from reproducibility to security to fairness, that has received over two thousand signatures from data scientists.[2] DJ Patil, former chief data scientist in the U.S. Office of Science and Technology Policy, and colleagues Hilary Mason and Mike Loukides released a thirteen-point data ethics checklist with items like these:

- Have we studied and understood possible sources of bias in our data?
- What kind of user consent do we need to collect to use the data?
- Have we tested for fairness with respect to different user groups?
- Do we have a plan to protect and secure user data?
- Do we have a mechanism for redress if people are harmed by the results?[3]

"Across all these oaths and checklists, I think there are four key concepts to understand: (1) fairness, (2) privacy and security, (3) transparency and reproducibility, and (4) the social impact of data."

FAIRNESS

Bias and Fairness in Machine Learning

"Now that we're starting to use machine learning to make decisions, we need to make sure that our models are designed appropriately so as not to introduce bias into the decision-making process," David suggested.

"David, my naive perspective was that using data to make decisions eliminates human bias. How can a machine learning model be biased if it's just finding patterns in the data?" Kamala asked.

David smiled. "It's easy to think that all data is objective, but if the underlying data or decisions made when collecting data were biased, then the machine learning model is going to reflect the same biases. You hit the nail on the head: a machine learning model does nothing more than recognize patterns in the data. All machine learning models are built by learning patterns within the training data and using those learned representations to make predictions about new data points. Issues can arise when the training data is biased."

Kamala scratched her head. "This is starting to ring a bell. Wasn't there an issue with training data bias in the early days of Google Images?"

"Yes," answered David, "that's a very famous example of what can go wrong if your training data is not representative. The Google Photos algorithm faced immense backlash when photos of people with dark skin were tagged as being photos of gorillas.[4] This is an egregious example of what can go wrong when the underlying data is biased. It's possible that the training data set that Google used did not include enough images of people with dark skin, so when the algorithm saw these images, it had no previously learned patterns to apply."

"This seems like a very avoidable problem," Kamala said. "How did something like this get past incredibly smart engineers at Google?"

David sat back in his chair. "Ultimately, machine learning models are designed by humans, so it's not a surprise that humans' biases could be baked into the machine learning models that they design. We don't know exactly what went wrong in this situation, but there are a number of possibilities. If you were a machine learning engineer at Google tasked with building this algorithm, where would you get your training data? A reasonable way to get it would be by scraping together images that are available online. The issue with this approach is that photos available online may not be representative of the people in the world. Google Images probably has a lot more photos of people from the United States and western Europe than it does from other parts of the world. In other words, the biases and underrepresentation that are present in the media end up getting baked into the machine learning model. The machine learning engineer would have had to recognize that the training data was not representative of all races and adjust accordingly. When you add on the fact that people of color are underrepresented in the tech industry, we can start to understand how these types of issues can arise.

"It reminds me of a similar incident a few years ago when Nikon came out with a camera with facial detection features. Users found that if they took a photo of an Asian person, the camera would often display a message asking "Did someone blink?" even if their eyes were wide open.[5] You'd think Nikon—a Japanese company—would have been able to catch this, but we know from experience that these issues can easily arise unless you're actively aware of them."

Kamala nodded. "When I was in medical school, all of our textbooks showed images of light-skinned patients. When we got to dermatology rotations, it was tough for us to understand how skin conditions presented in people with dark skin because all the images in the dermatology textbooks were of people with light skin. It's almost similar to the machine learning situation, where the biases of the people who wrote the medical textbooks get baked into the education system, and you end up with doctors treating people with dark skin without enough knowledge of how certain conditions present in these patients."

"It's funny you bring up that example, Kamala. In fact, there have been a number of papers published recently about whether algorithms can diagnose conditions like skin cancer better than dermatologists. The issue is that a lot of these algorithms were trained on images of patients with light skin, and they end up performing much worse on people with dark skin."[6]

Kamala's eyes widened. "That sounds dangerous—not only because some patients are less likely to have their skin cancer diagnosed but also because that sort of algorithm may exacerbate the inequities across racial lines that we see in health care. Are there any quality checks that we can do to quantitatively prove whether our model is performing equitably?"

"You're right about the danger," David agreed. "This concern has led to the emergence of a new field in artificial intelligence that's focused on establishing fairness and minimizing bias in machine learning. Researchers have developed a number of ways to recognize and address inequities and biases in machine learning models.

"One way to quantify the fairness of a machine learning model is to measure the performance of the model across groups of interest. Often in fairness analysis, we are interested in the performance of a model across certain demographic groups, some of which may be disadvantaged or of special interest: Black people, women, people of lower socioeconomic status, etc. One metric is called group fairness.[7] It measures whether subjects in each group have an equal probability of being assigned to a certain outcome class. For example, if we used a machine learning algorithm to help decide which candidates we should hire, we would want to make sure that our model does not perpetuate biases that may disadvantage women or people of color. We could use group fairness to see whether our model suggests hiring a similar percentage of women versus men or people of color versus white people. If we saw that the model thinks that 20 percent of all male applicants should be hired but that only 4 percent of all female applicants should be hired, that may warrant investigation as to whether the model has a gender bias.

"Another measure of model fairness is whether the accuracy of the model is comparable across groups of interest. If we built a model to recommend who should receive a certain treatment, we would want to make sure that the accuracy of the model is comparable between white people and people of color. We can define accuracy as the positive predictive value or the negative predictive value. We want to know "If we use this model, will it improve outcomes for patients of color just as much as it will for white patients?" This is an important question because we know patients of color generally have poorer health outcomes and more barriers to accessing health care compared to their white counterparts.[8] We want to make sure that implementing this algorithm will not exacerbate existing inequities in the health care system. Using the results from the test set, we can see whether the model had differential accuracy across racial groups. If we find out the model is performing more accurately for white patients, we may want to reconsider whether it's ready for deployment."

Kamala was furiously jotting down notes. "These sound like incredibly important steps to take before model deployment. What happens if we find there is bias in a model's performance? How can you fix that?"

David took his post at the whiteboard. "There are several ways we might address model bias. One way is to identify potentially biased sources of data, remove those data elements, and retrain the model.[9] For instance, in our model for spine surgery prior authorization, our outcome is defined as health expenditure following a spine surgery. We know that health care expenditure is a potentially biased data element: patients of color tend to have lower levels of health care expenditure due to a variety of factors, including mistrust of the health care system, unequal treatment performed or administered by physicians, and lack of insurance coverage. We were aware of this limitation when we built the model, and we did the appropriate analyses and follow-ups to make sure that we did not deploy a harmful model.

"Suppose we performed a fairness analysis and found that our model behaved differently for white patients compared to patients of color. Maybe the model recommended spine surgery for Black patients less frequently than it did for white patients just because in the training data set, Black patients had lower levels of health expenditure compared to white patients. In this case, we might strongly consider using a different outcome that is less biased or modifying the way the model makes predictions for different racial groups.[10]

"There are other ways of addressing model bias such as adversarial debiasing, fair representation learning, and fairness-constrained optimization.[11] All these methods involve baking considerations of fairness into the model development and training process."

Building Models with Sensitive Variables

"David, let's say we want to build a prediction model that performs equally well for patients of color and white patients. Why not just take out the race variable from the prediction model? Won't that help the model be agnostic to the patient's race?"

"Kamala, you've touched on a hot debate within the machine learning community: Should race be included in prediction models? The concern is that by including race in a model, the model will recapitulate the same racial biases and inequities that we see in the real world. On the other hand, if race is truly a strong predictor of the outcome, how can you justify not including it?[12]

"These are tough questions, but there are some best practices for dealing with race and other sensitive variables in predictive modeling. First, you should always check the performance of your model across racial groups.[13] Here using the fairness metrics that we talked about may be a good starting point. Whether or not you include race in the model, it is an important step to check how your model is performing across groups.[14]

"Second, you want to think about whether race is a proxy variable or whether there is a legitimate reason to believe that race is predictive of the outcome.[15] If we were using race in a model to determine whether or not a candidate should be hired, we should ask ourselves whether we truly believe that people of certain races should be hired at different frequencies. In this case, including race in the model may recapitulate biases that we see in the real world, such as people of certain racial groups not having access to opportunities that may make hiring them for a job more desirable. Third, we should consider where our data on race is coming from and whether the race variable that we're using is high-quality."

Kamala jumped in. "We see low-quality racial data a lot in the health care field. "Different races will be grouped into the same bucket. Asians may include Indian Asians, Chinese Asians, Korean Asians, Vietnamese Asians, and Cambodian Asians. Even though all these groups are technically Asian, they have very different health care needs. Indian Asians have a higher risk of cardiovascular disease than Chinese Asians, and Cambodian and Vietnamese Asians on average face greater socioeconomic barriers than Chinese and Indian Asians. You always see health data reported for all Asians, but that's not useful information because Asians are such a diverse group of people."[16]

David nodded. "Exactly, that's an example of where your race data is not of high enough quality to provide a valuable signal. These are exactly the types of pitfalls we want to be aware of when considering what sensitive variables to include in operation models."

Particular industries may have legal restrictions on modeling. Credit scoring[17] and actuarial modeling[18] are situations where the use of sensitive variables like gender and race may be prohibited in the model development process. In these applications, models may be evaluated for proxies by seeing if the variables in the model can predict variables like gender or race. If the variables in the model cannot accurately predict the sensitive variable, it suggests that the model does not contain any proxies for the sensitive variable that could lead to disparate performance across groups.

"So how can we prevent this at our company, David? What systems can we put in place to ensure that our machine learning models are trained on an unbiased data set?"

"You said it right, Kamala. We need a system. In other words, ensuring that the data is representative cannot be solely the responsibility of the data scientist who's building the model. We need a comprehensive approach. Of course, the model builder has some responsibility, but we need to put in place a system such that we bring together a diverse group of stakeholders who ask critical questions about the way the model is built. We need people from your team to keep us honest and help us think through the way the model will be used and the implications for training.

Data Drift

"It's essential to ask whether the training data is representative of the population that the model will be used on," David advised.[19] For example, if we're building a model that we are going to use for every patient across the country, then we shouldn't train the model just on patients from Florida. It seems obvious, but sometimes the most convenient training data set is not always the best."

"That makes sense," Kamala said. "We talked about the same idea of representativeness when it comes to evaluating decision-making based on data analysis. As we saw with the ClaroMax study, they tested the drug on patients being treated at five community cancer clinics in Texas, whereas we treat cancer patients from all over the country. Ultimately, we decided that the findings from the study may not be generalizable to our entire patient population.

"What happens if the population we're applying the model to changes over time? We see periodic shifts in the demographics of our patients over the years. Let's say we build a model today and it works well for the next year or two. Then we notice a demographic shift in the patient population: maybe we are attracting a younger pool of patients or a sicker pool of patients. Is it still safe to use the same model?"

"You're ahead of the game, Kamala. You just described the idea of data drift. Data drift refers to changes in the underlying distribution of data over time.[20] It can have serious ethical implications because changes in data can negatively affect the performance of a model. If a model to recommend specific treatments to patients performs worse over time due to data drift, there's an ethical imperative to recognize the dip in model performance and address it so that patients are not harmed.

"There are different types of data drift. There's concept drift, which refers to a change in the outcome variable over time or a change in the relationship between the outcome and the predictors over time.[21] Imagine you built a model to predict the incidence of an infectious disease. When there's an outbreak, the incidence of that disease may increase compared to nonoutbreak times. If the model was trained on data from a nonoutbreak period, it may not perform as well during an outbreak because of concept drift: the outcome (instance of the disease) is happening more frequently than expected according to the training data. You can also imagine that the factors that predict the probability of an infection during an outbreak may be different than the factors that predict an infection during a nonoutbreak period. These differences all contribute to concept drift.

"There's also feature drift, where the distribution of the predictor variables or features changes over time.[22] This is exactly what you were describing with the demographic shift. Suppose that age is a predictor variable in your model and the model was trained on a population where everyone was between the ages of 20 and 50. If the same model is used as the population ages, the model may not perform well when the population ages range from 40 to 70."

"This all seems straightforward. The model learns patterns based on the training data. If the state of the world does not match the patterns in the training data, the model isn't going to perform well," Kamala reasoned.

"Couldn't have said it better myself!"

"So how do you deal with data draft?" Kamala asked.

"The first step in dealing with data drift is to realize that it's happening. When a model is deployed, there should be a system for monitoring data drift.[23] There are many ways to monitor data drift, and most of them boil down to comparing the new input data with the original training data. We don't need to get into the specifics, but the point is that this type of monitoring should be conducted on a recurring basis. It may be useful to set up a recurring report that quantifies the extent of data drift. In addition to monitoring data drift, it's important to monitor the performance of your model over time. This can be trickier because it requires knowing the truth, but it's also important to do in order to catch things like calibration drift, which is when the calibration of your model changes over time."

Kamala was doing her best to synthesize David's explanation. "So we set up a recurring system to monitor data drift and model performance over time. Let's say we noticed that there is some data drift going on or that the performance of the model is decreasing over time. What do we do?"

"The devil is in the details, but one simple approach is to retrain the model. If you retrain the model on more recent data, you may find that it performs better. Depending on the amount of data drift, you can even consider periodic model retraining, where the model is evaluated every so often and retrained as needed."

PRIVACY AND SECURITY

"David, we've been spending a lot of time talking about using the data properly to do analysis and build models, but what about handling the data itself? At the end of the day, we're dealing with sensitive health information. How can we avoid lapses in data security that our peer companies are struggling with? Our competitor clearly didn't have strong enough data security systems to keep out hackers. With the sensitive patient information stored on our servers, a hack could expose personal data for millions of patients. Legal issues notwithstanding, our patients trust us to safeguard their data, and we have an ethical obligation to do all that we can to protect their health information."

"The data science team takes many measures to keep our data systems secure," David pointed out. "The first thing to recognize is that we're dealing with protected health information, which is subject to a number of legal regulations that normal data is not. Protected health information is covered under the Health Information Portability and Accountability Act, or HIPAA for short.[24] We work closely with our security team to ensure that our data infrastructure is secure and HIPAA compliant. Not only that—it is our ethical obligation to our patients to maintain their sensitive data as securely as possible.

"All of our computers and laptops are encrypted, our emails have an option to send encrypted messages when we're attaching data files, and our data is stored in highly secure servers with restricted access. Whenever we need to use the data for analysis, we make sure that people use a virtual private network and that they have access only to the minimum information needed for their role. This means that if you need to know only how many patients received a certain type of procedure, we won't give you access to patients' names, dates of birth, addresses, etc. We call this operating on a need-to-know basis. Sometimes this involves deidentifying the data or removing all possible data elements that can be used to link a data point back to an individual."

Depending on the industry, data may be subject to different laws and regulations. It's important to understand these constraints and develop the appropriate data infrastructure from day one. All industries need to protect the data of their customers or clients. Data breaches in any industry can decrease trust, lead to lawsuits, and hurt the bottom line. Engaging a data security expert or building a data security team can be an important step in ensuring the security of your data.

Data collection is another important consideration. In the health care context, where data can be extremely sensitive and confidential, it is critical to obtain consent for data collection and use. In the research context, informed consent is a prerequisite, both ethically and legally. For research that will eventually be published, informed consent procedures often need to be reviewed and approved by a board of ethics or an institutional review board.

TRANSPARENCY AND REPRODUCIBILITY

Why Reproducibility?

Reproducibility means that two scientists studying the same question should be able to design independent experiments and generate results that are concordant.[25] If researchers in the United States found that consuming large amounts of broccoli led to *lower* risk of heart attack, while researchers in India found that consuming large amounts of broccoli led to *higher* risk of heart attack, the findings are not reproducible. Related concepts are repeatability and replicability. Repeatability means that a specific scientist repeating an experiment should get nearly identical results every time. Replicability means that independent scientists following the same experimental methodology should arrive at the same result.[26]

Lack of reproducibility can mean a number of things. At best, it can indicate genuine scientific uncertainty. Perhaps there is active debate among experts as to what methodology is most appropriate to answer the question. Over time, debate and reexperimentation can spawn better scientific approaches and reduce uncertainty. Some of the most fundamental truths that we take for granted today—like the force of gravity, the shape of the earth, and the orientation of the solar system—began as findings that were irreproducible, sparking debate that led to further research and eventually to reproducible results in which we have high confidence. Reproducibility is not just a scientific concern; it also has ethical implications.[27] Ultimately, trustworthy science is defined by results that are reproducible by different scientists. Reproducibility of data science promotes credibility, encourages trust in data-driven analysis, and engenders trust with those who consume the results.

Lack of reproducibility can also indicate some source of error in the scientific process. For example, it could indicate human error—maybe a researcher mistakenly replaced a "9" with a "0" when writing some code—or measurement error—maybe a weighing scale that a scientist was using was faulty, leading to systematic undermeasurements.

At worst, lack of reproducibility can indicate misconduct or bad science. Maybe a researcher modified or fabricated data. Maybe a corporate sponsor of academic research exerted undue influence on which results were published and which were not. One notorious example of this is a debunked and retracted study linking the measles, mumps, and rubella (MMR) vaccine to autism, where the researcher was eventually found to have fabricated data.[28] To date, no other studies have reproduced a link between the MMR vaccine and autism.

Improving Reproducibility and Transparency in Data Science

"I have a naive question for you, David. In medicine, reproducibility can be difficult because scientific experiments are complex and have a lot of moving pieces. In animal research, each animal is different. In biology research, each lab may use slightly different types of equipment. When we describe how we performed an experiment, it can be difficult to describe every detail such that it can be reproduced. In data science, though, shouldn't reproducibility be a piece of cake? At the end of the day, you have data, and you have some code that works with that data. Both the data and the code can be saved as static computer files. Isn't it as simple as sharing your data and your code for others to repeat?"

David chuckled. "You're not wrong, Kamala. If people shared their data and their code, a lot of issues would be solved. First off, we would be able to check each other's code. Just like we make typos when writing essays, everyone makes mistakes when writing code. We'd also be able to cross-check the code with the methodology they described. For example, if someone reported replacing missing data values with the median, but their code uses the mean, that could be an important discrepancy to note."

"So why don't people share their code and data?" Kamala asked.

"More and more, the sharing of code and data is becoming standard practice," said David. "Tools like Github make it easy for people to collaboratively write code, review others' code, and share code with the world. There are also efforts to improve data sharing. For example, the Harvard Dataverse is a repository where researchers can store and share their data so that other researchers can reproduce their analyses.[29] There are some cases where sharing code or data may not be possible—for example, due to intellectual property or privacy reasons. In these cases, we can rely only on how analysts describe their data and methods."

Kamala shook her head. "If there's anything I learned from my short stint in research, it's that trying to replicate an experiment from a written description of the methods can be a nightmare. People leave out key steps, they omit details about key decisions they made, and the end result is something totally different than what was originally reported."

"Sounds like me whenever I try to follow a new baking recipe!" David joked. "You're absolutely right. Data science is both a science and an art. There are so many decisions that need to be made and so many possible approaches. It takes a lot of effort to write a truly comprehensive description of the analysis methods, but it's what we need to strive for to do good science."

"I imagine adequately documenting the analysis approach saves time as well," Kamala reasoned. "If someone on your team wants to leverage an analysis you did 6 months ago, you want it to be as easy as possible for them to recreate your approach. It would be a waste of company resources to have them struggling to figure out what was done in the absence of clear documentation."

SOCIAL IMPACT

Potential for Harm

"My son showed me a video the other day of Obama saying things that you would never imagine a president saying. Turns out it was a 'deep fake'—a computer-generated video that looks extremely realistic."

"That's really concerning, David. I've heard of deep fakes and always wondered what could happen if the wrong person got their hands on that technology."

"Unfortunately, Kamala, that's a big concern for artificial intelligence, or AI, developers these days. We have to be aware of the possibility that the technology we develop could be used to harm others.[30] Recently, leading AI researchers developed a suite of tools that can generate not only fake videos but also fake images and fake text. While normally researchers release their code to the public, this group chose not to release its work, recognizing that the technology was powerful enough to do serious harm in the wrong hands."

"I know we're not developing fake images at Stardust Health, but this is something I want us to consider in our data ethics strategy. The way we use our data could ultimately impact millions of patients." Kamala was intent on exploring this point further.

"Definitely," David agreed. "Just because we're not developing cutting-edge AI doesn't mean that our data and technology can't harm people. Take our spine surgery model, for example. We're using that model to determine who we think should receive spine surgery. What if, after deploying the model, we noticed a spike in the number of spine surgery complications among our patients? The reality is that our model is being used to shape real-world decisions that have an impact on real people. We need to consider how to respond if we notice people are being harmed by our model."

"I liked what we did when we developed that model," Kamala started. "We got a group of stakeholders together and brainstormed all the possible ways it could go wrong. We set up systems to monitor adverse events, and we're reviewing that data regularly to ensure our model is not causing any negative consequences. We should bake this sort of deliberation into our model development workflows so that we are proactive about monitoring potential harms."

Ethics in Data Analysis and Interpretation

"I often see decision makers going into an analysis with a preconceived conclusion," Kamala noted. "In other words, they'll ask the data science team to do an analysis, but it's as if they already know what the outcome of the analysis is going to be. At the last company where I worked, I remember one of the managers asking for data showing that increasing prices would improve patient outcomes in the long run. It seemed like a backward approach to data analysis to me. How can you ask for data that shows your conclusion? How can you have formed a conclusion without seeing the data first?"

"You're absolutely right, Kamala. If you ever hear someone ask for data that shows X without having looked at the data first, you have to be on the lookout for cherry-picking data analyses. The scary reality is that data can be very easily manipulated. If I gave you a data set on people's diets and their health outcomes and asked you to find me data that shows that eating broccoli increases your risk of heart disease, I guarantee you there are ways you could slice and dice the data to arrive at that conclusion. We've all seen this in the media with unethical journalism and fake news. There are ways to skew the facts to support your narrative, and data analysis is no different.

"Not only can you slice and dice data to support almost any conclusion, but also if you gave the same data set with the same question to ten different analysts, you may end up getting many different results. There is no single best approach to answer a given question. As data scientists and data consumers, we need to be aware of the fact that data can be easily manipulated. One way to prevent this is to prespecify your research question and your analysis plan.[31] This avoids the scenario where a data scientist does an analysis, gets results that don't support the original hypothesis, and then goes back and changes the analysis approach until the results align with the original hypothesis."

Kamala jumped in. "This is exactly what happened at my last company. The data science team found that raising coinsurance would actually lead to worse health outcomes because fewer people would access health care. Patients sought less health care because they knew that each time they received services, they would have to pay a greater share of the cost. When the manager saw this data, he told the team to look only at people in a higher socioeconomic bracket, where this behavior wasn't seen. In other words, he had them change the analysis approach to arrive at his desired result."

David shook his head in disapproval. "This is where both the data science team and the data consumer can work together to ensure that analysis is conducted with integrity. First, when we do an analysis, we should make sure that we don't have any preconceived conclusions or, at the very least, that our preconceived conclusions don't influence the objectivity of the analysis plan. Second, we should make sure that we document our analysis plan before doing it and ensure that any changes to the analysis plan are communicated and reviewed. Third, we should be OK with the fact that sometimes the data doesn't support our initial hypothesis."

CONCLUSION

From the way data is collected and stored to the way it's analyzed, interpreted, and used in machine learning models, there are many opportunities for bias, misinterpretation, and breaches in security and ethics. While having a team devoted to data security can address potential dangers, a system for ethical data analysis and interpretation should be adopted by all stakeholders within an organization. Building a culture of ethical data stewardship, where analysis plans are prespecified and documented, potential biases are called out and explored, and data is not manipulated to suit a certain narrative, is a responsibility that all team members should accept.

KEY QUESTIONS

Data Ethics:

- Could this project be used in malicious ways?
- Could this project result in unintended consequences?
- Was this data collected with consent from relevant parties?
- Do we have a system in place to monitor potential adverse effects of this project?
- Are we adequately and transparently documenting the analysis approach and results interpretation?
- Are we saving the code and data to ensure future reproducibility?
- Have we prespecified our analysis approach to avoid cherry-picking?
- Are there special measures we need to take to secure our data?
- Does this model perform fairly in marginalized groups?

- How will we monitor changes in the data and model performance over time?
- What variables should we avoid including in the model?
- What variables may bias the output of our model?
  - Which laws and regulations might be applicable to our project?
  - How might individuals' privacy and anonymity be impinged by our storage and use of the data?

CONCLUSION

W inston Churchill famously said, "Now this is not the end. It is not even the beginning of the end. But it is, perhaps, the end of the beginning."

And so this chapter is the end of the beginning of our journey together in becoming great data science customers. Our exploration spanned several important areas of data science while focusing on what is critical to the data science customer rather than what a data engineer or a machine learning specialist might need to understand. The strength in our approach of exposing readers to a large number of topics is that it enables them to explore more deeply the ones they are most interested in as they choose their future learning paths while developing new career interests.

We began our exploration by reviewing the tools of the trade. This included an overview of the typical data workflow, such as extract, transform, and load, as well as an introduction to the different methods of data storage. The breadth of data sources has expanded significantly over time along with the velocity and variety of data that can be readily analyzed. While there is a large number of coding languages used by data scientists, we emphasized the use of common languages, such as SQL, Python, and R. Finally, we examined the different data products that can be produced, which range from raw data to structured data sets that can be readily analyzed to an advanced product such as automated decision-making.

Working on the data science project, we emphasized that a data science project is just that—a project. The best practices of project management, such as establishing milestones, timelines, and roles and responsibilities and identifying risks, are critical to ensuring project success. A challenge that we acknowledge in data science is that people's titles are often misleading, so someone's official title may be quite different from the tasks they perform or their actual skill sets. We identified a mechanism for prioritizing projects as well as providing guidance on how to measure success.

We then introduced some basic statistics, the kind often used in exploratory data analysis. This is critical, since exploratory data analysis is a common first step before developing predictive models. We brought in the concepts of effect sizes and p-values, leading up to a basic understanding of linear regression, one of the oldest and still most useful methods of analyzing data.

Unsupervised machine learning is a set of commonly used techniques that is often overlooked by data science customers. It focuses on how observations can be grouped or clustered together using the data rather than relying on preset rules or expert opinion. Besides generating useful insight, it can often be a data processing step before developing a final predictive model.

Supervised machine learning is a topic that gets a lot of press and one that is likely to gain attention in most companies and organizations. Predicting sales, charge-offs, risk, product utilization, spam, or any other outcome is useful across all industries. While the techniques can range from simple linear regression models to deep learning neural networks, the basic principles of data science remain the same, and they often use many of the same key steps, including cleaning and preparing the data, identifying the features used as inputs in the prediction, training and testing the model, and taking steps to improve model performance. In applications spanning the range from natural language processing to network analysis to spatial analysis to computer vision, we demonstrated how customers can ask their data science team good questions and derive valuable insights.

A basic question when implementing any program is "Did it make a difference?" This speaks to the concept of measuring impact. The simplest approach to assessing impact is to implement randomized studies where all of the key features are similar in the two groups except that one receives the program and the other doesn't. This classic A/B testing is seen throughout many industries and, when implemented successfully, makes it easy to draw conclusions about the program impact. In situations where randomization cannot be implemented, there are other ways to assess impact (though we need to be careful that we do not confuse biases with the effects of the program).

We finished our tour of data science with a discussion of ethical considerations. For too long, ethical considerations were not sufficiently emphasized to data scientists or their customers. Now there is a better understanding of the importance of analyzing the moral problems related to data, algorithms, and their implementation in order to ensure that solutions are not only good solutions scientifically but also good solutions morally—that, simply put, they do the right things and not the wrong things.

This book touched on a large number of topics, many of which you may wish to learn about in more depth depending on your interests and how they relate to your career considerations. With that in mind, let's catch up with Kamala and Steve to understand the next steps in their journey.

KAMALA AND STEVE: CAREER PATHS

Annie called Kamala into her office for her annual review. Kamala was a little nervous as she sat down, but she saw Annie's relaxed smile and felt confident that things were going to go well.

"Kamala, you arrived here with an impressive educational background, both an MD and an MBA. We rarely see someone arriving here with such a broad background, yet you really hit the ground running the moment we hired you. Four years ago you came to Stardust, and you are already a director. How do you feel about your career growth and this past year's work?" Annie asked.

Kamala was ambitious but didn't want to sound too aggressive. "I am proud of the past year's collaborations, especially the work with the data science team. The prior authorization modeling work saved the company millions. Our work on ClaroMax saved lives and helped Stardust's bottom line."

Annie nodded her head. "I agree. You have found the right level of skills in data science so you are able to understand the problems, discuss potential solutions, and then let the data science team do what it does best. You showed how to be both a good customer and a leader. With that in mind, are there specific items you want to work on for your development next year?"

"Now that I have a good grasp of how to leverage data science to generate value for the company, I would love to expand the scope of my team to include not only folks from the clinical and business teams but also folks from the data science teams. I believe forming an interdisciplinary team can help kick-start more innovative data-driven initiatives, and I would be excited to lead that team. As part of those increased responsibilities, it might be good to continue building my skills as a project leader. Perhaps I can get more training in how to be a good project manager as well as how to lead effectively."

"These are great suggestions. There are some good online courses, but you can also look into some executive education courses. And we have a nice corporate program where our vice presidents receive intensive training on leadership, communications, and team building. Would that interest you?"

"Well, yes. But like you said, that is for vice presidents, and I am still a director."

Annie smiled broadly. "Yes. But I am looking at the new vice president of clinical strategy. Congratulations. Keep up the good work. Pretty soon I will be calling you boss."

At the same time as Kamala received the good news about her promotion, Steve was looking for some career advice from his data science mentor and friend, Brett.

"Got to admit that at first I was dreading working with the team, but I really got into the analytics," Steve said.

Brett gave him a thumbs up. "See, we aren't all a boring set of nerds. What did you like best?"

"Toward the end of our last project, I was doing some basic Python coding myself, and it was great being able to build my own simple models. Given the choice, I think I would rather focus more on programming than on managing projects or teams."

"Nothing wrong with becoming a data science guru. There are great opportunities to grow here at Shu Financial, and nearly every week a headhunter is calling me about a position somewhere else," Brett replied.

"What would I need to do to dig more deeply into the data and programming side? Last thing I want to do is get another degree. I am still paying off the debt from my Wharton MBA."

Brett nodded. "That is what makes data science such a great career. You don't need to go back to school. You can learn from tons of great online resources. Dive into Kaggle, and you can learn a ton. Coursera and Edx have plenty of free content, and if you are OK paying a little, there are many excellent online courses."

"Courses are fun, but what I really need to do is get more real-world experience."

"You can do it here. If you really are thinking about making a shift, we can talk with your boss about doing a hybrid role where you get more into the programming while you also keep some of your current responsibilities. Believe me, you wouldn't be the first Shuster to make this transition, and you won't be the last."

Steve hesitated for a second. "This really would take me down a different path than I had planned out of school."

Brett responded immediately, "We both know, if you don't know where you are going . . ."

" . . . then any road will take you there. OK. I know I want to test the data science programming waters more deeply, so let's set up a chat with my boss and we can see what is possible."

YOUR NEXT STEPS

What about you, the reader? You aren't Kamala and you aren't Steve.

You should make a conscious choice about your next step in the world of data science. What do you want to do next? Will you seek Kamala's path, enhancing your management skills as you lead larger teams, manage bigger budgets, and take a bigger role in your organization? Will you seek Steve's path, going more deeply into the technical aspects of data science? Will you create a different path—one that speaks to your interests and desires as it relates to your career and data? Will you be a mentor to others on how to be a good data science customer or how to work effectively with technical teams? Will you be satisfied with your knowledge and skill in data science and move on to another topic to broaden your skill set and increase your capability to add value to your company?

The choice is yours.

NOTES

1. TOOLS OF THE TRADE

1. "Debt Collection," Consumer Financial Protection Bureau, accessed September 21, 2022, https://www.consumerfinance.gov/consumer-tools/debt-collection/.
2. Ernst and Young, *The Impact of Third-Party Debt Collection on the US National and State Economies in 2016*, November 2017, https://www.acainternational.org/assets/ernst-young/ey-2017-aca-state-of-the-industry-report-final-5.pdf.
3. Mokhamad Hendayun, Erwin Yulianto, Jack Febrian Rusdi, Awan Setiawan, and Benie Ilman, "Extract Transform Load Process in Banking Reporting System," *MethodsX* 8 (2021): 101260.
4. "Differences Between Excel and Sheets," Google, accessed September 21, 2022, https://support.google.com/a/users/answer/9331278?hl=en.
5. Brian Hayes, "Cloud Computing," *Communications of the ACM* 51, no. 7 (2008): 9–11.
6. "Global Cloud Services Market Q1 2021," Canalys, https://www.canalys.com/newsroom/global-cloud-market-Q121. Updated 2020. Accessed 9/21/22.
7. Inge Grønbæk, "Architecture for the Internet of Things (IoT): API and Interconnect," in *2008 Second International Conference on Sensor Technologies and Applications* (Piscataway, NJ: IEEE, 2008), 802–807.
8. Hadley Wickham, "Data Analysis," in *ggplot2: Elegant Graphics for Data Analysis*, 2nd ed. (London: Springer, 2016), 189–201.
9. Natalia Miloslavskaya and Alexander Tolstoy, "Big Data, Fast Data and Data Lake Concepts," *Procedia Computer Science* 88 (2016): 300–305.

10. K. R. Chowdhary, "Natural Language Processing," in *Fundamentals of Artificial Intelligence* (New Delhi: Springer, 2020), 603–649.
11. Donald D. Chamberlin and Raymond F. Boyce, "SEQUEL: A Structured English Query Language," in *Proceedings of the 1974 ACM SIGFIDET (now SIGMOD) Workshop on Data Description, Access and Control* (New York: ACM, 1974), 249–264.
12. Guido van Rossum, "An Introduction to Python for UNIX/C Programmers," in *Proceedings of the NLUUG najaarsconferentie* (Dutch UNIX Users Group, 1993), https://citeseerx.ist.psu.edu/doc/10.1.1.38.2023; Ross Ihaka, "R: Past and Future History: A Draft of a Paper for Interface '98" (unpublished manuscript, January 1998), accessed June 12, 2023, https://www.stat.auckland.ac.nz/~ihaka/downloads/Interface98.pdf.
13. P. P. Uhrowczik, "Data Dictionary/Directories," *IBM Systems Journal* 12, no. 4 (1973): 332–350.

2. THE DATA SCIENCE PROJECT

1. J. N. Salapatas, "Best Practices—the Nine Elements to Success" (paper presented at the Project Management Institute Annual Seminars and Symposium, Houston, 2000).
2. D. Kahneman, *Thinking, Fast and Slow* (New York: Farrar, Straus and Giroux, 2011).
3. Project Management Institute, https://www.pmi.org/.
4. A. S. Grove, *High Output Management* (New York: Vintage, 2015).
5. G. T. Doran, "There's a S.M.A.R.T. Way to Write Management's Goals and Objectives," *Management Review* 70, no. 11 (1981): 35–36.
6. J. Meredith and O. Zwikael, "When Is a Project Successful?," *IEEE Engineering Management Review* 47, no. 3 (2019): 127–134.
7. R. S. Kaplan and D. P. Norton, "The Balanced Scorecard: Measures That Drive Performance," *Harvard Business Review* 83, no. 7 (2005): 172.

3. DATA SCIENCE FOUNDATIONS

1. R. Sanders, "The Pareto Principle: Its Use and Abuse," *Journal of Services Marketing* 1, no. 2 (1987): 37–40.
2. H. L. Stuckey, "The First Step in Data Analysis: Transcribing and Managing Qualitative Research Data," *Journal of Social Health and Diabetes* 2, no. 1 (2014): 6.

3. B. Efron, "Missing Data, Imputation, and the Bootstrap," *Journal of the American Statistical Association* 89, no. 426 (1994): 463–475.

4. C. M. Norris, W. A. Ghali, M. L. Knudtson, C. D. Naylor, and L. D. Saunders, "Dealing with Missing Data in Observational Health Care Outcome Analyses," *Journal of Clinical Epidemiology* 53, no. 4 (2000): 377–383.

5. R. R. Wilcox and H. J. Keselman, "Modern Robust Data Analysis Methods: Measures of Central Tendency," *Psychological Methods* 8, no. 3 (2003): 254.

6. E. A. Hanushek and J. E. Jackson, *Statistical Methods for Social Scientists* (New York: Academic Press, 2013).

7. M. J. Fisher and A. P. Marshall, "Understanding Descriptive Statistics," *Australian Critical Care* 22, no. 2 (2009): 93–97.

8. S. Manikandan, "Measures of Central Tendency: Median and Mode," *Journal of Pharmacology and Pharmacotherapeutics* 2, no. 3 (2011): 214.

9. J. M. Shaughnessy and M. Pfannkuch, "How Faithful Is Old Faithful? Statistical Thinking: A Story of Variation and Prediction," *Mathematics Teacher* 95, no. 4 (2002): 252–259.

10. P. Mishra, C. M. Pandey, U. Singh, A. Gupta, C. Sahu, and A. Keshri, "Descriptive Statistics and Normality Tests for Statistical Data," *Annals of Cardiac Anaesthesia* 22, no. 1 (2019): 67.

11. A. Papoulis, *Probability and Statistics* (Englewood Cliffs, NJ: Prentice Hall, 1990).

12. D. L. Whaley III, "The Interquartile Range: Theory and Estimation" (master's thesis, East Tennessee State University, 2005).

13. J. Benesty, J. Chen, Y. Huang, and I. Cohen, "Pearson Correlation Coefficient," in *Noise Reduction in Speech Processing* (Dordrecht, Netherlands: Springer, 2009), 35–40.

14. D. G. Altman, "Categorising Continuous Variables," *British Journal of Cancer* 64, no. 5 (1991): 975.

15. E. B. Andersen, *The Statistical Analysis of Categorical Data* (Berlin: Springer, 2012).

16. P. W. Laud and J. G. Ibrahim, "Predictive Model Selection," *Journal of the Royal Statistical Society: Series B (Methodological)* 57, no. 1 (1995): 247–262.

17. L. Myers and M. J. Sirois, "Spearman Correlation Coefficients, Differences Between," in *Encyclopedia of Statistical Sciences*, ed. S. Kotz, C. B. Read, N. Balakrishnan, B. Vidakovic, and N. L. Johnson (Hoboken, NJ: Wiley, 2004), 12.

18. D. A. Keim, M. C. Hao, U. Dayal, H. Janetzko, and P. Bak, "Generalized Scatter Plots," *Information Visualization* 9, no. 4 (2010): 301–311.

19. Y. Kim, T. Kim, and T. Ergün, "The Instability of the Pearson Correlation Coefficient in the Presence of Coincidental Outliers," *Finance Research Letters* 13 (2015): 243–257.

20. J. W. Tukey, *Exploratory Data Analysis*, vol. 2 (Reading, MA: Addison-Wesley, 1977).

21. E. L. Lehmann, *Testing Statistical Hypotheses*, 2nd ed. (New York: Wiley, 1986).

22. G. M. Sullivan and R. Feinn, "Using Effect Size—or Why the P Value Is Not Enough," *Journal of Graduate Medical Education* 4, no. 3 (2012): 279–282.

23. R. Rosenthal, H. Cooper, and L. Hedges, "Parametric Measures of Effect Size," in *The Handbook of Research Synthesis*, ed. H. Cooper and L. Hedges (New York: Russell Sage Foundation, 1994), 231–244.

24. E. Burmeister and L. M. Aitken, "Sample Size: How Many Is Enough?," *Australian Critical Care* 25, no. 4 (2012): 271–274.

25. Websites like https://clincalc.com/stats/samplesize.aspx can be used to perform sample size calculations based on statistical power.

26. J. O. Berger and T. Sellke, "Testing a Point Null Hypothesis: The Irreconcilability of *p* Values and Evidence," *Journal of the American Statistical Association* 82, no. 397 (1987): 112–122.

27. T. Dahiru, "P-Value, a True Test of Statistical Significance? A Cautionary Note," *Annals of Ibadan Postgraduate Medicine* 6, no. 1 (2008): 21–26.

28. J. A. Berger, "A Comparison of Testing Methodologies," in *PHYSTAT LHC Workshop on Statistical Issues for LHC Physics* (Geneva: CERN, 2008), 8–19; J. P. Ioannidis, "The Proposal to Lower P Value Thresholds to. 005," *JAMA* 319, no. 14 (2018): 1429–1430.

29. R. Rosenthal, R. L. Rosnow, and D. B. Rubin, *Contrasts and Effect Sizes in Behavioral Research: A Correlational Approach* (Cambridge: Cambridge University Press, 2000).

30. L. G. Halsey, D. Curran-Everett, S. L. Vowler, and G. B. Drummond, "The Fickle *P* Value Generates Irreproducible Results," *Nature Methods* 12, no. 3 (2015): 179–185.

31. X. Fan, "Statistical Significance and Effect Size in Education Research: Two Sides of a Coin," *Journal of Educational Research* 94, no. 5 (2001): 275–282.

32. T. Vacha-Haase and B. Thompson, "How to Estimate and Interpret Various Effect Sizes," *Journal of Counseling Psychology* 51, no. 4 (2004): 473.

33. D. A. Prentice and D. T. Miller, "When Small Effects Are Impressive," in *Methodological Issues and Strategies in Clinical Research*, ed. A. E. Kazdin (Washington, DC: American Psychological Association, 2016), 99–105.

34. E. Flores-Ruiz, M. G. Miranda-Novales, and M. Á. Villasís-Keever, "The Research Protocol VI: How to Choose the Appropriate Statistical Test; Inferential Statistics," *Revista Alergia México* 64, no. 3 (2017): 364–370.

35. M. M. Mukaka, "A Guide to Appropriate Use of Correlation Coefficient in Medical Research," *Malawi Medical Journal* 24, no. 3 (2012): 69–71.

36. D. York, N. M. Evensen, M. L. Martínez, and J. De Basabe Delgado, "Unified Equations for the Slope, Intercept, and Standard Errors of

the Best Straight Line," *American Journal of Physics* 72, no. 3 (2004): 367–375.

37. R. A. Philipp, "The Many Uses of Algebraic Variables," *Mathematics Teacher* 85, no. 7 (1992): 557–561.

38. H. R. Varian, "Goodness-of-Fit in Optimizing Models," *Journal of Econometrics* 46, no. 1–2 (1990): 125–140.

39. K. L. Pearson, "LIII. On Lines and Planes of Closest Fit to Systems of Points in Space," *London, Edinburgh, and Dublin Philosophical Magazine and Journal of Science* 2, no. 11 (1901): 559–572.

40. O. Fernández, "Obtaining a Best Fitting Plane Through 3D Georeferenced Data," *Journal of Structural Geology* 27, no. 5 (2005): 855–858.

41. M. K. Transtrum, B. B. Machta, and J. P. Sethna, "Why Are Nonlinear Fits to Data So Challenging?," *Physics Review Letters* 104, no. 6 (2010): 060201.

42. R. B. Darlington and A. F. Hayes, *Regression Analysis and Linear Models* (New York: Guilford Press, 2017), 603–611.

43. T. Hastie, R. Tibshirani, and J. H. Friedman, *The Elements of Statistical Learning: Data Mining, Inference, and Prediction*, 2nd ed. (New York: Springer, 2009; G. Shmueli, "To Explain or to Predict?," *Statistical Science* 25, no. 3 (2010): 289–310.

44. A. Gandomi and M. Haider, "Beyond the Hype: Big Data Concepts, Methods, and Analytics," *International Journal of Information Management* 35, no. 2 (2015): 137–144.

45. P. A. Frost, "Proxy Variables and Specification Bias," *Review of Economics and Statistics* 61, no. 2 (1979): 323–325.

46. P. Velentgas, N. A. Dreyer, and A. W. Wu, "Outcome Definition and Measurement," in *Developing a Protocol for Observational Comparative Effectiveness Research: A User's Guide*, ed. P. Velentgas, N. A. Dreyer, P. Nourjah, S. R. Smith, and M. M. Torchia (Rockville, MD: Agency for Healthcare Research and Quality, 2013). 71–92.

47. D. G. Altman and P. Royston, "The Cost of Dichotomising Continuous Variables," *BMJ* 332 (2006): 1080.

48. M. L. Thompson, "Selection of Variables in Multiple Regression: Part I. A Review and Evaluation," *International Statistical Review* 46, no. 1 (1978): 1–19.

49. G. Heinze, C. Wallisch, and D. Dunkler, "Variable Selection–a Review and Recommendations for the Practicing Statistician," *Biometrical Journal* 60, no. 3 (2018): 431–449.

50. L. Kuo and B. Mallick, "Variable Selection for Regression Models," *Sankhyā: The Indian Journal of Statistics, Series B* 60, no. 1 (1998): 65–81.

51. T. Mühlbacher and H. Piringer, "A Partition-Based Framework for Building and Validating Regression Models," *IEEE Transactions on Visualization and Computer Graphics* 19, no. 12 (2013): 1962–1971.

4. MAKING DECISIONS WITH DATA

1. M. A. Hernán and J. M. Robins, *Causal Inference: What If* (Boca Raton, FL: Chapman & Hall/CRC, 2010).
2. P. W. Holland, "Statistics and Causal Inference," *Journal of the American Statistical Association* 81, no. 396 (1986): 945–960.
3. G. W. Imbens and D. B. Rubin, *Causal Inference in Statistics, Social, and Biomedical Sciences* (New York: Cambridge University Press, 2015).
4. P. Spirtes, "Introduction to Causal Inference," *Journal of Machine Learning Research* 11 (2010): 1643–1662.
5. J. B. Holland, "Genetic Architecture of Complex Traits in Plants," *Current Opinion in Plant Biology* 10, no. 2 (2007): 156–161.
6. T. J. VanderWeele and I. Shpitser, "On the Definition of a Confounder," *Annals of Statistics* 41, no. 1 (2013): 196.
7. R. M. Mickey and S. Greenland, "The Impact of Confounder Selection Criteria on Effect Estimation," *American Journal of Epidemiology* 129, no. 1 (1989): 125–137.
8. O. S. Miettinen, "The Need for Randomization in the Study of Intended Effects," *Statistics in Medicine* 2, no. 2 (1983): 267–271.
9. L. J. Schulman and P. Srivastava, "Stability of Causal Inference," in *UAI'16: Proceedings of the Thirty-Second Conference on Uncertainty in Artificial Intelligence* (New York: ACM, 2016).
10. R. H. Groenwold, O. H. Klungel, D. G. Altman, Y. van der Graaf, A. W. Hoes, and K. G. Moons, "Adjustment for Continuous Confounders: An Example of How to Prevent Residual Confounding," *CMAJ* 185, no. 5 (2013): 401–406.
11. N. E. Breslow, "Statistics in Epidemiology: The Case-Control Study," *Journal of the American Statistical Association* 91, no. 433 (1996): 14–28.
12. C. M. Patino and J. C. Ferreira, "Inclusion and Exclusion Criteria in Research Studies: Definitions and Why They Matter," *Jornal Brasileiro de Pneumologia* 44, no. 2 (2018): 84.
13. This is a simplification of how causal effects are estimated. The analysis of randomized experiments has many nuances that are beyond the scope of this book. S. Greenland, "Randomization, Statistics, and Causal Inference," *Epidemiology* 1, no. 6 (1990): 421–429.
14. M. A. Hernán and J. M. Robins, "Using Big Data to Emulate a Target Trial When a Randomized Trial Is Not Available," *American Journal of Epidemiology* 183, no. 8 (2016): 758–764.
15. M. Petticrew, S. Cummins, C. Ferrell, A. Findlay, C. Higgins, C. Hoy, A. Kearns, and L. Sparks, "Natural Experiments: An Underused Tool for Public Health?," *Public Health* 119, no. 9 (2005): 751–757.
16. C. Brown, C. Gilroy, and A. Kohen, "The Effect of the Minimum Wage on Employment and Unemployment," *Journal of Economic Literature* 2o, no. 2 (1982): 487–528.

17. J. Hahn, P. Todd, and W. Van der Klaauw, "Identification and Estimation of Treatment Effects with a Regression-Discontinuity Design," *Econometrica* 69, no. 1 (2001): 201–209.
18. J. M. Bland and D. G. Altman, "Statistics Notes: Matching," *BMJ* 309 (1994): 1128.
19. B. Lu, R. Greevy, X. Xu, and C. Beck, "Optimal Nonbipartite Matching and Its Statistical Applications," *American Statistician* 65, no. 1 (2011): 21–30.
20. M. A. Mansournia, N. P. Jewell, and S. Greenland, "Case-Control Matching: Effects, Misconceptions, and Recommendations," *European Journal of Epidemiology* 33, no. 1 (2018): 5–14.
21. J. Heckman, "Varieties of Selection Bias," *American Economic Review* 80, no. 2 (1990): 313–318.
22. J. M. Bland and D. C. Altman, "Measurement Error," *BMJ* 312 (1996): 1654.
23. D. L. Paulhus, "Measurement and Control of Response Bias," in *Measures of Personality and Social Psychological Attitudes*, ed. J. P. Robinson, P. R. Shaver, and L. S. Wrightsman (San Diego, CA: Academic Press, 1991), 17–59.
24. P. E. Shrout and J. L. Fleiss, "Intraclass Correlations: Uses in Assessing Rater Reliability," *Psychological Bulletin* 86, no. 2 (1979): 420.
25. K. L. Gwet, "Intrarater Reliability," in *Wiley Encyclopedia of Clinical Trials*, ed. R. D'Agostino, J. Massaro, and L. Sullivan (Hoboken, NJ: Wiley, 2008), 4.
26. P. E. Fischer and R. E. Verrecchia, "Reporting Bias," *Accounting Review* 75, no. 2 (2000): 229–245.
27. C. B. Begg, "Publication Bias," in *The Handbook of Research Synthesis*, ed. Harris Cooper and Larry V. Hedges (New York: Russell Sage Foundation, 1994), 399–409.
28. M. L. Head, L. Holman, R. Lanfear, A. T. Kahn, and M. D. Jennions, "The Extent and Consequences of P-Hacking in Science," *PLOS Biology* 13, no. 3 (2015): e1002106.
29. N. Barrowman, "Correlation, Causation, and Confusion," *New Atlantis*, Summer/Fall 2014, 23–44.
30. P. D. Bliese and J. W. Lang, "Understanding Relative and Absolute Change in Discontinuous Growth Models: Coding Alternatives and Implications for Hypothesis Testing," *Organizational Research Methods* 19, no. 4 (2016): 562–592.
31. Bliese and Lang, "Understanding Relative and Absolute Change."
32. L. Wartofsky, "Increasing World Incidence of Thyroid Cancer: Increased Detection or Higher Radiation Exposure?," *Hormones* 9, no. 2 (2010): 103–108.
33. P. R. Rosenbaum, *Design of Observational Studies* (New York: Springer, 2010).
34. A. S. Detsky, C. D. Naylor, K. O'Rourke, A. J. McGeer, and K. A. L'Abbé. "Incorporating Variations in the Quality of Individual Randomized Trials

Into Meta-Analysis," *Journal of Clinical Epidemiology* 45, no. 3 (1992): 255–265.

35. A. Haidich, "Meta-Analysis in Medical Research," *Hippokratia* 14, no. S1 (2010): 29–37.

36. J. D. Harris, C. E. Quatman, M. M. Manring, R. A. Siston, and D. C. Flanigan, "How to Write a Systematic Review," *American Journal of Sports Medicine* 42, no. 11 (2014): 2761–2768.

37. L. K. Henderson, J. C. Craig, N. S. Willis, D. Tovey, and A. C. Webster, "How to Write a Cochrane Systematic Review," *Nephrology* 15, no. 6 (2010): 617–624.

5. CLUSTERING, SEGMENTING, AND CUTTING THROUGH THE NOISE

1. M. Usama, J. Qadir, A. Raza, H. Arif, K. A. Yau, Y. Elkhatib, A. Hussain, and A. Al-Fuqaha, "Unsupervised Machine Learning for Networking: Techniques, Applications, and Research Challenges," *IEEE Access* 7 (2019): 65579–65615.

2. L. I. Smith, *A Tutorial on Principal Components Analysis* (Dunedin, New Zealand: Department of Computer Science, University of Otago, 2002).

3. J. A. Lee and M. Verleysen, *Nonlinear Dimensionality Reduction* (New York: Springer, 2007).

4. K. Pearson, "LIII. On Lines and Planes of Closest Fit to Systems of Points in Space," *London, Edinburgh, and Dublin Philosophical Magazine and Journal of Science* 2, no. 11 (1901): 559–572.

5. V. Audigier, F. Husson, and J. Josse, "Multiple Imputation for Continuous Variables Using a Bayesian Principal Component Analysis," *Journal of Statistical Computation and Simulation* 86, no. 11 (2016): 2140–2156.

6. S. Vyas and L. Kumaranayake, "Constructing Socio-economic Status Indices: How to Use Principal Components Analysis," *Health Policy Planning* 21, no. 6 (2006): 459–468.

7. H. Abdi and L. J. Williams, "Principal Component Analysis," *Wiley Interdisciplinary Reviews: Computational Statistics* 2, no. 4 (2010): 433–459.

8. W. W. Hsieh, "Nonlinear Principal Component Analysis by Neural Networks," *Tellus A* 53, no. 5 (2001): 599–615.

9. Hsieh, "Nonlinear Principal Component Analysis."

10. G. W. Milligan and M. C. Cooper, "A Study of Standardization of Variables in Cluster Analysis," *Journal of Classification* 5, no. 2 (1988): 181–204.

11. G. H. Dunteman, *Principal Components Analysis* (Newbury Park, CA: SAGE, 1989).

12. J. E. Jackson, *A User's Guide to Principal Components* (Hoboken, NJ: Wiley, 2005).

13. S. Sousa, F. G. Martins, M. C. Alvim-Ferraz, and M. C. Pereira, "Multiple Linear Regression and Artificial Neural Networks Based on Principal Components to Predict Ozone Concentrations," *Environmental Modelling & Software* 22, no. 1 (2007): 97–103.

14. H. Kargupta, W. Huang, K. Sivakumar, and E. Johnson, "Distributed Clustering Using Collective Principal Component Analysis," *Knowledge and Information Systems* 3, no. 4 (2001): 422–448.

15. Kargupta et al., "Distributed Clustering."

16. F. Murtagh and P. Contreras, "Algorithms for Hierarchical Clustering: An Overview," *Wiley Interdisciplinary Reviews: Data Mining and Knowledge Discovery* 2, no. 1 (2012): 86–97.

17. M. E. Celebi, ed., *Partitional Clustering Algorithms* (Cham, Switzerland: Springer, 2014).

18. S. A. Alasadi and W. S. Bhaya, "Review of Data Preprocessing Techniques in Data Mining," *Journal of Engineering and Applied Sciences* 12, no. 16 (2017): 4102–4107.

19. A. Likas, N. Vlassis, and J. J. Verbeek, "The Global k-Means Clustering Algorithm," *Pattern Recognition* 36, no. 2 (2003): 451–461.

20. V. K. Dehariya, S. K. Shrivastava, and R. C. Jain, "Clustering of Image Data Set Using K-Means and Fuzzy K-Means Algorithms," in 2010 International Conference on Computational Intelligence and Communication Networks (November 2010): 386–391.

21. W. H. Day and H. Edelsbrunner, "Efficient Algorithms for Agglomerative Hierarchical Clustering Methods," *Journal of Classification* 1, no. 1 (1984): 7–24.

22. P. C. Besse, B. Guillouet, J. Loubes, and F. Royer, "Review and Perspective for Distance-Based Clustering of Vehicle Trajectories," *IEEE Transactions on Intelligent Transportation Systems* 17, no. 11 (2016): 3306–3317.

23. M. Roux, "A Comparative Study of Divisive and Agglomerative Hierarchical Clustering Algorithms," *Journal of Classification* 35 (2018): 345–366.

24. B. S. Everitt, S. Landau, and M. Leese, *Cluster Analysis*, 4th ed. (London: Arnold, 2001).

6. BUILDING YOUR FIRST MODEL

1. Marcus Dillender, "What Happens When the Insurer Can Say No? Assessing Prior Authorization as a Tool to Prevent High-Risk Prescriptions and to Lower Costs," *Journal of Public Economics* 165 (2018): 170–200.

2. Richard A. Deyo, Sohail K. Mirza, Judith A. Turner, and Brook I. Martin, "Overtreating Chronic Back Pain: Time to Back Off?," *Journal of the American Board of Family Medicine* 22, no. 1 (2009): 62–68.

3. John D. Kelleher and Brendan Tierney, *Data Science* (Cambridge, MA: MIT Press, 2018).

4. Kelleher and Tierney, *Data Science*, 99–100.

5. Health Insurance Portability and Accountability Act of 1996, Pub. L. 104-191.

6. Justin, Cummins, Jon D. Lurie, Tor Tosteson, Brett Hanscom, William A. Abdu, Nancy J. O. Birkmeyer, Harry Herkowitz, and James Weinstein, "Descriptive Epidemiology and Prior Healthcare Utilization of Patients in the Spine Patient Outcomes Research Trial's (Sport) Three Observational Cohorts: Disc Herniation, Spinal Stenosis and Degenerative Spondylolisthesis," *Spine* 31, no. 7 (2006): 806.

7. Nathan Douthit, Sakal Kiv, Tzvi Dwolatzky, and Seema Biswas, "Exposing Some Important Barriers to Health Care Access in the Rural USA," *Public Health* 129, no. 6 (2015): 611–620.

8. Daniel B. Neill, "Auditing Black Box Algorithms for Fairness and Bia," Workshop on Accountable Decision Systems, New York, February 2018, https://cs.nyu.edu/~neill/papers/accountable2018.pdf.

9. Qianyu Yuan, Tianrun Cai, Chuan Hong, Mulong Du, Bruce E. Johnson, Michael Lanuti, Tianxi Cai, and David C. Christiani, "Performance of a Machine Learning Algorithm Using Electronic Health Record Data to Identify and Estimate Survival in a Longitudinal Cohort of Patients with Lung Cancer," *JAMA Network Open* 4, no. 7 (2021): e2114723.

10. Kelleher and Tierney, *Data Science*, 47.

11. Kelleher and Tierney, *Data Science*, 48.

12. Benjamin Shickel, Patrick James Tighe, Azra Bihorac, and Parisa Rashidi, "Deep EHR: A Survey of Recent Advances in Deep Learning Techniques for Electronic Health Record (EHR) Analysis," *IEEE Journal of Biomedical and Health Informatics* 22, no. 5 (2017): 1589–1604.

13. Kelleher and Tierney, *Data Science*, 49–51.

14. Shunji Mori, Hirobumi Nishida, and Hiromitsu Yamada, *Optical Character Recognition* (New York: Wiley, 1999).

15. Alice Zheng and Amanda Casari, *Feature Engineering for Machine Learning: Principles and Techniques for Data Scientists* (Sebastopol, CA: O'Reilly Media, 2018).

16. Mark Andrew Hall, "Correlation-Based Feature Selection for Machine Learning" (PhD thesis, University of Waikato, 1999).

17. Mark A. Hall and Lloyd A. Smith, "Feature Selection for Machine Learning: Comparing a Correlation-Based Filter Approach to the Wrapper," in *Proceedings of the Twelfth International Florida Artificial Intelligence Research Society Conference*, ed. Amruth N. Kumar and Ingrid Russell (Menlo Park, CA: AAAI Press, 1999), 235–239.

18. Girish Chandrashekar and Ferat Sahin, "A Survey on Feature Selection Methods," *Computers & Electrical Engineering* 40, no. 1 (2014): 16–28.

19. Lukas Meier, Sara Van De Geer, and Peter Bühlmann, "The Group Lasso for Logistic Regression," *Journal of the Royal Statistical Society: Series B (Statistical Methodology)* 70, no. 1 (2008): 53–71.
20. Arthur E. Hoerl and Robert W. Kennard, "Ridge Regression: Applications to Nonorthogonal Problems," *Technometrics* 12, no. 1 (1970): 69–82.
21. Kelleher and Tierney, *Data Science*, 145–148.
22. S. Kavitha, S. Varuna, and R. Ramya, "A Comparative Analysis on Linear Regression and Support Vector Regression," in *2016 Online International Conference on Green Engineering and Technologies* (Piscataway, NJ: IEEE, 2016).
23. Kelleher and Tierney, *Data Science*, 147.
24. Tom Dietterich, "Overfitting and Undercomputing in Machine Learning," *ACM Computing Surveys* 27, no. 3 (1995): 326–327.
25. Kelleher and Tierney, *Data Science*, 147–148.
26. Payam Refaeilzadeh, Lei Tang, and Huan Liu, "Cross-Validation," in *Encyclopedia of Database Systems*, ed. L. Liu and M. T. Özsu (Boston: Springer, 2009), 532–538.
27. Avrim L. Blum and Pat Langley, "Selection of Relevant Features and Examples in Machine Learning," *Artificial Intelligence* 97, no. 1–2 (1997): 245–271.
28. Gareth James, Daniela Witten, Trevor Hastie, and Robert Tibshirani, *An Introduction to Statistical Learning* (New York: Springer, 2013), 225–282.
29. Matthias Feurer and Frank Hutter, "Hyperparameter Optimization," in *Automated Machine Learning: Methods, Systems, Challenges*, ed. Frank Hutter, Lars Kotthoff, and Joaquin Vanschoren (Cham, Switzerland: Springer, 2019), 3–33.
30. Gary Brassington, "Mean Absolute Error and Root Mean Square Error: Which Is the Better Metric for Assessing Model Performance?," in *Geophysical Research Abstracts* (Munich: European Geophysical Union, 2017), 3574.
31. Antonio Bella, Cèsar Ferri, José Hernández-Orallo, and María José Ramírez-Quintana, "Calibration of Machine Learning Models," in *Handbook of Research on Machine Learning Applications and Trends: Algorithms, Methods, and Techniques*, ed. Emilio Soria Olivas, Jose David Martin Guerrero, Marcelino Martinez Sober, Jose Rafael Magdalena Benedito, and Antonio Jose Serrano Lopez (Hershey, PA: Information Science Reference, 2010), 128–146.
32. Sarah A. Gagliano, Andrew D. Paterson, Michael E. Weale, and Jo Knight, "Assessing Models for Genetic Prediction of Complex Traits: A Comparison of Visualization and Quantitative Methods," *BMC Genomics* 16, no. 1 (2015): 1–11.
33. Olivier Caelen, "A Bayesian Interpretation of the Confusion Matrix," *Annals of Mathematics and Artificial Intelligence* 81, no. 3 (2017): 429–450.
34. Anthony K. Akobeng, "Understanding Diagnostic Tests 1: Sensitivity, Specificity and Predictive Values," *Acta Paediatrica* 96, no. 3 (2007): 338–341.

7. TOOLS FOR MACHINE LEARNING

1. M. Lunt, "Introduction to Statistical Modelling: Linear Regression," *Rheumatology* 54, no. 7 (July 2015): 1137–40, https://doi.org/10.1093/rheumatology/ket146.

2. Shibing Sun, Huan Zhao, "Research on the Regression Algorithm Analysis and Its Application," *Data Science Journal* 6, no. 0 (August 22, 2007): S485–91, https://doi.org/10.2481/dsj.6.S485.

3. P. Karaca-Mandic, E. C. Norton, and B. Dowd, "Interaction Terms in Nonlinear Models," *Health Services Research* 47, no. 1 Pt 1 (February 2012): 255–74, https://doi.org/10.1111/j.1475-6773.2011.01314.x.

4. A. C. Gallagher, J. Luo, and W. Hao, "Improved Blue Sky Detection Using Polynomial Model Fit," in *2004 International Conference on Image Processing, 2004. ICIP '04.*, 4:2367-2370 Vol. 4, 2004, abstract, https://doi.org/10.1109/ICIP.2004.1421576.

5. F. E. Harrell, *Regression Modeling Strategies: With Applications to Linear Models, Logistic Regression, and Survival Analysis* (New York: Springer, 2001).

6. K. Chen, Z. Ying, H. Zhang, and L. Zhao, "Analysis of Least Absolute Deviation." *Biometrika* 95, no. 1 (March 1, 2008): 107–22, https://doi.org/10.1093/biomet/asm082.

7. R. Koenker, and K. F. Hallock, K. F. "Quantile Regression." *Journal of Economic Perspectives* 15, no. 4 (2001), 143–56.

8. S. Sun and R. Huang, "An Adaptive K-Nearest Neighbor Algorithm," in *2010 Seventh International Conference on Fuzzy Systems and Knowledge Discovery*, 1:91–94, 2010, https://doi.org/10.1109/FSKD.2010.5569740.

9. A. R. Lubis, M. Lubis, and Al-Khowarizmi, "Optimization of Distance Formula in K-Nearest Neighbor Method," *Bulletin of Electrical Engineering and Informatics* 9, no. 1 (February 1, 2020): 326–38, https://doi.org/10.11591/eei.v9i1.1464.

10. J. Wang, P. Neskovic, and L. N. Cooper, "Neighborhood Size Selection in the K-Nearest-Neighbor Rule Using Statistical Confidence," *Pattern Recognition* 39, no. 3 (March 1, 2006): 417–23, https://doi.org/10.1016/j.patcog.2005.08.009.

11. T. Bailey, J. Ak, "A Note on Distance-Weighted k-Nearest Neighbor Rules," *IEEE Transactions on Systems, Man, and Cybernetics* 8, no. 4 (April 1978): 311–13, https://doi.org/10.1109/TSMC.1978.4309958.

12. T. Kumar, "Solution of Linear and Non Linear Regression Problem by K Nearest Neighbour Approach: By Using Three Sigma Rule," in *2015 IEEE International Conference on Computational Intelligence & Communication Technology*, 197–201, 2015, https://doi.org/10.1109/CICT.2015.110.

13. W.-Y. Loh, "Classification and Regression Trees," *WIREs Data Mining and Knowledge Discovery* 1, no. 1 (2011): 14–23, https://doi.org/10.1002/widm.8.

14. S. C. Lemon, J. Roy, M. A. Clark, P. D. Friedman, and W. Rakowski, "Classification and Regression Tree Analysis in Public Health: Methodological Review and Comparison with Logistic Regression" *Annals of Behavioral Medicine* 26, no. 3 (December 2003): 172–81.

15. R. Siciliano and F. Mola, "Multivariate Data Analysis and Modeling through Classification and Regression Trees," *Computational Statistics & Data Analysis* 32, no. 3 (January 28, 2000): 285–301, https://doi.org/10.1016/S0167-9473(99)00082-1.

16. J. K. Jaiswal and R. Samikannu, "Application of Random Forest Algorithm on Feature Subset Selection and Classification and Regression," in *2017 World Congress on Computing and Communication Technologies* (WCCCT), 65–68, 2017, https://doi.org/10.1109/WCCCT.2016.25.

17. Loh, "Classification and Regression Trees."

18. Siciliano and Mola, "Multivariate Data Analysis and Modeling through Classification and Regression Trees."

19. Loh, "Classification and Regression Trees."

20. Siciliano and Mola, "Multivariate Data Analysis and Modeling through Classification and Regression Trees.

21. Jaiswal and Samikannu, "Application of Random Forest Algorithm on Feature Subset Selection and Classification and Regression."

22. T. G. Dietterich, "Ensemble Methods in Machine Learning," in *Multiple Classifier Systems* (Berlin: Springer, 2000).

23. Dietterich, "Ensemble Methods in Machine Learning."

24. T. Hothorn and B. Lausen. "Double-bagging: Combining Classifiers by Bootstrap Aggregation," *Pattern Recognition* 36, no. 6 (2003): 1303–9.

25. R. E. Schapire, "The Boosting Approach to Machine Learning: An Overview," in *Nonlinear Estimation and Classification*, ed. D. D. Denison et al. (New York: Springer, 2003), 149–71.

26. Y. Cao, Q.-G. Miao, J.-C. Liu, and L. Gao, "Advance and Prospects of AdaBoost Algorithm." *Acta Automatica Sinica* 39, no. 6 (June 1, 2013): 745–58, https://doi.org/10.1016/S1874-1029(13)60052-X.

8. PULLING IT TOGETHER

1. Alejandro Baldominos, Iván Blanco, Antonio José Moreno, Rubén Iturrarte, Óscar Bernárdez, and Carlos Afonso, "Identifying Real Estate Opportunities Using Machine Learning," *Applied Sciences* 8, no. 11 (2018): 2321, https://doi.org/10.3390/app8112321.

2. Bogdan Trawiński, Zbigniew Telec, Jacek Krasnoborski, Mateusz Piwowarczyk, Michał Talaga, Tadeusz Lasota, and Edward Sawiłow, "Comparison of Expert Algorithms with Machine Learning Models for Real Estate

Appraisal," in *2017 IEEE International Conference on INnovations in Intelligent SysTems and Applications* (INISTA) (Piscataway, NJ: IEEE, 2017), 51–54, https://doi.org/10.1109/INISTA.2017.8001131.

3. Tianrun Cai, Andreas A. Giannopoulos, Sheng Yu, Tatiana Kelil, Beth Ripley, Kanako K. Kumamaru, Frank J. Rybicki, and Dimitrios Mitsouras, "Natural Language Processing Technologies in Radiology Research and Clinical Applications," *Radiographics* 36, no. 1 (2016): 176–191, https://doi.org/10.1148/rg.2016150080.

4. Cai at al., "Natural Language Processing Technologies"; Anne Kao and Steve R. Poteet, eds., *Natural Language Processing and Text Mining* (Berlin: Springer), 2007.

5. Kao and Poteet, *Natural Language Processing and Text Mining*.

6. Nitin Hardeniya, Jacob Perkins, Deepti Chopra, Nisheeth Joshi, and Iti Mathur, *Natural Language Processing: Python and NLTK* (Birmingham, UK: Packt, 2016).

7. Hardeniya et al., *Natural Language Processing*.

8. Jasmeet Singh and Vishal Gupta, "Text Stemming: Approaches, Applications, and Challenges," *ACM Computing Surveys* 49, no. 3 (2017): 1–46, https://doi.org/10.1145/2975608.

9. Singh and Gupta, "Text Stemming"; Cai at al., "Natural Language Processing Technologies."

10. Taqwa Hariguna, "Chatbot Smart Assistant Using N-gram and Bi-gram Algorithm," *International Journal of Advanced Trends in Computer Science and Engineering* 9, no. 4 (2020): 4788–4793, htps://doi.org/10.30534/ijatcse/2020/86942020.

11. Wisam A. Qader, Musa M. Ameen, and Bilal I. Ahmed, "An Overview of Bag of Words; Importance, Implementation, Applications, and Challenges," in *2019 International Engineering Conference* (Piscataway, NJ: IEEE, 2019), 200–204, https://doi.org/10.1109/IEC47844.2019.8950616.

12. W. B. Croft and D. J. Harper, "Using Probabilistic Models of Document Retrieval Without Relevance Information," *Journal of Documentation* 35, no. 4 (1979): 285–295, https://doi.org/10.1108/eb026683.

13. Vladimir Vargas-Calderón and Jorge E. Camargo, "A Model for Predicting Price Polarity of Real Estate Properties Using Information of Real Estate Market Websites," arXiv, November 19, 2019, https://doi.org/10.48550/arXiv.1911.08382.

14. Vargas-Calderón and Camargo, "A Model for Predicting Price Polarity."

15. Vargas-Calderón and Camargo, "A Model for Predicting Price Polarity."

16. Walaa Medhat, Ahmed Hassan, and Hoda Korashy, "Sentiment Analysis Algorithms and Applications: A Survey," *Ain Shams Engineering Journal* 5, no. 4 (2014): 1093–1113, https://doi.org/10.1016/j.asej.2014.04.011.

17. Petr Hájek, "Combining Bag-of-Words and Sentiment Features of Annual Reports to Predict Abnormal Stock Returns," *Neural Computing and*

Applications 29, no. 7 (2018): 343–358, https://doi.org/10.1007/s00521-017 -3194-2.

18. Vargas-Calderón and Camargo, "A Model for Predicting Price Polarity."

19. Sebastian Santibanez, Marius Kloft, and Tobia Lakes, "Performance Analysis of Machine Learning Algorithms for Regression of Spatial Variables: A Case Study in the Real Estate Industry" (paper presented at the 13th International Conference on GeoComputation, Richardson, TX, May 20–23, 2015).

20. Süleyman Bilgilioğlu and H. Yilmaz, "Comparison of Different Machine Learning Models for Mass Appraisal of Real Estate," *Survey Review* 55, no. 388 (2023): 32–43, https://doi.org/10.1080/00396265.2021.1996799; Sebastian, Kloft, and Lakes, "Performance Analysis of Machine Learning Algorithms."

21. M. V. Eitzel, Maggi Kelly, Iryna Dronova, Yana Valachovic, Lenya Quinn-Davidson, Jon Solera, and Perry de Valpine, "Challenges and Opportunities in Synthesizing Historical Geospatial Data Using Statistical Models," *Ecological Informatics* 31 (2016): 100–111, https://www.sciencedirect.com /science/article/pii/S1574954115001922.

22. Eitzel et al., "Challenges and Opportunities in Synthesizing Historical Geospatial Data."

23. Eitzel et al., "Challenges and Opportunities in Synthesizing Historical Geospatial Data"; Trang VoPham, Jaime E. Hart, Francine Laden, and Yao-Yi Chiang, "Emerging Trends in Geospatial Artificial Intelligence (GeoAI): Potential Applications for Environmental Epidemiology," *Environmental Health* 17, no. 1 (2018): 40, https://doi.org/10.1186/s12940-018-0386-x.

24. Emerson M. A. Xavier, Francisco J. Ariza-López, and Manuel A. Ureña-Cámara, "A Survey of Measures and Methods for Matching Geospatial Vector Datasets," *ACM Computing Surveys* 49, no. 2 (2016): 1–34, https:// doi.org/10.1145/2963147.

25. Bruce K. Wylie, Neal J. Pastick, Joshua J. Picotte, and Carol A. Deering, "Geospatial Data Mining for Digital Raster Mapping," *GIScience & Remote Sensing* 56, no. 3 (2019): 406–429, https://doi.org/10.1080/15481603.2018 .1517445.

26. Wylie et al., "Geospatial Data Mining."

27. Santibanez, Kloft, and Lakes, "Performance Analysis of Machine Learning Algorithms."

28. Bilgilioğlu and Yilmaz, "Comparison of Different Machine Learning Models."

29. Kimberly Winson-Geideman, Andy Krause, Clifford A. Lipscomb, and Nicholas Evangelopoulos, "Software Tools for Real Estate Analysis," in *Real Estate Analysis in the Information Age: Techniques for Big Data and Statistical Modeling* (London: Routledge, 2017), 25–35.

30. Edward L. Glaeser, Michael Scott Kincaid, and Nikhil Naik, "Computer Vision and Real Estate: Do Looks Matter and Do Incentives Determine Looks" (Working Paper No. 25174, National Bureau of Economic Research, Cambridge, MA, October 2018), https://doi.org/10.3386/w25174.

31. Yoji Kiyota, "Frontiers of Computer Vision Technologies on Real Estate Property Photographs and Floorplans," in *Frontiers of Real Estate Science in Japan*, ed. Yasushi Asami, Yoshiro Higano, and Hideo Fukui (Singapore: Springer, 2021), 325–337, https://link.springer.com/chapter/10.1007/978-981 -15-8848-8_23.

32. Athanasios Voulodimos, Nikolaos Doulamis, Anastasios Doulamis, and Eftychios Protopapadakis, "Deep Learning for Computer Vision: A Brief Review," *Computational Intelligence and Neuroscience* 2018, art. 7068349 (2018), https://www.hindawi.com/journals/cin/2018/7068349/.

33. Ronald Tombe and Serestina Viriri, "Effective Processing of Convolutional Neural Networks for Computer Vision: A Tutorial and Survey," *IETE Technical Review* 39, no. 1 (2022): 49–62, https://doi.org/10.1080/02564602 .2020.1823252.

34. Voulodimos et al., "Deep Learning for Computer Vision."

35. Voulodimos et al., "Deep Learning for Computer Vision"; Jing Li and Nigel M. Allinson, "A Comprehensive Review of Current Local Features for Computer Vision," *Neurocomputing* 71, no. 10–12 (2008): 1771–1787, https:// www.sciencedirect.com/science/article/abs/pii/S0925231208001124.

36. Garima Anand, Shilpa Srivastava, Anish Shandilya, and Varuna Gupta, "Recurrent Neural Networks in Predicting the Popularity of Online Social Networks Content: A Review," *ECS Transactions* 107, no. 1 (2022): 19991.

37. Sandeep Kumar and Viswanath Talasila, "A Combined Data Analytics and Network Science Approach for Smart Real Estate Investment: Towards Affordable Housing," in *Smart Governance for Cities: Perspectives and Experiences*, ed. Nuno Vasco Moreira Lopes (Cham, Switzerland: Springer, 2020), 153–176, https://link.springer.com/chapter/10.1007/978-3-030-22070-9_8; Melissa Marsh, "Frontiers in Social Data for Real Estate," *Corporate Real Estate Journal* 9, no. 2 (2019): 159–170, https://hstalks.com/article/5275 /frontiers-in-social-data-for-real-estate/.

38. Anand et al., "Recurrent Neural Networks in Predicting the Popularity of Online Social Networks Content"; Sagar S. De, Satchidananda Dehuri, and Gi-Nam Wang, "Machine Learning for Social Network Analysis: A Systematic Literature Review," *IUP Journal of Information Technology* 8, no. 4 (2012): 30–51.

39. De, Dehuri, and Wang, "Machine Learning for Social Network Analysis"; Younghee Hong and Choongrak Kim, "Recent Developments of Constructing Adjacency Matrix in Network Analysis," *Journal of the Korean Data and Information Science Society* 25, no. 5 (2014): 1107–1116, https://doi .org/10.7465/jkdi.2014.25.5.1107.

40. Hong and Kim, "Recent Developments of Constructing Adjacency Matrix in Network Analysis"; Pauli Miettinen and Stefan Neumann, "Recent Developments in Boolean Matrix Factorization," arXiv, December 5, 2020, https://doi.org/10.48550/arXiv.2012.03127.

41. Kiyota, "Frontiers of Computer Vision Technologies."

42. Leonardo Ermann, Klaus M. Frahm, and Dima L. Shepelyansky, "Google Matrix Analysis of Directed Networks," *Reviews of Modern Physics* 87, no. 4 (2015): 1261–1310, https://doi.org/10.1103/RevModPhys.87.1261; Brenton Prettejohn, Matthew Berryman, and Mark McDonnell, "Methods for Generating Complex Networks with Selected Structural Properties for Simulations: A Review and Tutorial for Neuroscientists," *Frontiers in Computational Neuroscience* 5 (2011), https://www.frontiersin.org/articles /10.3389/fncom.2011.00011.

43. Andrea Landherr, Bettina Friedl, and Julia Heidemann, "A Critical Review of Centrality Measures in Social Networks," *Business & Information Systems Engineering* 2, no. 6 (2010): 371–385, https://doi.org/10.1007/s12599-010-0127-3.

44. Mathijs de Vaan and Dan Wang, "Micro-Structural Foundations of Network Inequality: Evidence from a Field Experiment in Professional Networking," *Social Networks* 63 (2020): 213–230, https://doi.org/10.1016/j .socnet.2020.07.002.

45. Baldominos et al., "Identifying Real Estate Opportunities."

46. De, Dehuri, and Wang, "Machine Learning for Social Network Analysis."

47. De, Dehuri, and Wang, "Machine Learning for Social Network Analysis."

48. De, Dehuri, and Wang, "Machine Learning for Social Network Analysis."

49. Baldominos et al., "Identifying Real Estate Opportunities."

9. ETHICS

1. National Academies of Sciences, Engineering, and Medicine, *Data Science for Undergraduates: Opportunities and Options* (Washington, DC: National Academies Press, 2018).

2. "Data Values and Principles," Data Practices, accessed July 8, 2020, https:// datapractices.org/manifesto/.

3. DJ Patil, H. Mason, and M. Loukides, "Of Oaths and Checklists," O'Reilly, July 17, 2018, https://www.oreilly.com/radar/of-oaths-and-checklists/

4. M. Zhang, "Google Photos Tags Two African-Americans as Gorillas Through Facial Recognition Software," *Forbes*, July 1, 2015, https://www.forbes .com/sites/mzhang/2015/07/01/google-photos-tags-two-african-americans -as-gorillas-through-facial-recognition-software/?sh=44a3690e713d.

5. D. Hankerson, A. R. Marshall, J. Booker, H. Mimouni, I. Walker, and J. A. Rode, "Does Technology Have Race?," in *CHI EA '16: Proceedings of the 2016 CHI Conference Extended Abstracts on Human Factors in Computing Systems* (New York: ACM, 2016), 473–486.

6. Y. Liu, A. Jain, C. Eng et al., "A Deep Learning System for Differential Diagnosis of Skin Diseases," *Nature Medicine* 26, no. 6 (2020): 900–908.

7. S. Verma and J. Rubin, "Fairness Definitions Explained," in *FairWare '18: Proceedings of the International Workshop on Software Fairness* (New York: ACM, 2018), 1–7.

8. R. Yearby, "Racial Disparities in Health Status and Access to Healthcare: The Continuation of Inequality in the United States due to Structural Racism," *American Journal of Economics and Sociology* 77, no. 3–4 (2018): 1113–1152.

9. F. Kamiran and T. Calders, "Data Preprocessing Techniques for Classification Without Discrimination," *Knowledge and Information Systems* 33, no. 1 (2012): 1–33.

10. M. Du, F. Yang, N. Zou, and X. Hu, "Fairness in Deep Learning: A Computational Perspective," *IEEE Intelligent Systems* 36, no. 4 (2020): 25–34.

11. B. H. Zhang, B. Lemoine, and M. Mitchell, "Mitigating Unwanted Biases with Adversarial Learning," in *AIES '18: Proceedings of the 2018 AAAI/ACM Conference on AI, Ethics, and Society* (New York: ACM, 2018), 335–340; M. B. Zafar, I. Valera, M. G. Rodriguez, and K. P. Gummadi, "Fairness Constraints: Mechanisms for Fair Classification," *Journal of Machine Language Research* 20, no. 1 (2019): 2737–2778.

12. J. K. Paulus and D. M. Kent, "Race and Ethnicity: A Part of the Equation for Personalized Clinical Decision Making?," *Circulation: Cardiovascular Quality and Outcomes* 10, no. 7 (2017): e003823.

13. R. Jhala and R. Majumdar, "Software Model Checking," *ACM Computing Surveys* 41, no. 4 (2009): 1–54.

14. R. K. Bellamy, K. Dey, M. Hind et al., "AI Fairness 360: An Extensible Toolkit for Detecting and Mitigating Algorithmic Bias," *IBM Journal of Research and Development* 63, no. 4–5 (2019): 4:1–4:15.

15. J. D. Putzke, B. L. Hicken, and J. S. Richards, "Race: Predictor Versus Proxy Variable? Outcomes After Spinal Cord Injury," *Archives of Physical Medicine and Rehabilitation* 83, no. 11 (2002): 1603–1611.

16. A. T. Holland and L. P. Palaniappan, "Problems with the Collection and Interpretation of Asian-American Health Data: Omission, Aggregation, and Extrapolation," *Annals of Epidemiology* 22, no. 6 (2012): 397–405.

17. M. Hurley and J. Adebayo, "Credit Scoring in the Era of Big Data," *Yale Journal of Law & Technology* 18 (2016): 148.

18. B. E. Harcourt, "The Shaping of Chance: Actuarial Models and Criminal Profiling at the Turn of the Twenty-First Century," *University of Chicago Law Review* 70, no. 1 (2003): 105–128.

19. T. Borovicka, M. Jirina Jr., P. Kordik, and M. Jirina, "Selecting Representative Data Sets," in *Advances in Data Mining Knowledge Discovery and Applications*, ed. Adem Karahoca (Rijeka, Croatia: InTech, 2012), 43–70.

20. J. Gama, P. Medas, G. Castillo, and P. Rodrigues, "Learning with Drift Detection," in *Advances in Artificial Intelligence—SBIA 2004*, ed. A. L. C. Bazzan and S. Labidi (Berlin: Springer, 2004), 286–295.

21. J. Gama, I. Žliobaitė, A. Bifet, M. Pechenizkiy, and A. Bouchachia, "A Survey on Concept Drift Adaptation," *ACM Computing Surveys* 46, no. 4 (2014): 1–37.
22. J. P. Barddal, H. M. Gomes, F. Enembreck, and B. Pfahringer, "A Survey on Feature Drift Adaptation: Definition, Benchmark, Challenges, and Future Directions," *Journal of Systems and Software* 127 (2017): 278–294.
23. M. Baena-García, J. del Campo-Ávila, R. Fidalgo, A. Bifet, R. Gavalda, and R. Morales-Bueno, "Early Drift Detection Method," in *Proceedings of the 4th ECML PKDD International Workshop on Knowledge Discovery from Data Streams* (Berlin: Springer, 2006), 77–86; J. Lu, A. Liu, F. Dong, F. Gu, J. Gama, and G. Zhang, "Learning Under Concept Drift: A Review," *IEEE Transactions on Knowledge and Data Engineering* 31, no. 12 (2018): 2346–2363.
24. G. J. Annas, "HIPAA Regulations: A New Era of Medical-Record Privacy?," *New England Journal of Medicine* 348, no. 15 (2003): 1486–1490.
25. S. N. Goodman, D. Fanelli, and J. P. Ioannidis, "What Does Research Reproducibility Mean?," *Science Translational Medicine* 8, no. 341 (2016): 341ps12.
26. National Academies of Sciences, Engineering, and Medicine, *Reproducibility and Replicability in Science* (Washington, DC: National Academies Press, 2019).
27. P. Diaba-Nuhoho and M. Amponsah-Offeh, "Reproducibility and Research Integrity: The Role of Scientists and Institutions," *BMC Research Notes* 14, no. 1 (2021): 451, https://doi.org/10.1186/s13104-021-05875-3.
28. T. S. Rao and C. Andrade, "The MMR Vaccine and Autism: Sensation, Refutation, Retraction, and Fraud," *Indian Journal of Psychiatry* 53, no. 2 (2011): 95–96, https://doi.org/10.4103/0019-5545.82529.
29. Harvard Dataverse, https://dataverse.harvard.edu/.
30. "OpenAI Releases GLIDE: A Scaled-Down Text-to-Image Model That Rivals DALL-E Performance," Synced, December 24, 2021, https://syncedreview .com/2021/12/24/deepmind-podracer-tpu-based-rl-frameworks-deliver -exceptional-performance-at-low-cost-173/; Cale Weissman, "Elon Musk-Funded AI Text Generator Was Too Dangerous for the Public," Fast Company, February 15, 2019, https://www.fastcompany.com/90308169/openai -refuses-to-release-software-because-its-too-dangerous.
31. J. Pallant, *SPSS Survival Manual: A Step by Step Guide to Data Analysis Using IBM SPSS* (London: Open University Press, 2020).

INDEX